THINKING ABOUT

AD 70

CHALLENGING REALIZED ESCHATOLOGY

BY KYLE POPE

Truth
Publications

Taking His hand,
helping each other home.
™

ISBN 10: 1-58427-480-8

ISBN 13: 978-1-58427-480-3

Truth Publications, Inc.
CEI Bookstore
220 S. Marion St., Athens, AL 35611
855-492-6657
sales@truthpublications.com
www.truthbooks.com

TABLE OF CONTENTS

I dedicate this book to my wonderful wife Toni, for her patience and longsuffering during the many long hours I spent preparing this material and talking through the issues discussed within these pages. I also thank her for her idea for the title, which was clean, concise, and far less cumbersome and confusing than the original ideas that I considered. Thank you for being my wife and friend.
I love you very much!

INTRODUCTION

*I*n the summer of AD 70, following a four-month siege mounted by three Roman legions under the command of the future emperor Titus, the ancient city of Jerusalem was captured and its glorious Herodian temple burned. As unlikely as this event must have seemed at the time, forty years earlier when Jesus was asked about the beautiful buildings associated with it, He had prophesied that a time would come when, "not one stone shall be left here upon another, that shall be thrown down" (Matt. 24:2, NKJV). The Lord's words were fulfilled just as He had foretold.

No student of Scripture will deny the significance of this monumental event. The fulfillment of Christ's word demonstrated God's utter rejection of this rebellious people whom God once considered His own "special treasure" (Exod. 19:5; Deut. 7:6; 14:2). Yet, for some this important event has come to be viewed as the focal point of all redemption history. To some, it surpasses even the death of Jesus, as they have concluded that all end-times prophecies find their fulfillment in the destruction of Jerusalem.

This view, known as the *AD 70 Doctrine, Full-Preterism,* or *Realized Eschatology* remains a minority view within churches of Christ (and the religious world generally), but there are important reasons that all Christians should become familiar with this dangerous false doctrine.

First, because growing numbers of Christians have accepted some fundamental tenets of this erroneous belief. For example, they may interpret the destruction of Jerusalem as the sole focus of the Mount of Olives discourse, even though they do not accept other tenets of full-preterism. Or, they may hold to an early date for the book of Revelation, in spite of the fact that they still believe in final judgment, heaven, hell, and the bodily resurrection. They are not yet properly full-preterists, but in their acceptance of some elements of its teaching they make themselves vulnerable to the logical consequences that follow. Many of these concepts build upon one another. Like Calvinism, if a few premises are granted, it is reasonable to accept all other elements of realized eschatology. This makes it important for the student of God's word to understand exactly what is at stake before accepting any of these beliefs.

Second, this view is often adopted by those who are highly intelligent and possess a great knowledge of the Scriptures. I fear that may be part of the appeal of this doctrine. It sets itself up as something most people just have "not yet realized." Yet, at the same time it asserts that its interpretations are actually the meaning God has intended all along. In this it reminds us of ancient Gnosticism, which claimed to possess a *secret knowledge* that others didn't have. This is very appealing to some who want to feel as if they've "got it," while everyone else just "can't yet see it." Truth is what matters, whether few or many accept it, but what determines truth is not how difficult, mysterious, or obscure it is. Truth is found in the solid teachings of God's word.

The material in the pages that follow was first prepared for private distribution to some Christians with whom I was studying. We have removed all personal elements that were applicable only to these individuals and have tried to make it more generally applicable to any reader and student of God's word.

This is not easy material because this is not an easy doctrine. It holds to principles that at first seem either innocent or absurd. It demands that the student reject clear and evident readings of Scripture and impose upon them redefinitions of terms. It makes applications of subject matter from vastly different contexts and draws conclusions far different from those long taught across a broad spectrum of religious backgrounds. This makes it hard for the one first exposed to it to understand it initially. Then, when one attains a preliminary knowledge, it is still difficult to see any danger in it. It is only when Christians grasp the full scope of the most extreme tenets of full-preterism that they will find in it a false doctrine that seeks to change the entire focus of Scripture and the hope that is set before us.

Perhaps you are reading this material because you are questioning some of the traditional doctrines regarding the resurrection, Christ's return, final judgment, and the end of the world. It may be that you have been exposed to some arguments that seem quite compelling. If so, you are exactly the person we hope will study this material. We want to persuade you to reject this doctrine and lovingly work to turn those away from it whom you encounter.

You may see these views as intriguing possibilities, or even new discoveries, but we beg you to consider that you may be painting yourself into a doctrinal corner. As you slowly explain away Scripture after Scripture that students of the New Testament have long applied to the Day of Judgment, a bodily resurrection, heaven and hell, and the literal destruction of the universe, you are left with no scriptural foundation to continue to believe in these things. Others have traveled the path you are on and it has led them in that direction. Dear reader, we do not want to see that happen to you. Very knowledgeable and well-versed students of Scripture have accepted some of these false premises and it has forced them to take trails of thought that could ultimately lead you in the same direction.

You will find in the pages that follow some arguments you may never encounter. In some areas you will find exhaustive detail, while others may not be addressed as comprehensively. The reason for this is simple. I have addressed what I have encountered. My aim was to persuade those with whom I was working. This material is not an attempt to address every possible argument advocates of this doctrine have made. We have, however, tried to address some matters in greater depth than I encountered as I was studying out these issues for myself. I ask the reader's forgiveness and indulgence for any shortcomings in either oversimplifying or over examining the questions before us. My aim is truth, and my prayer is that God may be glorified by this effort.

Acknowledgements

I offer my sincere thanks to the elders of Olsen Park church of Christ in Amarillo, Texas. When this material was first written the elders, Patrick Ledbetter, Brady McAlister, and Jeff Nunn, read through it to check for typographical and scriptural errors and to help me keep the tone as it ought to be. Also, after it was modified into the present form, I thank my fellow members of the Truth Publications publishing committee, Dan King, Mark Mayberry, and Mike Willis for their work bringing this to print. I extend special thanks to my brothers in Christ, Dan King and Brooks Cochran who did the final reading of this book and not only identified needed corrections other eyes had missed, but offered valuable suggestions I have incorporated into the text. Finally, thanks be to God for His grace, mercy, and love for me. To Him belongs all glory, honor, and praise.

Kyle Pope
Amarillo, Texas
August, 2019

Some Definitions

ood communication depends on a clear understanding of terms. Because of this, we must begin our study with some definitions. The doctrine addressed in this book can be identified by any of the following terms:

Full-Preterism. This designation is drawn from the Latin word *praeter* that can mean "past" or "before." It describes the view that all biblical prophecy is *past. Full-Preterism* must be distinguished from *Partial-Preterism,* which argues, that although most prophecy has been fulfilled, not everything taught in Scripture has been.

Realized Eschatology. This term shows the connection with eschatology, or the study of end times. In that it holds that *all* has been fulfilled, it is a view that the end times foretold in Scripture have now been "realized." Most advocates of this doctrine no longer look for any future act of judgment, Messianic coming, or destruction of the present universe.

The AD 70 Doctrine. Since most who accept the view that *all* prophecy has now been fulfilled look to the year AD 70 as the time in which this ultimately happened, perhaps the most common way this view is identified in the pulpit is to speak of it as the *AD 70 Doctrine.* This was the year that Jerusalem was destroyed by the Roman armies, and it is viewed by advocates of this doctrine as the "end of the age" in that they believe it was the end of the Jewish age. This term can be a little confusing in the fact that often those who identify some particular passages as applicable to AD 70 may incorrectly be said to hold the "AD 70 Doctrine." In this study, while we oppose the application some brethren may have made of some particular passages to AD 70, if we speak of those holding the "AD 70 Doctrine" we are talking about those who accept all aspects of full-preterism or realized eschatology.

Covenant Eschatology. This is the preferred term for this position used by Dr. Don K. Preston, one of the most vocal proponents of this doctrine. Preston is a former evangelist for churches of Christ, who now speaks passionately against the teachings of churches of Christ. In explaining Covenant Eschatology he writes:

> . . . It is an extensive treatment of ALL of Israel's promises concerning her hope of restoration under Messiah . . . . it should be seen as the uncovering of the eternal purpose of God. It affects an extensive range of biblical doctrines and promises, and sees the NT as being the announcement, warning, and prompting concerning the fulfillment of those promises.[1]

Because it is less familiar (and subject to confusion with the *One Covenant Doctrine,* which argues that there has not really been a change in covenants) we will not use the term *Covenant Eschatology.* Instead, we will use the first three of these terms synonymously, applying the term "preterists" to the full-preterist position (without distinguishing it from *partial preterism*).

Among members of churches of Christ, prior to the rise of premillennialism (also called *dispensationalism* or *futurism*) many associated with the Restoration Movement took a largely futurist view of the book of Revelation and other end times prophecies. They sought to identify particular visions in the book with specific historic events that have taken place since the first century. As a result of battles fought against premillennialism in the early twentieth century by men like Foy Wallace, most members of churches of Christ (especially among non-institutional brethren) now hold that most of the book of Revelation was fulfilled in Rome's persecution of the church. This can be seen in commentaries on the book by Homer Hailey (*Revelation: An Introduction and Commentary.* Louisville, KY: Religious Supply Inc., 1992), Robert Harkrider (*Truth Commentaries: Revelation.* Bowling Green, KY: Guardian of Truth Foundation, 1997), and a recently released thematic commentary by Dan King ("*I Saw the Heaven Opened*" A Commentary on Revelation. Athens, AL: Truth Publications Inc., 2018).

Properly, much of the religious world would consider most members of churches of Christ *partial-preterists,* because we believe much has already been fulfilled in the Roman persecution of Christians. Even some who argue for an early date of the book of Revelation (like Art Ogden) or who apply all of the Olivet Discourse to AD 70 (like Kenneth Chumbley) are not full-preterists because they still believe some prophecies have not yet been fulfilled. My fear is that many Christians are standing right on the line, if they have not already crossed over, to accept full-preterism. This study is an effort to pull such souls away from that line altogether.

---

[1] Don K. Preston, "Why the Study of Covenant Eschatology Is Important," *Bible Prophecy,* November 28, 2012, http://www.bibleprophecy.com/why-the-study-of-covenant-eschatology-is-important-guest-article/.

So What Do Full-Preterists Believe?

Before we look at some key tenets of this doctrine in depth, let's consider an overview of the theory as a whole. This is a bit like trying to define *denominationalism,* in that it is a fluid and ever-changing concept with different interpretations taken by different people. Even so, we can summarize the doctrine in this way:

1. God has used figures of speech throughout His dealings with mankind that used dramatic judgment language to describe important events.

2. These were never intended to be taken literally, but as figurative or spiritual figures of speech.

3. New Testament writers used this same language and first taught a Jewish audience who would have been familiar with this use of figurative, end-times language.

4. New Testament teachings, when viewed in light of Old Testament language will be understood to apply to the glorious nature of the Lord's church here on earth, not to future conditions.

5. Christ will not literally return in judgment. The dead will not literally rise from the death, and the universe will not literally be destroyed. All of these concepts were spiritual in nature and not literal.

6. There are different teachings among preterists regarding the afterlife. Some find nothing in Scripture that actually addresses the afterlife. Others believe that judgment will occur when a person dies and immediately after death, one will either go to heaven or to hell—there will be no universal Judgment Day.

My Objective

While we agree that God has used end-times language to describe significant acts of judgment in ways that were spiritual or figurative, we wholly reject the conclusions of full-preterism that all end-times language must be interpreted in that way. In the pages that follow we will challenge the validity of these assertions in light of careful scriptural analysis of key issues.

THE SONG OF MOSES

One of the first Christians I met who accepted some of these views believed strongly that the Song of Moses in Deuteronomy 32 was a prophetic declaration that pointed specifically to the destruction of Jerusalem in AD 70. While this is not a passage commonly incorporated into arguments used by preterists, there are some who draw the same conclusions. Let's consider how this text is handled in order to set the stage for other issues we will address. The argument is that the correlations between the warning statements it contains and the descriptions of first century Judaism in the New Testament are so close that it must be a specific prophecy that the end of the Mosaic Covenant would be accomplished when Jerusalem was destroyed. Let's consider some specifics about this argument and test these conclusions.

The Song of Moses in Revelation

A connection between the Song of Moses and eschatology might be demonstrated by the statement we find in Revelation 15:3. After the vision of the Lamb standing on Mount Zion with the 144,000 in the previous chapter (14:1), John is shown seven angels with the "seven last plagues" (15:1), and those who "have the victory over the beast" standing on a sea of glass with harps (15:2). The text then declares:

> They sing the song of Moses, the servant of God, and the song of the Lamb, saying: "Great and marvelous are Your works, Lord God Almighty! Just and true are Your ways, O King of the saints! Who shall not fear You, O Lord, and glorify Your name? For You alone are holy. For all nations shall come and worship before You, For Your judgments have been manifested" (NKJV).

We notice that they are said to sing two songs: (1) the "song of Moses" and (2) the "song of the Lamb." This second song, may refer to what has already been mentioned twice in the book of Revelation. In the throne scene immediately after the letters to the seven churches, the twenty-four elders and four living creatures fall down before the Lamb with harps and the prayers of the saints (5:8), and the text records:

And they sang a new song, saying: "You are worthy to take the scroll, and to open its seals; for You were slain, and have redeemed us to God by Your blood out of every tribe and tongue and people and nation, and have made us kings and priests to our God; and we shall reign on the earth" (5:9-10).

This is then echoed by multitudes of angels who proclaim, "Worthy is the Lamb who was slain to receive power and riches and wisdom, and strength and honor and glory and blessing!" (5:12), followed by a declaration from every living creature in heaven and earth, saying, "Blessing and honor and glory and power be to Him who sits on the throne, and to the Lamb, forever and ever!" (5:13).

Before our text in 15:3, we are told of the 144,000—"They sang as it were a new song before the throne, before the four living creatures, and the elders; and no one could learn that song except the hundred and forty-four thousand who were redeemed from the earth" (14:3). Is this the "song of the Lamb" mentioned in 15:3? Or, is this something different from what is described in 5:9? Both are called *new* songs, but the song in 14:3 is said to be one that only the 144,000 could learn. Is that a way of describing the blessings that will be unique to those who overcome? Unfortunately, none of these questions are answered directly or conclusively. We should note, however, the theme of the song addressed to the Lamb in 5:9—"You are worthy" and "worthy is the Lamb" (5:12). We can conclude that the "song of the Lamb" is . . .

1. This song of praise to Christ for His worthiness in bringing salvation,
2. It is the song only the 144,000 will learn, or
3. It is some symbolic combination of both (since those also victorious over the beast on the sea of glass are also allowed to sing it, cf. 15:1-3).

Whatever the case, it appears to be a song of praise to God for the victory He has brought through Jesus Christ, the Lamb.

So, what then is the "song of Moses"? There are at least two passages that could be described in this way. Deuteronomy 31:30 describes the verses that follow as a "song" that "Moses spoke in the hearing of all the assembly of Israel." Before this, Moses had restated the Mosaic Law and explained that God had declared that "this song" would be "a witness for Me against the children of Israel" (Deut. 31:19). The text then records that, "Moses wrote this song the same day, and taught it to the children of Israel" (31:22), but it then records that he "completed writing the words of this law" (31:24). Is the song that would stand as God's witness the law itself or the song that follows in 32:1-43? Every seven years the law was to be read before the people

(31:10-11). So either way, the people would regularly hear the entire law and 32:1-43 (which was a part of the law), but the wording is interesting. If it is not talking about the whole law itself, it seems to assume that the reader is already familiar with the song that will follow.

There is also another passage that could be called the "song of Moses." After the crossing of the Red Sea, and the overwhelming of the Egyptian armies in the sea, Exodus 15:1-19 records another song that was also sung by Moses. The text begins:

> Then Moses and the children of Israel sang this song to the LORD, and spoke, saying: "I will sing to the LORD, For He has triumphed gloriously! The horse and its rider He has thrown into the sea! The LORD is my strength and song, and He has become my salvation; He is my God, and I will praise Him; My father's God, and I will exalt Him. The LORD is a man of war; the LORD is His name. Pharaoh's chariots and his army He has cast into the sea; His chosen captains also are drowned in the Red Sea" (Exod. 15:1-4).

At the conclusion of additional similar words of praise for God's victory, like the "song of the Lamb" in Revelation 5:8-13, Miriam echoes, "Sing to the LORD, for He has triumphed gloriously! The horse and its rider He has thrown into the sea!" (Exod. 15:21).

Like the song in praise of the Lamb in Revelation, this is a song of praise to God for a victory. In Revelation it is victory over sin. In Exodus it is victory over the Egyptian army. Like the song of the Lamb in Revelation, there is a responsive echoing of the themes that God is worthy of praise and victorious. These similarities lend great support to identifying Exodus 15:1-21 as the "song of Moses" described in Revelation 15:3, rather than the Song of Moses in Deuteronomy 32:1-43. Unlike Deuteronomy 32, it is not a song of warning, but a song praising God for His deliverance.

Connections between Deuteronomy 32 and First Century Judaism

That means we can't necessarily assume an eschatological connection between the "song of Moses" in Deuteronomy 32 and Revelation 15. However, those who argue that Deuteronomy 32 points specifically to AD 70 don't necessarily appeal to Revelation 15, but to what they see as significant similarities in its wording and New Testament descriptions of New Testament Judaism. Consider a chart showing these similarities offered by a preacher who made this argument:[1]

---

[1] Out of respect for this brother in Christ, and a hope that he may one day change his mind, I do not cite the specific source of this chart. However, let the reader

Description of Israel Deuteronomy 32	First Century AD Israel Matthew – Revelation
Not God's Children 32:5	Not God's Children John 8:41-47
Perverse / Crooked Generation 32:5	Perverse / Crooked Generation Acts 2:40; Phil. 2:15
Foolish / Unwise 32:6	Foolish Matt. 7:26; 23:16-22; Luke 11:37-41
Perverse Generation, Faithless 32:20	Perverse Generation, Faithless Matt. 17:17; Mark 9:19; Luke 9:41
Made Jealous / Angry by a "No People" 32:21	Made Jealous / Angry by Gentiles Luke 4:14-30; Rom. 10:19
Lack Counsel / Understanding and Unable to Discern Their End 32:28-29	Unable to Discern the Signs of the Times That Pointed to Their End Matt. 16:1-4; Luke 19:41-44
Vine of Sodom 32:32	Spiritual Sodom Rev. 11:8
Poison / Venom of Serpents 32:33	Serpents, Brood of Vipers Matt. 3:7; 12:34; 23:33
God's Enemy 32:27	God's Enemy John 8:31-41; 1 Thess. 2:14-16; Rev. 2:9; 3:9
Hate God 32:41	Hate God John 8:42; 15:18-25
God's Wrath, Vengeance Coming Against His Enemy 32:22, 35, 43	God's Wrath, Vengeance on "This People" to Fulfill What Was Written Luke 21:22-23, 32; Heb. 10:30
Blood of God's Servants to Be Avenged at Israel's End 32:20, 36, 43	Blood of God's Servants Avenged upon "This Generation" Matt. 23:29-36; Rev. 6:9-11; 16:4-7

Many of these comparisons are quite compelling. Certainly, God brought the Old Testament system to an end in the first century, but advocates of this view go too far in two areas:

1. When they interpret the Song of Moses as a specific prophecy directed at first century Judaism (rather than a general warning that applied to Israel throughout its entire history), and . . .
2. When they argue that New Testament texts address AD 70 rather than a final judgment and the end of the universe.

---

understand that I am not presenting this as my own work, and I have personally shared my analysis of his work with him before presenting it in this study.

To address my first concern, let's notice what is said in the chapter before the song begins. If it is correct that the song that God sets forth as a "witness" (31:19) against Israel is 32:1-43, notice how the Lord says it was to be used:

> When I have brought them to the land flowing with milk and honey, of which I swore to their fathers, and they have eaten and filled themselves and grown fat, then they will turn to other gods and serve them; and they will provoke Me and break My covenant. Then it shall be, when many evils and troubles have come upon them, that this song will testify against them as a witness; for it will not be forgotten in the mouths of their descendants, for I know the inclination of their behavior today, even before I have brought them to the land of which I swore to give them (31:20-21).

To what timeframe does the Lord say this applies? He says, first it is when He has brought them to the "land flowing with milk and honey." This is the common way the Promised Land is described (cf. Exod. 3:8, 17; 13:5; 33:3; Lev. 20:24; Num. 13:27; et al.). So, it is to apply to when they have come into Canaan. Yet, He says further, "this song will testify against them" when "many evils and troubles have come upon them." Unfortunately, that would not be a one-time tendency on their part. They would repeatedly become complacent and idolatrous and the Lord set this song forth as a continual reminder of the consequences of such behavior. They could never accuse God of failing to warn them. This song was a "witness" to them of what they would face if they disobeyed God.

In arguing that this specifically points to first century Judaism, advocates of this view may be saying that the warnings offered in Deuteronomy 32:1-43 find fulfillment in the behavior of the Jews of that time in ways that they had not prior to that. That may be true, but we must be careful not to assume that simply because similar wording is used to rebuke the conditions of the people of this time period it *necessarily* means that it demonstrates the song as a specific prophecy of AD 70.

For example, let's consider some elements from the chart above. We can find descriptions of those who were no longer considered (or behaving like) God's children from the eighth century BC (Isa. 1:4; 30:1; Hos. 4:6) and from the seventh through the sixth centuries BC (Jer. 3:19-22; 16:1-5). We find rebukes of "perverse" people from the eighth century (Isa. 19:14; 30:12) and the eighth to the seventh centuries (Hab. 1:4). They are said to be "foolish" as far back as the eleventh and tenth centuries BC (Ps. 74:18), the tenth century BC (Prov. 14:2) and the seventh to sixth centuries BC (Jer. 4:22). People were also rebuked for failing to discern their "end" throughout all major periods of Israelite history, including the eleventh to the tenth centuries BC (Ps. 73:17), the tenth century BC (Prov. 19:20), the eighth century BC (Isa. 47:7), and the seventh through the sixth centuries BC (Lam. 1:9). The figure of "Sodom" is used to describe Israelites in the eighth century BC (Isa. 1:10; Amos 4:11) and possibly in the sixth century BC (Ezek. 16:46).[2] The chilling figure of those with the poison of serpents is applied all the way back into the eleventh and tenth centuries BC (Ps. 140:3) and in the eighth century BC (Micah 7:17). Israel is figured as an enemy of God in texts describing the eighth century BC (Isa. 1:24; Micah 2:8) as well as the seventh to the sixth centuries BC (Lam. 2:4-5). People of the seventh to sixth centuries were said to hate God (Jer. 23:17) as well as those from the sixth century (Mal. 1:6). Even pronouncements of God avenging "the blood of His servants" span from the ninth century BC (2 Kings 9:7) to the eighth century BC (Isa. 34:8; Hos. 1:4) to the seventh through the sixth centuries BC (Jer. 5:9, 29; 9:9 [Jerusalem]; 46:10 [Egypt]). We could apply these to a modified version of the chart as seen on the next page. While this is not an exhaustive list, it illustrates the problem with assuming that the Song of Moses is intended as a specific prophecy against first century Judaism because of the similarity of wording used. The Lord does not say that is its purpose or limit its application in that way. These are general rebukes that apply to Israel throughout its history.

Specificity and Frequency

Part of the argument rests on how frequent and specific these warnings and similarities are. We have already seen that in declaring its purpose, the song was intended to act as a "witness" against Israel 32:19-21 throughout its history when evils came upon them as a result of turning from God's law. Should we change our understanding of its purpose if we see instances in which it applies specific wording used in the song?

If so, we should note a few examples that may be even more specific than those offered in the first chart. Isaiah begins with wording that is almost exactly the same as the song of Moses—"Hear, O heavens, and give ear, O earth! For the LORD has spoken: 'I have nourished and brought up children, and they have rebelled against Me'" (Isa. 1:2). Just like Deuteronomy 32, there is an address to heaven and earth and a rebuke of rebellious children. Does that indicate we should apply the Song of Moses specifically to the time of Isaiah? In 2 Kings 9:7, in the time of Jehoshaphat, the Lord says Jehoshaphat is to act so, "that I may avenge the blood of My servants the prophets, and the blood

---

[2] It is unclear if the figure is applied to Moab and Ammon or Israelite cities on the eastern side of the Jordan.

Description of Israel Deuteronomy 32	11th Century BC	10th Century BC	9th Century BC	8th Century BC	7th Century BC	6th Century BC
Not God's Children 32:5				Isa. 1:4; 30:1; Hos. 4:6	Jer. 3:19-22; 16:1-5	
Perverse / Crooked Generation 32:5				Isa. 19:14; 30:12	Hab. 1:4	
Foolish / Unwise 32:6	Ps. 74:18	Prov. 14:2				
Lack Counsel / Understanding and Unable to Discern Their End 32:28-29	Ps. 73:17	Prov. 19:20		Isa. 47:7	Lam. 1:9	
Vine of Sodom 32:32				Isa. 1:10; Amos 4:11		Ezek. 16:46
Poison / Venom of Serpents 32:33	Ps. 140:3			Micah 7:17		
God's Enemy 32:27				Isa. 1:24; Micah 2:8	Lam. 2:4-5	
Hate God 32:41					Jer. 23:17	Mal. 1:6
Blood of God's Servants to Be Avenged at Israel's End 32:20, 36, 43			2 Kings 9:7	Isa. 34:8; Hos. 1:4	Jer. 5:9, 29; 9:9 46:10	

of all the servants of the LORD." That is the same language as Deuteronomy 32:43, which promised, "He will avenge the blood of His servants." Should we conclude that the song applies to Jehoshaphat's time? Finally, in Jeremiah 46:10 the Lord declares, "For this is the day of the Lord GOD of hosts, a day of vengeance, that He may avenge Himself on His adversaries. The sword shall devour; it shall be satiated and made drunk with their blood." That is a declaration of judgment against Egypt (Jer. 46:1-2), not Jerusalem in AD 70, but it parallels Deuteronomy 32:42 almost perfectly. The Lord promised, "I will make My arrows drunk with blood, and My sword shall devour flesh, with the blood of the slain and the captives" (Deut. 32:42). Clearly, parallel wording does not change the general purpose of the song to make it specifically apply to only one period of Israelite history.

As noted above and in the first chart, there are numerous ways in which the warnings of Deuteronomy 32 *did* apply to first century Judaism, but does frequency of application change a general warning to a specific prophecy? If so, we might note how many similar statements apply to the condition of Israel in the eighth century. Should that lead us to identify it as the time to which the song is pointing? No, the song is a general "witness" that would be applicable throughout the entire history of Israel.

Why Are There So Many Parallels?

So, why is it that so many parallels exist between first century Judaism and the warnings in the Song of Moses if it is not intended to specifically indicate the time of Israel's end?

1. Vocabulary of Rebuke. As a witness against Israel, the Song of Moses established a vocabulary of rebuke. Just as it was used throughout its history, Jesus (and New Testament writers) used it to explain the severity of Israel's rejection of her Messiah. This has a cumulative effect. Centuries of use allowed it to become common and understandable speech to a Jewish audience, but it is interesting to note some of the wording in the song that does not directly apply to first century Judaism, or that will even be used to describe those outside of Israel.

Several times in the song reference is made to "foreign gods" (Deut. 32:16; cf. 32:12) and sacrificing to "new gods" (32:17). Now, we might argue that the close association some of the Jewish leaders had to Rome created a type of idolatry and worship of foreign gods, but first century Judaism was far less given to literal idolatry than was true at other periods of her history (see 1 Kings 11:7; Jer. 32:35, etc.). In the time of Pilate Jews were so opposed to idolatry that they successfully persuaded him not to bring the standards into the city that had an eagle on the tops, because the Romans worshipped these images (Josephus, *Antiquities* 18.3.1-3). So, while many elements of the Song of Moses match descriptions of first century Judaism, how can we explain that this rebuke of idolatry does not—especially if this is intended to specifically point to first century Judaism?

We see a similar problem in some applications that are drawn from the song, but which do not apply to first century Judaism, but to the world in general. In Philippians 2:15, Paul urged the Christians in Philippi to "become blameless and harmless, children of God without fault in the midst of a crooked and perverse generation, among whom you shine as lights in the world." The first chart cites this in fulfillment of Deuteronomy 32:5— "They have corrupted themselves; they are not His children, because of their blemish: a perverse and crooked generation." We will address later in our study the argument some make that the phrase "this generation" in Luke 11:49-51 points specifically to those who would suffer in Jerusalem in AD 70. There, advocates of this view use this promise of *requiring* of "this generation" the blood of the prophets to argue that Jerusalem is the Babylon of Revelation 18:24, rather than Rome. We believe this reasoning creates an inconsistency if you try to apply Philippians 2:15 as a specific fulfillment of the Song of Moses. Paul says they are "in the midst of" a "crooked and perverse generation." The phrase *in the midst of* translates the Greek *en mesō* (ἐν μέσῳ),meaning literally "in the middle of." Philippi was a Roman colony 1500 miles away from Jerusalem. The city could hardly be considered to be *in the middle of* first century Judaism. Now if we are including all of the ancient world within the term "generation" We would agree, but that changes how one can apply Luke 11:49-51 to Revelation 18:24—we would have to include Rome within "this generation." The point is that Philippians 2:15 is actually an example of using language from the Song of Moses to apply to those outside of Israel, not specifically to first century Jerusalem.

2. "The fullness of the times." Another reason for so many parallels could be the fact that the first century was the time towards which all of the Old Testament pointed. Paul called it "the fullness of the times" (Eph. 1:10). It was the time of Daniel's promise—"in the days of these kings the God of heaven will set up a kingdom which shall never be destroyed" (Dan. 2:44). We might expect that in the time when God had promised a New Covenant, that He would use the warnings He had offered as a "witness" to characterize the nature of the rebellious people who refused to accept His Messiah. Does that mean it specifically points to AD 70? No. We can acknowledge that the conditions of rebellion described in the song *especially* apply to first century Judaism without trying to limit its focus to specific events of AD 70.

References to "the End" in the Song

The fact that similar descriptions of Israel are also applied at other times in its history precludes us from saying that Deuteronomy 32 is *only* talking about first century Judaism. However, proponents of this view put strong emphasis upon the two references to the "end" in the song, arguing it specifically points to AD 70. This in turn influences how they interpret New Testament passages that concern the "end of the age," the "latter days," or "the last day."

This concept is addressed twice in the song and once in the previous chapter that explains the purpose of the song. In Deuteronomy 31:29, after commanding the elders and officers to assemble to hear the song, Moses says, "For I know that after my death you will become utterly corrupt, and turn aside from the way which I have commanded you; and evil will befall you in the LATTER days, because you will do evil in the sight of the LORD, to provoke Him to anger through the work of your hands" (emphasis mine). Then in the song, first in 32:20 the song says of God, "And He said: 'I will hide My face from them, I will see what their END will be, For they are a perverse generation, Children in whom is no faith'" (emphasis mine). Then in 32:29 he bemoans, "Oh, that they were wise, that they understood this, that they would consider their LATTER END!" (emphasis mine).

In all three of these passages the word (or words) that we capitalized are translated from the same Hebrew word. It is the word *'acharith* (אַחֲרִית) defined, "after part, end; (a) end, issue, event; (b) latter time (prophetic for future time); (c) posterity; (d) last, hindermost" (BDB). The KJV translates it "end" thirty-one times, "latter" twelve times, "last" seven times, and "posterity," "reward," "hindermost," "uttermost parts," "at the length," "remnant," or "residue" in the other instances of its sixty-one uses in the Old Testament.

As with all words, the specific application of its meaning is influenced (if not determined) by its context. Let's notice this throughout the Old Testament and observe what the context tells us about how this word must be interpreted.

The first example of its use comes in Genesis 49:1. Before Jacob offered blessings to his sons in the form of predictive prophecies of the role their descendents would play in Israelite history, he declared, "And Jacob called unto his sons, and said, 'Gather yourselves together, that I may tell you that which shall befall you in the last (*'acharith*) days.'" Within these blessings we find the powerful Messianic prophecies concerning "Shiloh" coming forth from Judah, to whom shall be "the obedience of the people" (49:8-12). While this points to Christ and those who would follow Him, the use of *'acharith* describes all that would come upon the tribes of Israel. It is not a specific word pointing to AD 70.

The word is used three times in the prophecies of Balaam, but none of them have anything to do with AD 70. The first refers to Balaam's end—" Let me die the death of the righteous, and let my last end (*'acharith*) be like his!" (Num. 23:10, KJV). The next to Israel's treatment of Moab during its history as a nation—"I will advise you what this people will do to your people in the latter (*'acharith*) days" (Num. 24:14, NKJV). And finally, the end of Amalek—"Amalek was the first of the nations; but his latter end (*'acharith*) shall be that he perish for ever" (Num. 24:20, KJV).

Earlier in Deuteronomy we see the same thing. The Lord promised Israel, "When you are in distress, and all these things come upon you in the latter (*'acharith*) days, when you turn to the LORD your God and obey His voice" (Deut. 4:30). This could not apply to AD 70 because the Lord promised to hear them when they turned to Him. By AD 70 (and really before that time) Israel's opportunity to repent as a nation had ended. In Deuteronomy 8:16 it applies to the blessings God brought to Israel in the wilderness. He tells them He had allowed their trial that, "He might test you, to do you good in the end (*'acharith*)." In Deuteronomy 11:12 it is used simply of the "end (*'acharith*) of the year."

In the books of Poetry it is used of the latter days of Job's life (Job 8:7; 42:12). In the Psalms it is used of the fate of the upright (Ps. 37:37; 73:17) as opposed to the fate of the wicked (Ps. 37:38), the "posterity (*'acharith*)" of the wicked (Ps. 109:13) or even the "uttermost parts (*'acharith*) of the sea" (Ps. 139:9). This word is what is used in the verse repeated twice in Proverbs— "There is a way that seems right to a man, but its end (*'acharith*) is the way of death" (Prov. 14:12; 16:25). This describes the general outcome of sinful behavior, as seen in numerous examples of its use in Proverbs and Ecclesiastes (see Prov. 5:4, 11; 23:32; 25:8; Eccl. 10:13), or simply the consequences of different actions in general (Prov. 19:20; 20:21; 29:21; Eccl. 7:8).

In trying to apply references in the Song of Moses to "the end" as specific prophecies of AD 70, the assumption seems to be that it is the *end* and nothing after that has yet to be fulfilled. Some interesting examples of *'acharith* in Proverbs challenge that assumption. Proverbs 23:17-18 teach, "Do not let your heart envy sinners, but be zealous for the fear of the LORD all the day; for surely there is a HEREAFTER, and your hope will not be cut off" (emphasis mine). The term the NKJV renders "hereafter" is *'acharith*. The KJV puts it more literally, "For surely there is an end ('*acharith*)." This is not saying that life will *terminate* with nothing after it. Instead, the reader is assured that the righteous will have hope in the '*acharith*. Two other texts reflect the same idea. Proverbs 24:14, from a positive perspective declares, "So shall the knowledge of wisdom be to your soul; if you have found it, there is a prospect ('*acharith*), and your hope will not be cut off." By contrast, from a negative perspective Proverbs 24:20 teaches, "For there will be no prospect ('*acharith*) for the evil man; the lamp of the wicked will be put out." Other translations put it "no hereafter shall be to the evil" (GLT), "there is not a posterity to the evil" (YLT), "there will be no future for the evil man" (NASB), or "the evil man has no future hope" (NIV). This is not teaching annihilation. In both cases it is talking about the *after-times* (so to speak) of the righteous and the wicked. In the same way, even if we apply Deuteronomy 32 to "the end" of Judaism it does not indicate that every reference in Scripture to the end points to AD 70, or that nothing was prophesied after that time.

We conclude that this sense of *after-times* may be the best way to conceptualize the meaning of '*acharith*. In the prophets, Isaiah wrote, "Let them bring forth and show us what will happen; let them show the former things, what they were, that we may consider them, and know the latter end ('*acharith*—"outcome" NASB) of them; or declare to us things to come" (Isa. 41:22). Also, "You did not take these things to heart, nor remember the latter end ('*acharith*—"outcome" NASB) of them" (Isa. 47:7). While it can point to the ultimate *latter time* (e.g., "Declaring the end ('*acharith*) from the beginning, and from ancient times things that are not yet done," Isa. 46:10), its conceptual sense is just *the things that come after*.

The remaining examples of its use illustrate what we have already seen, but let's categorize them so as not to appear to be avoiding anything. We will address Daniel in a later portion of our study, but in the remaining Scriptures we see '*acharith* used of the general consequences of behavior (Jer. 17:11); of the fate of Jews at the time being discussed (Jer. 5:31; 12:4); of the Babylonian destruction of Jerusalem (Lam. 1:9), and the return of the Jews after the Babylonian exile (Jer. 29:11). Jeremiah prophesied, "There is hope in your future ('*acharith*—"latter end" ASV), says the LORD, That your children shall come back to their own border" (Jer. 31:17). Captives of Moab return "in the latter ('*acharith*) days" (Jer. 48:47). Babylonian exiles return "in the latter ('*acharith*) days" (Jer. 49:39). '*Acharith* is used of the last portion of nations under Babylon's control (Jer. 50:12), of Gog's assault upon Israel (Ezek. 38:8), of someone's "posterity"—those who come *after* them (Amos 4:2), and the last portion of people slain in battle (Ezek. 23:25; Amos 9:1).

There are only three texts to which one could even remotely appeal in support of the argument that the "end" of the Song of Moses refers to AD 70, but let's consider them carefully. Two are virtually identical. Jeremiah writes, "The anger of the Lord will not turn back Until He has executed and performed the thoughts of His heart. In the latter (*'acharith*) days you will understand it perfectly" (Jer. 23:20), and later, "The fierce anger of the Lord will not return until He has done it, And until He has performed the intents of His heart. In the latter days (*'acharith*) you will consider it" (Jer. 30:24). The first text comes after Jeremiah explains that many were saying, "you shall have peace" while each was following the "dictates of his own heart" telling each other, "no evil shall come upon you" (Jer. 23:17), to which Jeremiah warned them "Behold, a whirlwind of the Lord has gone forth in fury—A violent whirlwind! It will fall violently on the head of the wicked" (23:19). While this is clearly the language of judgment, it is talking about Babylon's destruction of Jerusalem in 586 BC—not AD 70. The second text comes in the context of promising, "Thus says the Lord: 'Behold, I will bring back the captivity of Jacob's tents, and have mercy on his dwelling places; the city shall be built upon its own mound, and the palace shall remain according to its own plan'" (Jer. 30:18). Most likely, the Lord is restating the promise of 23:20 describing what the people will recognize when the exile is completed—they will "consider it" or "understand" in the *after times*. If it points beyond this, it is only in a sense that is generally Messianic. Chapter 31 will, of course, bring the great promise of the New Covenant (Jer. 31:31ff), but the direct application of 23:20 and 30:24 is to the Babylonian Captivity and Return.

The third text comes in Amos. The prophet writes, "I will turn your feasts into mourning, and all your songs into lamentation; I will bring sackcloth on every waist, and baldness on every head; I will make it like mourning for an only *son*, and its end (*'acharith*) like a bitter day" (Amos 8:10). The book of Amos is a warning to the wicked northern kingdom of Israel of its impending fate. After this text the passage rebukes, "those who swear by the sin of Samaria" (8:14). Samaria was one of the capitals of the northern kingdom of Israel. It fell in 721 BC, not AD 70. So, even these texts do not use "end" in reference to AD 70.

"The End" in the First Century

Are there instances of its use that clearly point to the first century? Yes. Hosea declared, "Afterward the children of Israel shall return and seek the Lord their God and David their king. They shall fear the Lord and His goodness in the latter (*'acharith*) days" (Hos. 3:5). Does this apply to AD 70? We should note this is said to come *after* a time when Israel is "without king or prince, without sacrifice or sacred pillar, without ephod or teraphim" (Hos. 3:4). If AD 70 is "the end," how can Hosea apply the term to a period *after* there is no sacrifice or priestly service? Now, one might argue that AD 70 was "the end" which included the kingdom that would follow it within the "latter days," yet that would concede that some of what is prophesied comes *after* AD 70. We would agree—we are still living in the "latter days." At any rate, it is clear that the *'acharith* for Hosea is the time in which God's people (having been disciplined) will return to Him, either under Christ or following the Babylonian Exile.

Isaiah 2:2-3 and Micah 4:1-3 both quote the same prophecy—"Now it shall come to pass in the latter (*'acharith*) days that the mountain of the LORD's house shall be established on the top of the mountains, and shall be exalted above the hills; and peoples shall flow to it" (Isa. 2:2; Micah 4:1, KJV). So, is this AD 70? The text continues, "And many nations shall come, and say, Come, and let us go up to the mountain of the LORD, and to the house of the God of Jacob; and He will teach us of His ways, and we will walk in His paths: for the law shall go forth of Zion, and the word of the LORD from Jerusalem" (Isa. 2:3; Micah 4:2-3). When did the *law go forth* from Jerusalem? Jesus explained to His disciples, "Thus it is written, and thus it was necessary for the Christ to suffer and to rise from the dead the third day, and that repentance and remission of sins should be preached in His name to all nations, beginning at Jerusalem" (Luke 24:46-47). This began with the Great Commission (Matt. 28:19-20; Mark 16:15-16) and started in earnest on the Day of Pentecost—Jesus told them, "But you shall receive power when the Holy Spirit has come upon you; and you shall be witnesses to Me in Jerusalem, and in all Judea and Samaria, and to the end of the earth" (Acts 1:8). This makes it clear that Isaiah and Micah did not apply *'acharith* to AD 70, but to the time during which the law would go forth from Jerusalem—37 years earlier.

Conclusion

We may conclude, therefore, that *'acharith* is used in a variety of ways in Scripture to refer to things that come in the *after-times*. This is also true of its use in the Song of Moses. If we read into the word "end" a specific application to AD 70 we are bringing an assumption to the text that cannot be sustained by the passage itself. Let's demonstrate this by going back to Deuteronomy 31:29. Before the song, Moses said, "For I know that after my death you will become utterly corrupt, and turn aside from the way which I have commanded you; and evil will befall you in the latter (*'acharith*) days." Did these words have application to the people immediately after Moses' death? Absolutely. Were there ways they became "utterly corrupt"? Yes—if not the generation of

Joshua, then those during the times of the judges, kings, and later prophets (including first century Judaism). Did evil befall them when this happened? Yes, and in each case it befell them in their own *after-times* or "latter days." To apply it only to AD 70 makes the warning (and the witness this song would serve) meaningless to the people it was intended to teach.

So, while we would agree that the Song of Moses had general application to first century Judaism, we have seen that the evidence precludes applying it too specifically to the destruction of Jerusalem in AD 70. We will see in later studies that this also precludes us, therefore, from interpreting New Testament references to final things in such a limited and narrow fashion.

THE HEAVENS AND THE EARTH

The Song of Moses is prefaced with the words, "Then Moses spoke in the hearing of all the assembly of Israel the words of this song until they were ended" (Deut. 31:30), then begins with the words, "Give ear, O heavens, and I will speak; and hear, O earth, the words of my mouth" (Deut. 32:1). Preterists assert that this text demonstrates Israel being addressed as the *heavens* and the *earth,* and then argue that this sets the stage for the same interpretation throughout Scripture—especially in New Testament texts usually applied to final judgment. We believe this conclusion is seriously flawed and has led its proponents to adopt several additional erroneous views.

"Hear, O Heavens"

To test this let us begin by seeing if there are parallels to this type of address in Scripture. In Job, in anguish he cried out, "Although no violence is in my hands, and my prayer is pure. O earth, do not cover my blood, and let my cry have no resting place! Surely even now my witness is in heaven, And my evidence is on high" (Job 16:17-19). Job is pleading his innocence by appealing to the earth not to conceal his blood. He trusts that the One who has witnessed his innocence—likely using "heaven" as a personification of God or His dwelling place—may stand as his "witness." This is not saying that Israel is heaven and earth—some date Job to the Patriarchal Period. It is appealing to things that are stable and unmovable to act as his witness.

Now we might argue that Job lived before the Law of Moses. What do we find elsewhere? Psalm 114 begins, "When Israel went out of Egypt, the house of Jacob from a people of strange language, Judah became His sanctuary, and Israel His dominion." (Ps. 114:1-2). The psalmist then calls on different inanimate things within nature to proclaim what it had witnessed. These include the sea, the Jordan, the mountains, and the hills, which the psalmist questions (114:3-6). He ends with the charge, "Tremble, O earth, at the presence of the Lord, at the presence of the God of Jacob, who turned the rock into a pool of water, the flint into a fountain of waters" (114:7-8). It would be pure supposition to imagine that after personifying other elements of nature to act as witness, the Holy Spirit then addresses the "earth," but actually means Israel. This is a poetic way of describing the reality of what God did for Israel that is figuratively planted in the memory of nature, no matter how much man forgets the works of God.

The prophets frequently do the same thing and it becomes even clearer that this is not intended as a figurative way of speaking of Israel, but a poetic form of address. Isaiah begins, "Hear, O heavens, and give ear, O earth! For the LORD has spoken: 'I have nourished and brought up children, And they have rebelled against Me; The ox knows its owner And the donkey its master's crib; but Israel does not know, My people do not consider'" (Isa. 1:2-3). According to the preterist argument we must conclude that the prophet is speaking to Israel with the words "O heavens" and "O earth," but notice the prophet quotes the Lord to say, "Israel does not know." Now, if the Lord intended, and the Jews would have automatically understood that they were being addressed in the words *heaven* and *earth* (as preterists argue), shouldn't the text read, "YOU do not know"? This makes it clear that the heavens and the earth are poetically being told what Israel has done.

The same is seen later in Isaiah: "Sing, O heavens, for the LORD has done it! Shout, you lower parts of the earth; Break forth into singing, you mountains, O forest, and every tree in it! For the LORD has redeemed Jacob, And glorified Himself in Israel" (Isa. 44:23). And, "Sing, O heavens! Be joyful, O earth! And break out in singing, O mountains! For the LORD has comforted His people, and will have mercy on His afflicted" (Isa. 49:13). If preterists are correct that heaven and earth are Israel, who are the "mountains" or the "forest and every tree in it"? Who should we identify as the "lower parts of the earth"? In these passages we must note the same thing we observed above. It doesn't say "the LORD has redeemed YOU" or "the LORD has comforted YOU," He is rhetorically proclaiming to the natural world what He has and will do for Israel.

This can be seen in many other texts (Isa. 8:9; Jer. 2:12; 6:19; 22:29), including the book of Revelation—"Therefore rejoice, O heavens, and you who dwell in them! Woe to the inhabitants of the earth and the sea! For the devil has come down to you, having great wrath, because he knows that he has a short time" (Rev. 12:12). This cannot be Israel (spiritually or physically). The heaven and earth are given different admonitions. The heavenly condition can rejoice, while the earthly condition must fear.

John Gill, in his *Exposition on the Entire Bible,* commenting on Deuteronomy 32:1, helps us understand that these texts use a figure of speech known as *prosopopoeia* meaning, "a figure of speech in which an abstract thing is personified" (*New Oxford American Dictionary*). Gill explains that this is:

> ... A figure frequently used in Scripture, things of great moment and importance are spoken of; and these are called upon to hearken, either to rebuke the stupidity and inattention of men, or to show that these would shed or withhold their influences, their good things, according to the obedience or disobedience of Israel; or because these are durable and lasting, and so would ever be witnesses for God and against His people.

Prosopopoeia is a Greek term used to explain this figure of speech going back into ancient history. The first century Roman rhetorician Quintilian claimed that, "In this kind of figure, it is allowable even to bring down the gods from heaven, evoke the dead, and give voices to cities and states" (*Institutes of Oratory* 9.2).

We see a taste of this in Micah's opening words, "Hear, all you peoples! Listen, O earth, and all that is in it! Let the Lord God be a witness against you, The Lord from His holy temple" (Micah 1:2). Other peoples, the earth and God Himself are called upon as witnesses (in this case) for what God will figuratively do to the earth. Now, in this text it does say "against YOU" (emphasis mine). Why? Because the Lord is proclaiming to the earth what He is about to do to it (1:3-4). "Earth" is not a figure for Israel, because the text continues, "All this is for the transgression of Jacob and for the sins of the house of Israel" (Micah 1:5). He doesn't say "YOUR transgressions" or "YOUR sins" even though the earth is being addressed.

In Deuteronomy 32:1 we can demonstrate that the same thing is true. Although the Song of Moses begins with the words, "Give ear, O heavens, and I will speak; and hear, O earth, the words of my mouth" (Deut. 32:1), before this Moses calls all of the elders and officers of Israel before him to proclaim this song, explaining that in doing so he will "call heaven and earth to witness against THEM" (Deut. 31:28, emphasis mine). Now, if the phrase "heaven and earth" stands for Israel and the Mosaic system we would have to say they are called upon as their own witness. If we say "heaven and earth" stands for the people, we would have to say that the elders and officers are pictured as standing *outside of* Israel, but the song is addressed to Israel and its leaders. Instead, the "heaven and earth" (fixed, unchanging things) are called upon metaphorically and poetically to witness God's unchanging warning to the people.

So, if we have demonstrated that Deuteronomy 32:1 doesn't set down a pattern that *heaven* and *earth* automatically refer to Israel, how does this affect the interpretation preterists have drawn from other Scriptures?

Preterists assert that Joseph's dream in Genesis 37:9-10 supports their position by using the sun, moon, and stars as figures of kings, leaders, and people in apocalyptic language. We must remember that there were two dreams. The first involved sheaves (37:6-8). Now, we would agree that in one dream the heavenly bodies represent Joseph's family later bowing to him in his position of leadership in Egypt. We know this because of its fulfillment in the account in Genesis. Does that mean that we should interpret every reference in Scripture to "sheaves" as a reference to "kings, leaders, and peoples"? Of course not. This is the problem with saying that anytime something is used in a figurative sense in one passage it necessarily means it should be interpreted that way in all of Scripture.

The End of the Universe in the Old Testament

Preterists assert that people in biblical times would have been unfamiliar with the concept of the destruction of the universe and the planet earth. They sometimes cite passages such as the entire book of Genesis, Psalm 148:4-6; 78:69; 119:90; and Ecclesiastes 1:4 in support of this claim. We must ask, *how do we know the concepts with which biblical characters were and were not familiar?* We can only know anyone's thoughts by what has been revealed about his or her thoughts. We would agree that less is revealed about these things in the Old Testament than in the New, but we firmly reject this assertion.

Let's consider a text from Genesis. After the flood, God declared, "While the earth remains, seedtime and harvest, cold and heat, winter and summer, and day and night shall not cease" (Gen. 8:22). Most English translations render this text with a dynamic equivalency rather than literal wording. The Hebrew uses the adverb *ad* (עַד) meaning "as long as," before the words "all the days" (YLT, DBY). God literally promises "as long as all the days of the earth" seasons and day and night will not cease. To refer to something with the qualifier "while" or "as long as" necessarily infers that there will be a time when the earth will not remain (or literally) when "all the days" of earth will be completed. This sets the stage for things that will be further revealed as time goes on. Clearly, that has to play a role in how we must interpret the wording in Daniel 12:13—"the end of the days." If the inference has been made as early as Genesis 8:22 that "all the days of the earth" is a limited number, Daniel can properly understand "the end of the days" to point to that time. We will address this further in later studies.

The four other texts mentioned above each make some statement about the heaven and earth being "established forever" (Ps. 148:4-6; 78:6-9); abiding "forever" (Eccl. 1:4); or having been established, the earth "abides" (Ps. 119:90). We must note of the text from Ecclesiastes, that the book as a whole is addressing things "under the sun" (Eccl. 1:3, et al.), that is, things as they appear. So, the Preacher speaks of the apparent vanity of all things throughout the book, but finally acknowledges that God will bring all things to judgment (Eccl. 12:13-14).

The other texts from the Psalms involve some different things we must consider. Psalm 148:4-6 reads, "Praise Him, you heavens of heavens, and you waters above the heavens! Let them praise the name of the LORD, For He commanded and they were created. He also established them forever and ever; He made a decree which shall not pass away." Preterists use of this passage to say the Jews thought the universe was unending actually contradicts their argument regarding the *heavens* and *earth*. Is the psalmist addressing Israel—he says, "Praise Him, you heavens"? No, here clearly the psalmist is talking about the material heavens, but what is meant by declaring that it is "established forever"?

Psalm 148:6 and 78:69 both use the Hebrew world *ōlam* (עוֹלָם) and 148:6 adds the word *ad* (עַד) before it. These words express concepts difficult to bring into English. Gesenius tells us that *ōlam* refers, "properly to what is hidden; especially *hidden time.*" Strong explains it in terms of something whose vanishing point is concealed. It can be used of past time (e.g., "whose goings forth have been from of old, from everlasting [*ōlam*]"—Micah 5:2). It can be used of future endless time ("swore by Him who lives forever [*ōlam*]"—Dan. 12:7), or it can be used of that which only *seemed* as if it would last forever ("The earth with its bars closed behind me forever [*ōlam*]"—Jonah 2:6). Babylon was said to be an "ancient [*ōlam*] nation" (Jer. 5:15), but she had a beginning (Gen. 10:9-10). Clearly past time for Babylon is not equivalent to the past time of the Messiah in Micah 5:2. The freed servant who chooses to remain with a master is said to be "your servant forever [*ōlam*]" (Deut. 15:17), but all men die (Heb. 9:27). So, clearly future time is not the same for the servant as it is for God in Daniel 12:7. Similar points could be illustrated when the word *ad* is combined with *ōlam*. In any instance, the context and the nature of the things to which these words are applied must determine the scope of their meaning.

In the texts preterists cite, we cannot say that they prove (or even demonstrate) that the writers to whom the Holy Spirit revealed these words, or the Jewish audience who first read them interpreted them to mean that the universe and earth were endless. As we have seen, these words can be used of things that merely *seem* to be endless. We must take all that is said in Scripture about the heavens and the earth in order to make sound determinations of their nature.

Assuming that *heaven* and *earth* automatically refers to Israel, then interpreting *ōlam* as necessarily describing endless future time when applied to the physical heaven and earth, skews the manner in which preterists view the many instances of eschatological and cosmological language in the Old Testament. As a result, we fear they are ignoring some obvious allusions to the end of the universe on the Day of Judgment.

Examples of Apocalyptic and Cosmological Language

Preterists offer various Old Testament prophecies that they affirm demonstrate figurative descriptions of judgments upon various nations. These include judgments on Babylon (Isa. 13:1-17); Israel (Isa. 24:3-6); Egypt (Ezek. 30-32); Edom (Isa. 34:4-5); and Nineveh (Nahum 1:1-5). We actually agree with some of their conclusions that these are figurative in nature. Where we must differ with them is in their conclusion that these passages demand we interpret all New Testament prophecies figuratively.

In Isaiah 13 we find a prophecy, "against Babylon" (13:1). Her judgment is prefaced with the warning, "Wail, for the day of the LORD is at hand" (13:6). This is describing a day of Divine judgment, but it declares:

> Behold, the day of the LORD comes, cruel, with both wrath and fierce anger, to lay the land desolate; and He will destroy its sinners from it. For the stars of heaven and their constellations will not give their light; the sun will be darkened in its going forth, and the moon will not cause its light to shine. "I will punish the world for its evil, and the wicked for their iniquity; I will halt the arrogance of the proud, and will lay low the haughtiness of the terrible" (13:9-11).

He continues, "Therefore I will shake the heavens, and the earth will move out of her place, in the wrath of the LORD of hosts and in the day of His fierce anger" (13:13). Is this a literal description of what would happen in the Lord's judgment on Babylon? Yes and no. Yes, they would experience "wrath" and become "desolate," but the physical earth continued, the sun and moon continued to shine, and the stars did not fall. We see similar things regarding:

- **Israel** ("the world languishes and fades away"—Isa. 24:4; "the inhabitants of the world are burned"—Isa. 24:6)
- **Egypt** ("I will cover the heavens, and make its stars dark; I will cover the sun with a cloud, And the moon shall not give her light"—Ezek. 32:8)
- **Edom** ("All the host of heaven shall be dissolved, and the heavens shall be rolled up like a scroll; All their host shall fall down As the leaf falls from the vine, and as fruit falling from a fig tree"—Isa. 34:4)
- And **Nineveh** ("The mountains quake before Him, the hills melt, and the earth heaves at His presence"—Nahum 1:5)

Preterists look at these texts and conclude that since the cosmological apocalyptic language was figurative as it related to the judgment of these nations at the time, it must therefore be figurative any time it is used. In other words, since it didn't happen then it has no relationship to what will ever happen. *How do we know that?* Preterists look at these texts and argue that since the Jews could look at them and recognize these things had not happened literally, they would automatically interpret them as figurative references to world powers and systems falling and have no expectation of a literal fulfillment at any time in the future. Again, *how can we know that?*

We believe texts such as this utilize something William Hendrickson calls "prophetic foreshortening." He explains:

> By the process of prophetic foreshortening, by means of which before one's eyes the widely separated mountain peaks of historic events merge and are seen as one, two momentous events are . . . intertwined . . . .[1]

We can demonstrate what Hendrickson describes from Scripture. When Hannah conceived, she praised the Lord saying "The LORD will judge the ends of the earth" (1 Sam. 2:10). That didn't mean He did that in the conception of Samuel. It looked to what He would do in the future at the point at which He had done something great. When David brought the ark to Jerusalem, he wrote a psalm and gave it to Asaph (1 Chron. 16:1-7). The psalm is preserved in 1 Chronicles 16:8-36. In praising God for all that He has done, it declares "He is coming to judge the earth" (1 Chron. 16:33). That didn't mean that He judged the earth when the ark came to Jerusalem, but as this was being done, David considered what God would one day do in the future. If it be so in this regard, then we must accept the possibility that prophetic cosmological apocalyptic language does the same thing.

If this idea of prophetic foreshortening is correct what would it tell us about what Jews familiar with the Old Testament might expect? We believe Jews who heard declarations that "the world languishes and fades away," and "the host of heaven shall be dissolved," would anticipate a time when such judgments would be more than a foreshadowing, but a literal fulfillment. If this is so, then the Old Testament is filled with allusions to the destruction of the universe.

Think about a passage like Psalm 102:25-27, which reads:

> Of old You laid the foundation of the earth, and the heavens are the work of Your hands. They will perish, but You will endure; yes, they will all grow old like a garment; like a cloak You will change them, and they will be changed. But You are the same, and Your years will have no end.

---

[1] Hendrickson, William. *Exposition of the Gospel According to Matthew.* Grand Rapids: Baker Book House, 1973, 846.

Now, here we see reference to the "heavens" and the "earth," but can we argue that this means Israel? No, Israel's beginning was not "of old," its history only looked back to Moses or Jacob. So, if it is the physical universe, let's note, this is not in the genre of prophetic judgment language. This is talking about the *actual* nature of God and the *actual* nature of His creation. Yet, what does it say? Without qualification, without elaboration, but simply as a matter of fact it says, "They will perish." How can we claim that the Jews would have no concept of an end of the universe if in a psalm they might sing from Sabbath to Sabbath, they sang that the heavens and earth "will perish"? Moreover, this is quoted in Hebrews 1:10-12.

None of us can get into the minds of those who lived thousands of years ago, but what we must do is consider all that Scripture has to say on any subject and do our best to avoid assumptions that unjustifiably skew how we look at the Scripture as a whole. May God help us all to do that!

The New Heaven and the New Earth

All of this ultimately leads us to the question of how we are to understand New Testament promises of a New Heaven and a New Earth. As background for these texts we must begin with what is said at the end of Isaiah. The Lord declares, "For behold, I create new heavens and a new earth; and the former shall not be remembered or come to mind" (Isa. 65:17). Then after describing conditions in this new existence He concludes, "'For as the new heavens and the new earth which I will make shall remain before Me,' says the LORD, 'So shall your descendants and your name remain'" (Isa. 66:22). How are we to understand this?

This is likely a figurative description of some type of restoration of Israel following a judgment from the Lord. The imagery of the wolf feeding alongside the lamb, and the lion eating straw are common figures for peace and safety (66:25; cf. 11:6). At the same time, there is also nothing in the wording of the text that would preclude seeing an element of prophetic foreshortening regarding what *will* one day happen literally. In 65:17, the Lord uses the Hebrew Qal perfect verb form, expressing simple completed action—i.e., "I create new heavens and a new earth," leaving the time when this creation occurs unspecified. In Isaiah 66:22, although it is usually translated as a future, "I will make," the Lord actually uses a Hebrew Qal participle there, which also expresses simple completed action—i.e., "I make" (GLT) or "I am making" (YLT).

Our initial impulse might be to see this as an allusion to the spiritual kingdom under Christ, but the description offers some challenges to this conclusion. For example, in this "New Earth" eating of "swine's flesh" is still forbidden (66:17), worship from "Sabbath to Sabbath" continues (66:23), and there are "Levites" (66:21). In Christ all foods are clean (1 Tim. 4:4), the Sabbath is no longer binding (Col. 2:16), and all believers are priests (1 Pet. 2:9).[2]

These texts clearly set the stage for descriptions in the New Testament of a condition also called the *new heavens* and *new earth*, but we must notice some important differences that must be recognized. In the new earth of Isaiah there is death (Isa. 65:20). In the new earth of the New Testament there is no death (Rev. 21: 4). In the new earth of Isaiah there is a temple (Isa. 66:6). In the new earth of the New Testament there is no temple (Rev. 21:22). How much can we make of these differences? Some would say they are immaterial to the overall thrust of the text. Perhaps, but the Holy Spirit uses words for a purpose. We must discern that purpose. The fact that these differences exist makes it clear that the new heavens and earth of Isaiah cannot be absolutely equated with New Testament descriptions that are called by the same name.

The New Heavens and New Earth in the New Testament

The New Testament refers to the new heavens and earth in two passages:

1. Revelation 21:1-2. At the close of the vision John is shown in the book of Revelation, he writes, "Now I saw a new heaven and a new earth, for the first heaven and the first earth had passed away. Also there was no more sea. Then I, John, saw the holy city, New Jerusalem, coming down out of heaven from God, prepared as a bride adorned for her husband" (Rev. 21:1-2). Preterists have argued that this should be understood as a description of the church. It is true that Christians in the New Testament were told, "you have come to Mount Zion and to the city of the living God, the heavenly Jerusalem, to an innumerable company of angels, to the general assembly and church of the firstborn who are registered in heaven, to God the Judge of all, to the spirits of just men made perfect" (Heb. 12:22-23). We should note, however, that these are said to be "registered" or "enrolled" (NASB) in heaven. We should compare this with what is promised to the church in Philadelphia:

> He who overcomes, I will make him a pillar in the temple of My God, and he shall go out no more. And I will write on him the name of My God and the name of the city of My God, the New Jerusalem, which comes down out of heaven from My God. And I will write on him My new name (Rev. 3:12).

---

[2] At a preachers' study I attended earlier this year, some brethren who interpret this text as a reference to the church explained this use of Mosaic requirements as "accommodative language," utilizing elements required at the time to illustrate general obedience to God. While we find this explanation interesting, I don't think it fully explains all elements found in the text. See Appendix: The Eschatology of Ezekiel.

The use of the future tense is significant here. If the New Jerusalem *is* the church, the saints in Philadelphia would *be* the "New Jerusalem." Yet, Jesus speaks of this as a future reward that will be given to the faithful (i.e., "I will make"—"I will write"). There is another difference we should note. The Hebrew writer calls it the Jerusalem that is "Heavenly," from the Greek word *epouranios* (ἐπουράνιος) meaning, "existing in heaven" or "of heavenly origin or nature" (Thayer). It belongs to (or exists in) heaven, but enjoyment of the "New Jerusalem, which comes down out of heaven" is a future promise to those whose names are "enrolled in heaven."

We should also note some conditions promised in the "New Jerusalem, which comes down out of heaven" that do not apply to the saints in the church. In the church we are to "weep with those who weep" (Rom. 12:15) and death is still appointed to all (Heb. 9:27). In the New Jerusalem there is no more death or tears (Rev. 21:4). In the church saints can return to sin (2 Pet. 2:20-22) and lie (Col. 3:9). In the New Jerusalem, "there shall by no means enter it anything that defiles, or causes an abomination or a lie, but only those who are written in the Lamb's Book of Life" (Rev. 21:27). Perhaps preterists would argue that these conditions would only apply after the destruction of Jerusalem, but today, long after AD 70 we still face death, mourning, temptation, and dishonesty. To equate the church with the New Jerusalem does not exalt the relationship we now enjoy with Christ, it denies the promises He has made to us! If we can't trust these promises how can we believe any of them?

2. 2 Peter 3:13. After a graphic description of the destruction of the present universe, Peter assures the reader, "Nevertheless we, according to His promise, look for new heavens and a new earth in which righteousness dwells" (2 Pet. 3:13). The preterist view assumes that this is not talking about the physical universe, and asserts that it is speaking in figurative or spiritual terms of the new system that would come in Christ. As we have seen, this relies on the assumption that *heaven* and *earth* would have been understood by Jews as a way of referring to Israel. We have shown that this cannot be proven from Scripture.

This view also assumes that there was something about the kingdom of God under Christ that had not yet been inaugurated. That is exactly what premillennialism contends! That's not how Paul described it. He told the Colossians, "He has delivered us from the power of darkness and conveyed us into the kingdom of the Son of His love" (Col. 1:13). At the beginning of this very epistle, Peter himself declared, "His divine power has given to us all things that pertain to life and godliness, through the knowledge of Him who called us by glory and virtue" (2 Pet. 1:3). If this is describing the new system under Christ, but Christians were already in the kingdom and had already received "all things that pertain to life and godliness," why would Peter describe this as a future condition?

The context and wording of the text demonstrate that the preterist view of this passage is not correct. They argue that the "heavens" and "earth" in this passage are the old system under Moses and the new system under Christ. Peter declares, "But the day of the Lord will come as a thief in the night, in which the heavens will pass away with a great noise, and the elements will melt with fervent heat; both the earth and the works that are in it will be burned up" (2 Pet. 3:10). Is Peter discussing the physical universe or the old system under Moses? The answer is given three verses before this. After mentioning that some will scoff at the Divine promises, he writes, "For this they willfully forget: that by the word of God the heavens were of old, and the earth standing out of water and in the water, by which the world that then existed perished, being flooded with water" (2 Pet. 3:5-6). Of what world does this speak? This could not be talking about the Mosaic system. It is describing the flood. It happened long before the time of Moses. This is talking about the physical, material universe. It is described as "the world (*kosmos*) that then existed," and stands in contrast to what is mentioned in the next verse. Peter continues, "But the heavens and the earth which ARE NOW preserved by the same word, are reserved for fire until the day of judgment and perdition of ungodly men" (2 Pet. 3:7, emphasis mine). This is the same thing Peter calls "the heavens" and "the earth" in 3:10. To conclude otherwise we must twist this out of its context and read into the text an assumption that cannot be supported by the rest of Scripture.

"The Elements"

Within this context, Peter says, "the heavens will pass away with a great noise, and the elements (*stoicheion*) will melt with fervent heat; both the earth and the works that are in it will be burned up" (3:10). This is summarized in the next verse—"all these things will be dissolved" (3:11), and it is restated in the verse after that—"Looking for and hasting unto the coming of the day of God, wherein the heavens being on fire shall be dissolved, and the elements (*stoicheion*) shall melt with fervent heat?" (3:12). Preterists have appropriately compared this with Isaiah 34:4—"All the host of heaven shall be dissolved, and the heavens shall be rolled up like a scroll," with the assumption that since it did not happen in the judgment of Edom, it cannot be literal here. This disregards any possibility that Isaiah's prophecy involved prophetic foreshortening. Similarity does not mean equivalence.

Preterists have also addressed the use of the word *stoicheion*, translated "elements" in 3:10 and 12 arguing that the use of *stoicheion* throughout the New

Testament proves that its use in 2 Peter applies to the "elements" of the Old Testament system. In this argument they are misunderstanding the true meaning and use of this word elsewhere, and also assuming that the use of a word in one sense, in a given context necessitates understanding it that way in every context.

Let's first consider the meaning of this word. *Stoicheion* (στοιχεῖον) refers to, "any first thing, from which the others belonging to some series or composite whole take their rise, an element, first principal" (Thayer). It was a broad term used in many ways. It could apply to the basic sounds used in speech (Plato, *Cratylus* 424d), or even letters in the alphabet (Apollonius Dyscolus, *de Syntaxi* 313.7). In fact, the phrase *kata stoicheion* could mean "alphabetically" (*Greek Anthology* 11.15). To the ancients this was the term used in science and physics to describe the basic substances from which all things were composed (Plato, *Theatetus* 201e; et al.). This is how it is used in the Jewish apocryphal text, known as *The Wisdom of Sirach* (or *Ecclesiasticus*) written before the New Testament (7:17; 19:18). It could be used in mathematics and geometry of the elements of proof (Aristotle, *Metaphysics* 998a). It was used of fundamental principles of thought or philosophy (Xenophon, *Memorabilia* 2.1.1). It could be used to refer to the stars or planets (Manetho, 4.624), which is how the *Greek-English Lexicon,* edited by Liddell, Scott, and Jones classify its use in 2 Peter 3:10, Galatians 4:3, and Colossians 2:8. We don't necessarily agree with that classification, but find it interesting that the most respected lexicon of the ancient Greek language used throughout the world classifies it that way.

Stoicheion is used seven times in the New Testament; two of which are in 2 Peter. The first two come in Galatians, but possibly in two different ways. In speaking to the Jewish element among the churches in Galatia he explains, "the law was our schoolmaster to bring us unto Christ, that we might be justified by faith. But after that faith is come, we are no longer under a schoolmaster" (3:24-25). He then explains that now, in Christ, "there is neither Jew nor Greek" (3:28), explaining that all in Christ are "Abraham's seed" (3:29). He characterizes their condition before Christ (whether Jew or Gentile) as children "guardians and stewards" (4:1-2). He then uses *stoicheion,* in reference to this condition, explaining, "Even so we, when we were children, were in bondage under the elements (*stoicheion*) of the world (*cosmos*)" (4:3). Is this talking about the basic principles of Mosaic Law? Perhaps. The next point he makes is that Christ came, "to redeem those who were under the law, that we might receive the adoption as sons" (4:5). The problem is that Paul then uses the term again. He writes:

> But then, indeed, when you did not know God, you served those which by nature are not gods. But now after you have known God, or rather are

known by God, how is it that you turn again to the weak and beggarly elements (*stoicheion*), to which you desire again to be in bondage? (4:8-9).

It is true that the Galatians (both Jews and Gentiles) were trying to turn back to the old law, but only the Gentiles among them once "served those which by nature are not gods." Yet, Paul says to them as well that they were trying to return to the "weak and beggarly elements" that once held them in bondage. The Gentile was never under Mosaic Law, but the point Paul made earlier was that their condition before Christ (whether Jew or Gentile) was a childish, elementary state in which they were not yet mature and liberated by Christ. This suggests that *stoicheion* is not being used narrowly of the Mosaic Law alone, but rather of the "ABCs" (so to speak) of their childish state of bondage before coming to Christ.

The next two examples come in Colossians, where Paul likely uses it in a very similar way. Unlike the churches in Galatia, the problem was not as narrow as just turning back to Mosaic Law. It also included turning to worldly philosophies. He warns them, "Beware lest anyone cheat you through philosophy and empty deceit, according to the tradition of men, according to the basic principles (*stoicheion*) of the world, and not according to Christ" (Col. 2:8). Like Galatians, Paul speaks of the *stoicheion* "of the world," but also like Galatians there appears to be a Jew and Gentile element being addressed. The phrase "the traditions of men" may allude to Jewish rabbinical traditions (cf. "the tradition of the elders," Matt. 15:2; Mark 7:3, 5), but the warning against "philosophy" is likely more aimed at those tempted to follow after the itinerant Greek and Roman philosophers so common in the ancient world (cf. Acts 17:18).

In both Galatians and Colossians it would be too narrow to say that the use of *stoicheion* only means the elements of the Mosaic system. Both are talking about the elementary, now childish, weak, and insufficient condition the Jew and Gentile faced before coming to Christ. He challenges them not to return to such a condition by abandoning the gospel of Christ.

The final example appears in Hebrews. Like the epistle to the churches in Galatia, the audience of Jewish Christians to whom this book is addressed is also urged not to go back to Judaism. However, in the passage where *stoicheion* is used it has nothing to do with Mosaic Law. It is not even used as it was in Galatians and Colossians. In the course of explaining how the Old Testament pointed to Jesus, the writer offers a parenthetical rebuke to his readers, recognizing that they were too spiritually immature to grasp the things he was teaching them. Having just addressed Melchizedek, he writes, "of whom we have much to say, and hard to explain, since you have become dull of hearing. For though by this time you ought to be teachers, you need someone to teach you again the first principles (*stoicheion*) of the oracles of God; and you have come to need milk and not solid food" (Heb. 5:11-12). Notice, he says he can't tell them more because they don't yet know the basics— "the first principles (*stoicheion*) of the oracles of God." Preterists assert that what he means is the first principles of Mosaic Law, but we should note that he explains exactly what he means three verses later. He writes, "Therefore, leaving the discussion of the elementary principles of Christ, let us go on to perfection" (Heb. 6:1a). He does not use *stoicheion* here—the phrase is *tēs archēs tou Christou* (lit. "the beginning of the Christ"). This is talking about the elementary principles of faith in Christ. Remember, he describes them as babes (5:13). They were already in Christ.

How do we know that he is not talking about elements of the Mosaic Law that pointed to Christ? For one thing because that is what he has already been talking to them about. He is rebuking them because they don't understand the basics of the gospel, making it even harder for them to understand Old Testament principles that pointed to Christ. But, we also know this from the things he lists as "elementary principles of Christ." He urges them to move past the basics, which he calls the "foundation of"—(1) "repentance from dead works" and (2) "of faith toward God" (6:1b). Yes, Mosaic Law involved faith and repentance, but it is obedience to the gospel that involves "repentance from dead works" (i.e., repentance from sins, or works that offered no spiritual benefit). He lists further, (3) "of the doctrine of baptisms"; (4) "of laying on of hands"; (5) "of resurrection of the dead" and (6) "of eternal judgment" (6:2). Mosaic Law did not teach baptism except as seen in the teaching of John. We should note, however, that this is not the usual noun *baptisma* (βάπτισμα), but *baptismos* (βαπτισμός), leading some to translate this "of the doctrine of washings" (DBY). Most translators render this with some reference to baptism (or baptisms), but even if it alludes to old ceremonial washings, we think Thayer explains it correctly, "of washing prescribed by the Mosaic Law (Heb. 9:10) which seems to mean an exposition of the difference between the washings prescribed by the Mosaic Law and Christian baptism." While Mosaic Law said much about the priest laying hands on offerings (Lev. 3:2, 8, 13; 4:4, 15, 24, 29, 33; 16:21; 24:14; Num. 8:12) the Jewish people's involvement in laying on of hands was minimal (Num. 8:10). On the other hand, under Christ, during the age of miraculous spiritual gifts, the laying on of the apostles' hands was the way by which the Holy Spirit was given (Acts 8:18). The teaching concerning this is what allowed Christians taught by those who had received the laying on of hands to have confidence that their teachings were inspired by God (cf. 2 Tim. 1:6). Finally, as we discuss whether matters such as the resurrection and final judgment are literal or figurative, it is worth noting that the Hebrew writer calls these things "elementary principles." Clearly, obedience to Mosaic Law did not promise a resurrection from the dead—this was an elementary doctrine of Christ (cf. 1 Cor. 15:12-13). So we can conclude that the Hebrew writer is not using *stoicheion* as a reference to principles of the Law of Moses, but to the basic principles that constitute faith in Christ—the "ABCs" (so to speak) of being a Christian.

So how does this relate to its use in 2 Peter 3:10 and 12. We have shown that the immediate context shows clearly that he is talking about the present physical heavens and earth in contrast to the world before the flood (3:5-7). We have also shown that *stoicheion* is not used universally in Scripture to refer to the Mosaic system, but to the childish incomplete state of Jew and Gentile before coming to Christ (in Galatians and Colossians) and to basic principles of faith in Christ (in Hebrews). The most reasonable conclusion then, from the context of 2 Peter is that the apostle is talking about the material universe and therefore the most basic elements from which it is composed. Peter says these will "melt," be "burned up," be "dissolved," and "pass away." The similarity in wording shared with the Old Testament prophets allows us to see them as foreshadowing what will ultimately happen in the context of major judgments brought upon the enemies of God.

Conclusion

To understand 2 Peter as a prophecy of the end of the Jewish system depends on the assumption that Jews (or in this case Jewish Christians) would have automatically heard "Mosaic System" in the words "Heavens and Earth." This cannot be proven and rests on a faulty application of Scripture. It demands that we imagine that the Jewish system had not already come to an end. Paul said, "Christ is the end of the law for righteousness to everyone who believes" (Rom. 10:4). There is nothing further that needed to be given when Peter penned this epistle (2 Pet. 1:3). It also demands that we make an application of the word *stoicheion* that cannot be supported by Scripture. Because of this, the preterist view must be rejected and the scriptural references to the destruction of the *heaven* and *earth* be understood as clear, and unambiguous descriptions of the final destruction of the present material universe upon the Lord's final return.

Moses and the Prophets

O ne of the fundamental flaws of premillennialism is the position it takes towards the Jewish people and Mosaic Law. Misunderstanding passages such as Romans 11:26—"And so all Israel will be saved," they imagine that the physical descendents of Jacob still hold a place in God's plan. Many dispensationalists imagine that one day Christ will literally reign from earthly Jerusalem, and the Jews who have rejected Him as their Messiah are still under His grace awaiting that time. By holding this erroneous view, they miss the fact that Paul in the same book asserts, "they are not all Israel who are of Israel" (Rom. 9:6) and "he is not a Jew who is one outwardly, nor is circumcision that which is outward in the flesh; but he is a Jew who is one inwardly; and circumcision is that of the heart, in the Spirit, not in the letter; whose praise is not from men but from God" (Rom. 2:28-29). It is all of the *spiritual* Israel that Paul asserts will be saved. It is those who are of Abraham's faith that "are Abraham's seed, and heirs according to the promise" (Gal. 3:29).

While preterists are quick to reject this error, and speak aggressively against a political stance toward the modern nation of Israel based on this false conception, ironically they commit a very similar error in their own understanding of the Jewish people and Mosaic Law. On September 12, 2015, full-preterist Dr. Don K. Preston (the former evangelist among churches of Christ mentioned at the beginning of our study) had a debate with Jason Wallace, an Orthodox Presbyterian. Wallace asked Preston if the Jerusalem Council of Acts 15 and Paul's words in Colossians 2:16—"let no one judge you in food or in drink, or regarding a festival or a new moon or sabbaths" do not indicate that all of the Mosaic Law had "already passed away before 70 AD?" Preston replied, "No as a matter of fact it hadn't," going on to argue that both passages only stipulated that Gentiles were not required to keep *Torah* (i.e., Mosaic Law). He asserted, "Peter never said, James never said, in Acts 15 that Torah had been done away with," citing Acts 21:20, describing Jewish believers in Christ who were said to be "zealous for the law." He then explained that he believes there was a "transitional period" or a "tension" regarding "how much the Jews should continue to observe Torah," arguing that the Mosaic Law did not end for Jews until AD 70. After his comments,

Wallace properly pointed out that his view creates a "Jewish church and a Gentile church, when it's clear in Ephesians, of the two God 'has made one' (Eph. 2:14), we who were strangers and aliens from the commonwealth of Israel, now we have been brought near (cf. Eph. 2:17)."[1]

This is one of the most egregious flaws in the entire system of realized eschatology. While presenting itself as a view that takes *all* of Scripture into account, to accept this tenet of its theology requires that one ignore scores of clear and unequivocal statements in Scripture to the contrary. It sets forth the notion that after the cross, and before AD 70 there were two ways to salvation.[2] While we certainly hope for God's mercy, forbearance, and patience upon those who had faithfully followed God under Mosaic Law during this period, we cannot put ourselves in the place of God to judge souls who found themselves in such a condition. Our duty is to act as "stewards of the manifold grace of God" (1 Pet. 4:10), speaking only "the oracles of God" (1 Pet. 4:11). Just as premillennialism falsely sets forth another hope apart from obedience to the gospel of Jesus Christ, this preterist position does the same. It would be a small step for someone who accepts this view to say, "If God saved people who did not obey the gospel before AD 70, perhaps He will do the same today!"

Preterist Views of the Old Testament

Advocates of the AD 70 doctrine frequently point out that before the New Testament was written all Christians (and those whom they taught) could look to were the Old Testament Scriptures. They quote Paul's statement that he taught, "no other things than those which the prophets and Moses said would come" (Acts 26:22). They hold the firm conviction that Christians today should spend far more time studying the Old Testament, and are convinced that if believers would do that, they would reach the same conclusions they do regarding biblical eschatology.

We agree that there is great benefit in the study of the Old Testament, but as we are asserting in this study, we reject their premise that greater study of the Old Testament will lead all to accept their views of eschatology. Whether it

---

[1] "Don K Preston Debates Jason Wallace on the Validity of Preterism," September 12, 2015, https://www.youtube.com/watch?v=PjOMCLbPhvc.

[2] We should note that some argue that in order for Jews to be saved they had to obey the gospel, but still describe them as being "under" Mosaic Law. This doesn't work! The standard of law that one is "under" is what defines sin and righteousness (1 John 3:4-7). Paul told the Jewish Christians in Rome, "you are not under law but under grace" (Rom. 6:14). One cannot be "under" the system of grace dictated by the Law of Christ and "under" the system of service to God taught by Mosaic Law at the same time.

is their intention or not, they give the impression that the study of the Law and the Prophets gives believers today *all* that they need to follow God in Christ. That is a dangerous view that rejects the basic premise of the New Testament. It is the New Testament that now stands as the final rule of faith and practice in this age.

Jesus and the Law

Let's begin by considering what Jesus taught about the Mosaic Law and His relationship to it. From the beginning of His personal ministry, we see statements that point to a change in Mosaic Law.

In the Sermon on the Mount, Jesus said, "Do not think that I came to destroy the Law or the Prophets. I did not come to destroy but to fulfill" (Matt. 5:17). This fulfillment is understood in at least two ways.

1. Jesus fulfilled what was spoken about Him. After His resurrection, He told His disciples, "These are the words which I spoke to you while I was still with you, that all things must be fulfilled which were written in the Law of Moses and the Prophets and the Psalms concerning Me" (Luke 24:44). The life of Jesus fulfilled what had been promised regarding the Messiah.

2. Jesus "established" or empowered the Law to accomplish its purpose. Paul taught, "what the law could not do in that it was weak through the flesh, God did by sending His own Son in the likeness of sinful flesh" (Rom. 8:3). This pertained to the Law's role in defining and addressing sin. It brought the knowledge of sin (Rom. 3:20), but it was "not possible that the blood of bulls and goats could take away sins" (Heb. 10:4). Christ brought the ultimate means of forgiveness that the Law could not. Faith in Christ's sacrifice enabled one to attain the measure of forgiveness that the Law alone could not. Paul explained this, asking, "Do we then make void the law through faith? Certainly not! On the contrary, we establish the law" (Rom. 3:31).

Christ's teachings also showed the way to fulfill the moral intent of the Law. He identified love for God and one's neighbor as the greatest commandments on which "hang all the Law and the Prophets" (Matt 22:40). His disciples echoed this, explaining obedience to these principles as allowing one to have "fulfilled the law" (Rom. 13:8), since "love is the fulfillment of the law" (Rom. 13:10). Paul and James both cite the second of these commandments—"You shall love your neighbor as yourself," teaching that, "all the law is fulfilled in one word, even in this" (Gal. 5:14), calling it the "royal law according to the Scripture," which one will "do well" if he does (Jas. 2:8). Does that suggest that Paul and James were teaching that some were still *under* Mosaic Law? No. Mosaic Law had never explained love of one's neighbor as the fulfillment of "all the law." That is Christ's

Law, which modifies, explains, restates, and ratifies a new doctrine. James called it "the law of liberty" (Jas. 2:12), or the "perfect law of liberty," by which one will be "blessed in what he does" if he "continues in it" (Jas. 1:25). James equated it with holding "the faith of our Lord Jesus Christ" (Jas. 2:1). Mosaic Law was not *perfect* (or complete). The Hebrew writer said it made nothing "perfect" (Heb. 7:19) and was not "faultless" (Heb. 8:7). So, Christ fulfilled the Law in that He put forth that which was considered perfect, complete, and faultless Divine Law.

In the Sermon on the Mount Jesus went on to say, "For assuredly, I say to you, till heaven and earth pass away, one jot or one tittle will by no means pass from the law till all is fulfilled" (Matt. 5:18). Luke records this, "it is easier for heaven and earth to pass away than for one tittle of the law to fail" (Luke 16:17). We saw in our earlier study that "heaven and earth" cannot be understood as metaphors for the Mosaic system. Jesus was not saying, "When the Mosaic system ends the law ends." That misses the points we have just observed about Christ's teaching *empowering, establishing,* and thus *fulfilling* the Law. This is more like Isaiah's statement—"The grass withers, the flower fades, but the word of our God stands forever" (Isa. 40:8). Even when Mosaic Law passed away, it was not as if it had *failed.* Instead, as the Lord told Isaiah, His word will always, "accomplish what I please, and it shall prosper in the thing for which I sent it" (Isa. 55:11).

The gospels record other statements that make it clear that Jesus was predicting a move away from Mosaic Law. He taught, "The law and the prophets were until John. Since that time the kingdom of God has been preached, and everyone is pressing into it" (Luke 16:16). The kingdom would not come until Pentecost. When Jesus's disciples asked when He would "restore the kingdom to Israel" (Acts 1:6), He associated its coming with the time when He said they would "receive power when the Holy Spirit has come upon you" (Acts 1:8). Yet, Jesus during His ministry was already teaching "the gospel of the kingdom" (Matt. 4:23; 9:35). So, He described those who accepted His teaching as "pressing into it." We should note, however, that He said, "The law and the prophets were UNTIL John" (emphasis mine). Does that mean that the Law ended with His ministry? No. He told the Jews to continue to follow what their Jewish teachers taught (Matt. 23:2-3). Yet, this wording makes it clear that things were changing. If there was any "transitional period" this was it! As people were "pressing into" the kingdom by accepting the teaching of Jesus, they were moving from their old standard ("the law and the prophets") to a new standard.

John put it this way, "For the law was given through Moses, but grace and truth came through Jesus Christ" (John 1:17). That doesn't mean that before Christ there was no grace—Noah "found grace in the eyes of the LORD" which led to his salvation from the flood (Gen. 6:8). Yet, John's words show that Christ brought something that could no longer be provided by the law "given through Moses." In speaking to the Christians in Rome (who were largely from a Jewish background) Paul told them "you are not under law but under grace" (Rom. 6:14). Does that sound like Jewish Christians were still *under* Mosaic Law (as Preston asserts)? Absolutely not! John's words make it clear that in Christ "grace and truth" now rest in something that could no longer be provided by the law "given through Moses."

The Law and the Cross

Preterists agree that ultimately "grace and truth came through Christ," but the question is *when* did that happen? The clear testimony of Scripture is that this happened at the cross. Paul taught the Colossians, "And you, being dead in your trespasses and the uncircumcision of your flesh, He has made alive together with Him, having forgiven you all trespasses, having wiped out the handwriting of requirements that was against us, which was contrary to us. And He has taken it out of the way, having nailed it to the cross" (Col. 2:14-15). In the debate mentioned above, Preston argued that, "Colossians is a Gentile book." Certainly, in this passage Paul speaks of their past condition as characterized by the "uncircumcision of your flesh," but it is also clear that there were some members within the church in Colosse who came from a Jewish background, as seen from teachings regarding "sabbaths" (Col. 2:16) and the "worship of angels" (Col. 2:18). We should note that he speaks of Christ having taken "out of the way" and having nailed "to the cross" what he calls "the handwriting of requirements that was against us." What was that? Some translations bring out a different sense here, rendering it "the certificate of debt consisting of decrees" (NASB) or "the record that stood against us with its legal demands" (NRSV). It is true that the Gentiles were never under Mosaic Law, but "all are under sin" (Rom. 3:9) and "sin is not imputed when there is no law" (Rom 5:13). Paul is telling the Colossians that the Divine Law, which established them as sinners before God, was nailed "to the cross."

This is expressed even clearer earlier in Colossians. Paul writes, "For it pleased the Father that in Him all the fullness should dwell, and by Him to reconcile all things to Himself, by Him, whether things on earth or things in heaven, having made peace through the blood of His cross. And you, who once were alienated and enemies in your mind by wicked works, yet now He has reconciled in the body of His flesh through death, to present you holy, and blameless, and above reproach in His sight" (Col. 1:19-22). We should note two things from this text:

1. **God reconciled "all things to Himself" in both heaven and earth "through the blood of His cross."** This contradicts the preterist view that the *gathering* of Jews and Gentiles together didn't happen until AD 70—it happened at the cross.
2. **Those who once "were alienated and enemies"—"NOW He has reconciled in the body of His flesh through death"** (emphasis mine). Again, this was not something awaiting AD 70—it happened at the cross.

Let's look at another text that states this even more emphatically. It is clear that the church in Ephesus began from Jews who accepted Christ as the Messiah (cf. Acts 18:19; 18:24-28; 19:1-10), so we cannot claim that Ephesians is a "Gentile book." Paul told them, "For He Himself is our peace, who has made both one, and has broken down the middle wall of separation" (Eph. 2:14). This likely refers to the wall outside of the temple court that prevented Gentiles, under penalty of death from entering closer. We will discuss this more later in our studies (see chapter 7). Under Christ these distinctions end. Paul told the saints in Corinth, "For by one Spirit we were all baptized into one body—whether Jews or Greeks, whether slaves or free—and have all been made to drink into one Spirit" (1 Cor. 12:13). He told the Galatians, "There is neither Jew nor Greek, there is neither slave nor free, there is neither male nor female; for you are all one in Christ Jesus" (Gal. 3:28).

He continues, to the Ephesians, "having abolished in His flesh the enmity, that is, the law of commandments contained in ordinances, so as to create in Himself one new man from the two, thus making peace" (Eph. 2:15). Notice several things he makes clear in these words:

1. **Jesus "abolished in His flesh the enmity" which Paul then defines to be "the law of commandments contained in ordinances."** That is the Mosaic Law. Paul says Jesus *abolished* it "in His flesh." How can anyone claim it continued when Paul says Christ *abolished* it?
2. **In so doing, Christ created "one new man from the two."** After the cross, the Jew and the Gentile were no longer separate. Both were now considered a "new" type of identity in Christ (cf. Gal. 3:28—"There is neither Jew nor Greek").

He continues, "that He might reconcile them both to God in one body through the cross, thereby putting to death the enmity" (Eph. 2:16). Earlier, he defined "the enmity" as the Mosaic Law. Here he explicitly states that "through the cross" it has been put "to death." That leaves no question—if Mosaic Law died at the cross, it was no longer binding upon anyone, Jew or Gentile.

"Christ Is the End of the Law"

This fundamental premise of the gospel is taught throughout the entire New Testament. Paul explained his teaching in this way:

> Therefore, King Agrippa, I was not disobedient to the heavenly vision, but declared first to those in Damascus and in Jerusalem, and throughout all the region of Judea, and then to the Gentiles, that they should repent, turn to God, and do works befitting repentance. For these reasons the Jews seized me in the temple and tried to kill me (Acts 26:19-21)

Why did Paul teach those "throughout all the region of Judea" to "repent" and "turn to God"? Because the coming of Christ had left them in a position in which they were not right with God unless they repented. If they were still under Mosaic Law (and faithfully following it), there was nothing for which they needed to repent. Yet, Paul told those in Athens that God "now commands all men everywhere to repent" (Acts 17:30). This was before AD 70, and yet "all men everywhere" (Jew and Gentile alike) were commanded to "repent."

Paul made this clear in his letter to the Romans, another church composed of those from a Jewish background. He said unequivocally, "For Christ is the end of the law for righteousness to everyone who believes" (Rom. 10:4). Much of the epistle is devoted to explaining the superiority of the gospel to the Law of Moses. Consider some statements that illustrate that these Jewish Christians to whom Paul was writing were no longer *under* Mosaic Law. He told them, "Therefore, my brethren, you also have become dead to the law through the body of Christ, that you may be married to another" (Rom. 7:4). How could they be *under* the Law if they were "dead to the law"? Once again, this happened "through the body of Christ," that is, at the cross their obligation to Mosaic Law ended. He wrote further, "But now we have been delivered from the law, having died to what we were held by, so that we should serve in the newness of the Spirit and not in the oldness of the letter" (Rom. 7:6). If they were "delivered from the law" they were no longer under it in any binding sense.

Paul illustrates this further in discussing justification. He declared, "by the deeds of the law no flesh will be justified in His sight" (Rom. 3:20). That is a dramatic change in the view Jews were to have towards the Law. Under Moses, the Lord taught, "You shall therefore keep My statutes and My judgments, which if a man does, he shall live by them: I am the LORD" (Lev. 18:5). Yet, under Christ when Paul wrote to the Romans it is clear that after the cross, justification comes by the system of faith that rests in Jesus Christ. This side of the cross, "by the deeds of the law no flesh will be justified." The means of righteousness before God no longer had any relationship to Mosaic Law. Paul wrote, "But now the righteousness of God apart from the law is revealed, being witnessed by the Law and the Prophets" (Rom. 3:21). We should notice, this is "apart from the law." If the Law was still binding, then righteousness could not come "apart from the law." So what is the relationship of this new way of righteousness to the Old Testament Scriptures? It was "witnessed by the Law and the Prophets." In other words, it was foretold by the Old Testament Scriptures. What is this new means of righteousness? In the beginning of the epistle, Paul called it "the gospel" (Rom. 1:16). Later, like John's statement in John 1:17, Paul put it, "sin shall not have dominion over you, for you are not under law but under grace" (Rom. 6:14). The gospel is a system of grace to which all men are now responsible, and so Paul tells these Jewish Christians they are "not under law."

In the beginning of the epistle, to illustrate the sinfulness of both Jew and Gentile before God, Paul offers some powerful statements that make it clear that Mosaic Law was no longer binding upon anyone. After describing the sinful Gentile world, to demonstrate the sinfulness of the Jew as well, he asks, "Therefore, if an uncircumcised man keeps the righteous requirements of the law, will not his uncircumcision be counted as circumcision? And will not the physically uncircumcised, if he fulfills the law, judge you who, even with your written code and circumcision, are a transgressor of the law?" (Rom. 2:26-27). Paul speaks of an "uncircumcised man" keeping or *fulfilling* the law. If Paul is not considering a change in the law, this would be technically impossible, because the Law commanded circumcision. Even before the Mosaic code, the Law taught:

> This is My covenant which you shall keep, between Me and you and your descendants after you: Every male child among you shall be circumcised; and you shall be circumcised in the flesh of your foreskins, and it shall be a sign of the covenant between Me and you (Gen. 17:10-11).

Paul must be speaking of *fulfillment* of the Law in a way similar to what was discussed above—the fulfillment of the moral intent rather than the specific ordinances. This was itself a change of the nature and character of the Law. A Jew following such a sense of fulfilling the Law was not following Mosaic Law as it had been previously applied, so he could not be considered to be *under* Mosaic Law. It is at the end of this chapter that Paul redefines what truly identifies one as a Jew before God. He writes:

> For he is not a Jew who is one outwardly, nor is circumcision that which is outward in the flesh; but he is a Jew who is one inwardly; and circumcision is that of the heart, in the Spirit, not in the letter; whose praise is not from men but from God (Rom. 2:28-29).

Jesus echoes this, in speaking of "those who say they are Jews and are not" (Rev. 2:9; 3:9). This redefinition of who constitutes and what makes one a citizen of the "Israel of God" (Gal. 6:16) becomes a fundamental principle of the gospel, as we shall observe further below.

The Law in Galatians

In his epistle to the churches of Galatia Paul makes it even clearer that Mosaic Law had ended for all. He said of himself, "For I through the law died to the law that I might live to God" (Gal. 2:19). How did Paul die *through the Law?* The Law had pointed to Christ, and Paul continues, "I have been crucified with Christ; it is no longer I who live, but Christ lives in me; and the life which I now live in the flesh I live by faith in the Son of God, who loved me and gave Himself for me" (Gal. 2:20). Paul shows a connection here between his own death to the Law (and therefore sin) and Christ's death. He died to the Law that he might "live to God," but in this death to the Law, he was "crucified with Christ." That makes it clear that the one who has not "died to the law" has not, therefore, been "crucified with Christ." Paul explained further, "I do not set aside the grace of God; for if righteousness comes through the law, then Christ died in vain" (Gal. 2:21). We saw above that after the cross, righteousness could no longer come through the Law. We saw that the system under Christ was described as being "under grace." How could we argue that the Jews were still *under* Mosaic Law if Paul says that one who accepts the grace of God and is crucified with Christ has "died to the law"? That doesn't add up.

In Romans we noticed that Paul described the new standard under Christ as "the gospel" (Rom. 1:16) and as being "under grace" (Rom. 6:4). In Galatians, Paul describes this as being "led by the Spirit," of which he explains, "If you are led by the Spirit, you are not under the law" (Gal. 5:18). This is not saying, as our friends in the religious world try to argue, that the Holy Spirit just leads us directly, so we don't need any written law. Paul explained to the Romans what it means to be led by the Spirit. He wrote, "For those who live according to the flesh set their minds on the things of the flesh, but those who live according to the Spirit, the things of the Spirit" (Rom. 8:5). The soul who sets his or her mind on the things of the Spirit as revealed in the gospel of Christ, the system of grace, is "led by the Spirit." This was the sense of Jeremiah's promise of conditions under the New Covenant—"I will put My law in their minds, and write it on their hearts; and I will be their God, and they shall be My people" (Jer. 31:33).

To the Galatians, Paul explains in some of the most graphic terms the relationship between the Mosaic Law, and the New Covenant under Christ. He explains, "before faith came, we were kept under guard by the law, kept for the faith which would afterward be revealed. Therefore the law was our tutor to bring us to Christ, that we might be justified by faith" (Gal. 3:23-24). In light of these descriptions of the relationship, we must consider what it says about the condition of the Jews if it was true (as preterists claim) that they continued *under* the Law of Moses until AD 70. First, Paul says they had been, "kept under guard by the law"—"before faith came." So, if Jewish Christians were still *under* Mosaic Law, had faith not yet come? Then, why would they still be "kept under guard by the law"? Paul says the Law was their "tutor" to bring them to Christ, so that they "might be justified by faith." Were they still under this "tutor," and if so, would it not indicate that they had not yet been brought to Christ? If they were still under a "tutor," but the tutor could not bring justification (Gal. 2:16), isn't it clear that they could not yet be "justified by faith"? These conclusions are inescapable and make it clear that Paul is not teaching that Jewish Christians were still *under* Mosaic Law.

Paul taught them further about the purpose of Mosaic Law. He asks, "What purpose then does the law serve? It was added because of transgressions, till the Seed should come to whom the promise was made; and it was appointed through angels by the hand of a mediator" (Gal. 3:19). He explained this sense of the Law being "added because of transgressions" extensively to the Romans. While there was sin in the world before the Mosaic Law was given (Rom. 5:15), the commandment of the Law came "so that sin through the commandment might become exceedingly sinful" (Rom. 7:13). In other words, the Law brought "the knowledge of sin" (Rom. 3:20). But, Paul says the Law was added, "till the Seed should come." So, if we say Jewish Christians were still *under* the Mosaic Law, had "the Seed" (i.e., Christ) not yet come? If He had come, how could Mosaic Law still be in force?

Finally, let's think about this premise. Preterists argue that the Law was not binding upon Gentiles, but it continued to be in force for Jews until AD 70. We will see in later studies that much of the reason for this argument is because of the conclusions they draw about specific eschatological statements. If that is true, however, it means that Jewish Christians continued to carry out the *works of the Law*—not merely as matters of indifference before God, but as legal requirements before God. Let's notice what Paul told the Galatians about this. He wrote, "For as many as are of the works of the law are under the curse; for it is written, 'Cursed is everyone who does not continue in all things which are written in the book of the law, to do them'" (Gal. 3:10). Were Jewish Christians still "under the curse"? If so, they were not right with God. We noted above that the Law was the Jews' tutor "before faith came" (Gal. 3:23), but he explains further, "the law is not of faith, but 'the man who does them shall live by them'" (Gal. 3:12). Were they under faith? If so, Paul says that, "the law is not of faith." How then could redemption from the "curse" come? He explains, "Christ has redeemed us from the curse of the law, having become a curse for us (for it is written, 'Cursed is everyone who hangs on a tree')" (Gal. 3:13). This brings us back to the cross. The Law's power to put the Jew under the "curse" ended at the cross. After the cross, those who stood condemned before God were not condemned because of their violation of Mosaic Law, they were condemned for their failure to "obey the gospel of our Lord Jesus Christ" (2 Thess. 1:8).

"The Strength of Sin Is the Law"

In our next study we will consider what the Scriptures teach regarding the resurrection of the dead. A significant text in the study of the resurrection is 1 Corinthians 15. Preterists often look to the chronology of events described in that chapter in order to argue that it describes a spiritual collective (rather than a bodily, personal) resurrection. In that text, and yet crucial to our current discussion, is a statement in 15:56. After asserting in 15:26 that, "The last enemy that will be destroyed is death," when Paul returns to a discussion of this final conquest over death (15:51-55), he declares, "The sting of death is sin, and the strength of sin is the law" (15:56). The preterist argues, "If death's sting comes from sin, and the strength of sin is the law, it must mean that the Law of Moses was still in force until the final trumpet end" (which they interpret to have come in AD 70).[3]

So, does this prove that Mosaic Law continued after the cross? No. While it is true that "sin is not imputed when there is no law" (Rom. 5:13), the end of Mosaic Law did not mean the end of all accountability to Divine Law. Paul spoke of what he called the "Law of Christ" (Gal. 6:2). In seeking to influence all to obey Christ, he affirmed that all are "under law toward Christ" (1 Cor. 9:21). While the rule and reign of Christ will continue forever (Dan. 2:44), it is clear that after the final judgment there will be nothing that enters the New Jerusalem "that defiles, or causes an abomination or a lie" (Rev. 21:27). In that age something will obviously be far different than it is now, in that either the ability to sin, or the legal standard that allows for sin will be removed.

---

[3] This position, taken by preterists actually poses more challenges to their own doctrine than it does to that of their opponents. While they imagine that the New Jerusalem of Revelation 21 and 22 is the church, and argue that the conquest of death described in 1 Corinthians 15 has already occurred, they also argue that there is still sin (because it says "outside are dogs and sorcerers and sexually immoral and murderers and idolaters, and whoever loves and practices a lie"—Rev. 22:15). So, if they appeal to 1 Corinthians 15:56 to say Mosaic Law continued until AD 70, how can they explain their view that sin can still happen after the New Jerusalem is established if they define law so narrowly?

"Ready to Vanish Away"

A passage preterists often cite in defense of their position is the phrase in Hebrews 8:13 that speaks of the Law as "ready to vanish away." Interpreting this as if it is saying, "It was still in force, but *ready* to end," ignores the context and seriously misinterprets the force of the passage. The writer has just quoted the great promise of Jeremiah 31:31-34 of the coming of and conditions under the "New Covenant" (Heb. 8:8-12). The writer then refers to what he has just quoted, pointing out, "In that He says, 'A new covenant,' He has made the first obsolete. Now what is becoming obsolete and growing old is ready to vanish away" (Heb. 8:13). The writer is addressing what "He" (i.e., God) said through Jeremiah. When God spoke these words to Jeremiah the Law was still in force. The Hebrew writer is describing conditions *when* God spoke to Jeremiah, *not* conditions in the first century. In Jeremiah's time it was "ready to vanish away," but when the Hebrew writer wrote it had already *vanished away.* He is showing that this end had been foretold in the Old Testament Scriptures. This is clear from what is taught throughout the rest of the book.

For example, in the previous chapter he taught, "For the priesthood being changed, of necessity there is also a change of the law" (Heb. 7:12). Three chapters before this he taught, "Seeing then that we have a great High Priest who has passed through the heavens, Jesus the Son of God, let us hold fast our confession. For we do not have a High Priest who cannot sympathize with our weaknesses, but was in all points tempted as we are, yet without sin" (Heb. 4:14-15). Those to whom this epistle was addressed were also Jewish Christians, yet he identifies Christ as their High Priest. If the Law was still in force did they have *two High Priests?* No. So, either the Law had changed or Christ was not High Priest—but the Hebrew writer clearly says, "we HAVE a great High Priest" (emphasis mine). He doesn't say *we will have* (in AD 70). He says, "we HAVE A [singular] great High Priest" (emphasis mine). That means the Law had changed and was no longer in force.

He taught further, "For the law, having a shadow of the good things to come, and not the very image of the things, can never with these same sacrifices, which they offer continually year by year, make those who approach perfect" (Heb. 10:1). If the Law was still in force, it taught that those who offered sacrifices "shall be forgiven" (Lev. 4:20, 26, 31, 35; 5:10, 13, 16, 18; 6:7; 19:22). By contrast, the gospel teaches "in those sacrifices there is a reminder of sins every year" (Heb. 10:3). Christ became "the Mediator of the new covenant, by means of death, for the redemption of the transgressions under the first covenant" (Heb. 9:15). The fact that Christ had become the sacrifice and Mediator made the old sacrifices *imperfect* and useless. He explains, "for the law made nothing perfect; on the other hand, there is the bringing in of a better hope, through which we draw near to God" (Heb. 7:19). If the Law was still in force the "better hope" had not yet come. Preterists agree that the writer is urging his Jewish readers not to go back to the Law as the means of justification, but then try to argue that it was still binding upon these Jewish Christians. That doesn't add up.

When did this "better hope" come? The Hebrew writer also makes this clear. He writes, "For where there is a testament, there must also of necessity be the death of the testator. For a testament is in force after men are dead, since it has no power at all while the testator lives" (Heb. 9:16-17). The New Covenant, as noted above came into force at the cross—upon "the death of the testator." Yet, we should note the Hebrew writer explains that when he wrote, Christ had already "entered the holy places" which were in "heaven itself" (Heb. 9:24), at a time he identifies as "now, once at the end of the ages, He has appeared to put away sin by the sacrifice of Himself" (Heb. 9:26). Preterists argue that AD 70 was the "end of the ages.'" The Holy Spirit says Christ's death was "at the end of the ages." This is when the "better hope" came. This is when the Law changed—not at AD 70.

Let's note some final significant things the Hebrew writer taught. He speaks of the "annulling of the former commandment because of its weakness and unprofitableness" (Heb. 7:18). We have already discussed some ways in which Mosaic Law was *weak* and *unprofitable*, but note in this passage that he speaks of the "annulling of the former commandment." Remember, he is talking to Jewish Christians. The word translated "annulling" is *athetēsis* (ἀθέτησις) meaning "abolition, disannulling, put away, rejection" (Thayer). That which is *abolished, annulled,* or *put away* is no longer in force. He writes further, "For if that first covenant had been faultless, then no place would have been sought for a second" (Heb. 8:7). He refers to the New Covenant as "a second." Two chapters later he declares of Christ, "He takes away the first that He may establish the second" (Heb. 10:9). That suggests that in order to *establish* the "second" the "first" (i.e., the Mosaic Law) had to be *taken away.* If we argue that the first was still in place how can we say the second had come? Finally, in discussing ceremonial elements of Mosaic Law, he writes that they were, "concerned only with foods and drinks, various washings, and fleshly ordinances imposed UNTIL the time of reformation" (Heb. 9:10, emphasis mine). We should notice, they were "imposed until" what he calls "the time of the reformation." We assert that this happened at the cross (as we shall see below), preterists say it didn't happen until what they call "The Gathering," which they contend happened in AD 70.

Moses and the Prophets • 57

Why Did Paul "Keep" the Law?

So, if it is correct that the Law ended at the cross, some will immediately turn to Acts 21:24 and ask why Paul there was said to "keep the law." This was the key text to which Preston turned in the debate mentioned above. We should first observe some things about the context of this. First, it is after the controversy that had arisen in Acts 15 regarding Gentile circumcision. Luke prefaces that event writing, "But some of the sect of the Pharisees who believed rose up, saying, 'It is necessary to circumcise them, and to command them to keep the law of Moses'" (Acts 15:5). When the apostles and elders in Jerusalem respond to this, they write, "Since we have heard that some who went out from us have troubled you with words, unsettling your souls, saying, 'You must be circumcised and keep the law'—to whom we gave no such commandment" (Acts 15:24). We should note, this was not only a controversy over circumcision, but also the effort to bind Mosaic Law on Gentiles. The apostles and elders make it clear, they had given "no such commandment."

The events of Acts 21 come some time after this, although they will be mentioned in the discussion. Paul returns to Jerusalem, goes to James and the other elders and reports on his work among the Gentiles (21:17-19). James reports to Paul "how many myriads" (or "thousands" KJV, ASV, NASB) of "Jews there are who have believed" (21:20a). Both are rejoicing together about God's work among both Jews and Gentiles, but James further describes them by saying "they are zealous for the law" (21:20b). Preston assumes without any qualification that this is the Law of Moses. From the verses that follow, he is likely correct. However, we noted above that Jesus's teaching *fulfilled* or *established* the Law. It was James who had taught that holding to faith in Jesus fulfilled the "perfect law of liberty" (Jas. 1:25; 2:1). So, by the phrase "the law" he may not have meant the old form of Mosaic Law, but the fulfilled "royal law" of Christ.

We must also remember, that Jerusalem was still a Jewish city. To the extent that Rome allowed it, Mosaic Law was also civil law, so a visitor to or resident of Jerusalem would be expected to follow certain elements of Mosaic Law whether he considered them personally binding upon himself or not. The gospel always taught submission to civil authorities (Rom. 13:1-7; 1 Pet. 2:13), unless it required the violation of God's law (Acts 5:29).

In addition to this, Paul made it very clear that simply because one had obeyed the gospel did not mean that following *some* elements of Mosaic Law, was wrong. On the contrary, "in Christ Jesus neither circumcision nor uncircumcision avails anything, but faith working through love" (Gal. 5:6). In the matter of foods and feast days, he wrote, "He who observes the day, observes it to the Lord; and he who does not observe the day, to the Lord he does not observe it. He who eats, eats to the Lord, for he gives God thanks; and he who does not eat, to the Lord he does not eat, and gives God thanks" (Rom. 14:6). It only became sinful if someone sought to bind it on another person as if it was necessary to be right with God (cf. Gal 2:3-5), or if someone tried to compel one who struggled to put off old scruples about Mosaic Law to violate his conscience (cf. Rom. 14:14-21).

Paul also taught that in order to maintain influence with others, the Christian should be willing to adapt to the manners and customs of others. He wrote:

> For though I am free from all men, I have made myself a servant to all, that I might win the more; and to the Jews I became as a Jew, that I might win Jews; to those who are under the law, as under the law, that I might win those who are under the law; to those who are without law, as without law (not being without law toward God, but under law toward Christ), that I might win those who are without law; to the weak I became as weak, that I might win the weak. I have become all things to all men, that I might by all means save some. Now this I do for the gospel's sake, that I may be partaker of it with you (1 Cor. 9:19-23).

This didn't mean that he committed sin to win sinners, but he was willing to accommodate himself (within God's law) to influence others. Notice he said, "to the Jews I became as a Jew, that I might win Jews." What does that mean? He was already a Jew. If as a Jew he was still *under* Mosaic Law there would have been nothing for him to *become* in order to influence them. Does this not show that he acknowledged that he was no longer *under* Mosaic Law?

In Acts 21, after James told Paul about the Jews who had believed and were "zealous for the law," he then shares with Paul a concern that had arisen among these converts. Luke writes, "they have been informed about you that you teach all the Jews who are among the Gentiles to forsake Moses, saying that they ought not to circumcise their children nor to walk according to the customs" (Acts 21:21). Preterists want to assume that this means these Jews still considered themselves *under* Mosaic Law, but is that necessarily the issue? Perhaps these were new converts whose scruples did not yet allow them to see that these things were unnecessary. Perhaps their concern was the influence that believers would be able to have among Jews if Mosaic customs were not observed. It might even be that the fear was that such behavior on the part of Jews living among the Gentiles would compromise their ability to be able to freely return to Jerusalem and be received by other Jews. Whatever the reason, James urges Paul to act so as to settle the fears of these converts (Acts 21:22-23). Paul is to go with four men who have taken a vow and, "Take them and be purified with them, and pay their expenses so that they may shave their heads, and that all may know that those things of which they were informed concerning you are nothing, but that you yourself also walk orderly and keep the law" (Acts 21:24). James then referred to the letter that had been sent to Gentile Christians (21:25), and Paul did as James suggested (21:26).

Does that prove Paul considered himself *under* the Law? No. As noted above, he had "died to the law" (Gal. 2:9). However, following the suggestion of James would allow him to say, as he did later in his life, "Neither against the law of the Jews, nor against the temple, nor against Caesar have I offended in anything at all" (Acts 25:8). He taught Christians at all times, "Give no offense, either to the Jews or to the Greeks or to the church of God" (1 Cor. 10:32). We might compare this to what he later described to Timothy (in a different context) as using the law "lawfully" in accordance with "the glorious gospel of the blessed God" (1 Tim. 1:8, 11).

We should consider one final text that is sometimes used to argue that Paul was still under Mosaic Law. When Paul defends himself, he states, "But this I confess to you, that according to the Way which they call a sect, so I worship the God of my fathers, believing all things which are written in the Law and in the Prophets" (Acts 24:14). Does that mean that Paul still considered himself *under* the Law and Prophets? No. He *believed* "all things which were written in" them. Remember, Jesus didn't discredit, disregard, or disprove Old Testament Scriptures, He fulfilled them. That doesn't mean that Old Testament Scriptures give us all that is needed. It means that the Old Testament Scriptures pointed to Christ. Paul didn't reject Old Testament Scriptures. His faith in Christ was founded upon them. So it is today, those who believe in Christ do so standing upon the things "written in the Law and in the Prophets."

"The Gathering"

I was once teaching a class and heard an argument posed that was new to me. While studying the familiar passage in Hebrews 10:25 regarding "the assembling of ourselves together" a student in the class argued that the "Day approaching" was AD 70. He then argued that the focus is not on assembling together within local churches, but the assembling of Israel and the Gentiles under the Messiah. In studying this further after class it became clear to me that this is tied into a fundamental teaching espoused by preterists. The argument is that numerous passages in the Old Testament speak of God gathering Israel back together with the Gentiles under the Messiah. This is then tied into the wording in the Olivet Discourse promising, "And He will send His angels with a great sound of a trumpet, and they will gather together His elect from the four winds, from one end of heaven to the other" (Matt. 24:31). Concluding that this is AD 70, it is then asserted that this must be the *gathering* or *assembling* of Hebrews 10:25. Is that reasoning valid?

Old Testament Promises of a Gathering

A serious concern we have with the preterist approach to scriptural interpretation is the tendency to apply a chosen definition to a particular passage of Scripture that may (or may not) be correct. Little attention is given to context or background, but that definition is then applied throughout any other passages that use similar language—again giving little concern for context. If the original definition is valid, then the connections may also be valid. If, however, the original definition is flawed it carries the flawed application throughout any other passages that use similar language.

A number of preterist sources offer lists of Old Testament passages describing *gatherings*. Don Preston has written a series of seven articles entitled, "The Re-Gathering of Israel."[4] Another preterist author named Tina Rae Collins has published a book advocating this view, entitled *The Gathering in the Last Days* (New York: M. F. Sohn Publications, 2012).[5] Collins offers ten passages to defend her position. Let's consider each of these texts.

1. "The sceptre shall not depart from Judah, nor a lawgiver from between his feet, until Shiloh come; and unto him shall the gathering of the people be" (Gen. 49:10, KJV). This passage is clearly Messianic, and points to Jesus as the lawgiver and king descended from the lineage of Judah. In this text, however, Collins' use of the KJV has led her to make a faulty association. The word it translates "gathering" is the Hebrew word *yiqqahah* (יִקְּהַה), meaning, "obedience, cleansing, purging" (BDB). Most modern translations render this "obedience" (ASV, NASB, NKJV). Although it points to the reign of the Messiah, nothing is said in this text about His gathering of the people.

2. "When the peoples are gathered together, and the kingdoms, to serve the LORD" (Ps. 102:22, NKJV). This statement comes in a psalm that begins with an appeal to God, "Do not hide Your face from me in the day of

---

[4] This series started began April 29, 2013 and ran through May 14, 2013. They can be viewed on his website: http://donkpreston.com/articles/.

[5] In the introduction to her book Collins doesn't tell much about her religious background, but she does extend personal thanks to Arthur Ogden, whom she says started her on "this journey" and "patiently listened to my questions," and Sam Dawson whom she says "nudged me over a hump that was holding me back." She also thanks Dawson for proofreading her manuscript. Although brother Ogden did not embrace full-preterism, it is interesting that she says he *started* her in this direction. Sam Dawson, who used to preach where I now preach at Olsen Park in Amarillo, Texas, is now a full-preterist. This is a progressive path that begins with accepting a few faulty premises. When these are adopted the logical consequences follow. Dear reader, please do not take this same "journey."

my trouble" (102:2). This spans the first section of the psalm (102:1-11), with a final cry, "My days are like a shadow that lengthens, and I wither away like grass" (102:11). In contrast to this, the psalmist declares, "But You, O LORD, shall endure forever, and the remembrance of Your name to all generations." (102:12). Like the preterist argument about Deuteronomy 32, Collins argues that this is aimed at a specific future generation, appealing to the declaration, "This will be written for the generation to come" (102:18a). But, the verse continues, "That a people yet to be created may praise the LORD" (102:18b). Like verse 12 the psalmist is appealing to God's eternal nature in the face of the fleeting troubles of mortals who suffer as he has. Although the reference to "when the peoples are gathered together" could be Messianic or eschatological, that is not explicit in the psalm. In fact, in the middle of the psalm the writer appeals to the mercy God has shown to Zion (102:13), and His building of Zion (102:16), "So the nations shall fear the name of the LORD, and all the kings of the earth Your glory" (102:15). This reminds us of Solomon's prayer at the completion of the temple (1 Kings 8:12-53), that God would hear the prayers of His people, and foreigners "will hear of Your great name and Your strong hand and Your outstretched arm" (1 Kings 8:42). It is quite a stretch to conclude that this foretells a Messianic spiritual gathering in AD 70.

3. "He will set up a banner for the nations, And will assemble the outcasts of Israel, and gather together the dispersed of Judah From the four corners of the earth" (Isa. 11:12). This text is Messianic and we would agree that it looks to a future gathering of God's people under the Messiah. Before this Isaiah was told, "And in that day there shall be a Root of Jesse, Who shall stand as a banner to the people; For the Gentiles shall seek Him, and His resting place shall be glorious" (Isa. 11:10). Jesse, of course, was the father of David. Paul quotes this verse (Rom. 15:12), identifying Jesus and his own work among the Gentiles with its fulfillment (Rom. 15:8). Yet, while we would agree that it foreshadows a gathering under the Messiah, the question is when did this happen? Earlier in Romans Paul had taught, "For there is no distinction between Jew and Greek, for the same Lord over all is rich to all who call upon Him" (Rom. 10:12). As noted above, in Romans Paul made it clear "they are not all Israel who are of Israel" (Rom. 9:6), redefining a Jew as one inwardly circumcised (Rom. 2:29). Although Isaiah 11:11 had promised "To recover the remnant of His people who are left, from Assyria and Egypt, from Pathros and Cush, From Elam and Shinar, from Hamath and the islands of the sea," the gospel's redefinition of what constitutes an Israelite must be considered in the interpretation of this prophecy. That is not to say that Jews would not be included in this gathering. Paul said that those who were Israelites according to the flesh could be grafted in "if they do not continue in

unbelief" (Rom. 11:23), but he makes it clear that this *gathering* or *reconciliation* had already occurred. He wrote:

> For if when we were enemies we were reconciled to God through the death of His Son, much more, having been reconciled, we shall be saved by His life. And not only that, but we also rejoice in God through our Lord Jesus Christ, through whom we have now received the reconciliation (Rom. 5:10-11).

Paul does not describe the gathering of the remnant of Israel, or the reconciliation of Jew and Gentile to God as something that would come in AD 70. He claims that "through the death of His Son" they had "been reconciled," and already "received the reconciliation." This casting away of fleshly Israel had accomplished "the reconciling of the world" (Rom. 11:15).

4. "He will feed His flock like a shepherd; He will gather the lambs with His arm, and carry them in His bosom, And gently lead those who are with young" (Isa. 40:11). In this text we would also agree that it is Messianic and foretells a future "flock," gathered under a Divine "Shepherd." Earlier in the chapter we find the text that will be applied in the New Testament to the work of John the Baptist:

> The voice of one crying in the wilderness: "Prepare the way of the LORD; Make straight in the desert a highway for our God. Every valley shall be exalted and every mountain and hill brought low; the crooked places shall be made straight and the rough places smooth; the glory of the LORD shall be revealed, and all flesh shall see it together" (Isa. 40:3-5; cf. Luke 3:4-6).

Collins focuses on the phrase, "all flesh shall see it together" and tries to argue that it does not literally mean all who "ever lived, or ever will live" (4), going on to compare it to the promise of Revelation 1:7 that "every eye" will see Jesus, also discounting that statement as merely figurative. Her argument is odd. The prophecy of Isaiah is obviously speaking of the spiritual preparations leading to the glory of the Messiah's kingdom coming into reality. The text does not specify *when* all flesh would behold the Messiah's glory, but simply the reality that the Messiah's reign would affect all flesh. Paul declared, "at the name of Jesus every knee should bow, of those in heaven, and of those on earth, and of those under the earth" (Phil. 2:10). That sounds like all flesh to me!

What gathering does Isaiah 40:11 foreshadow? Is this an AD 70 gathering of Jews and Gentiles? The gathering is called a "flock" under a "shepherd." Clearly, before the destruction of Jerusalem, the church was already described as God's "flock" (Luke 12:32; John 10:9-16; Acts 20:28; 1 Pet. 5:2) and Jesus was already the "great Shepherd of the sheep, through the blood of the everlasting covenant" (Heb. 13:20). Yes, Peter spoke of a future time "when the Chief Shepherd appears" (1 Pet. 5:4a), but it is clear He is already the "Chief Shepherd" and His "flock" has already been *gathered by His arm.* If we connect this gathering with the flock that Isaiah foretells, we cannot read into it a delay until AD 70. When He "appears" Peter promises, "you will receive the crown of glory that does not fade away" (1 Pet. 5:4b). The flock already existed before AD 70, so we must conclude that Isaiah was not promising a gathering of the "flock" at that time.

5. "Hear the word of the LORD, O nations, and declare it in the isles afar off, and say, 'He who scattered Israel will gather him, and keep him as a shepherd does his flock'" (Jer. 31:10). The imagery of the "shepherd" and "flock" come again in this text, so the issues considered in the previous text apply here as well. As in the two previous texts, we would agree that this looks to the reign of the Messiah. Later in this chapter we find the promise of the New Covenant (Jer. 31:31-34). Before this text, Jeremiah is told, "Behold, I will bring them from the north country, and gather them from the ends of the earth, among them the blind and the lame, the woman with child and the one who labors with child, together; a great throng shall return there" (Jer. 31:8). Who are these whom the Lord promises to bring back? Before this verse was the appeal, "O LORD, save Your people, The remnant of Israel!" (Jer. 31:7).

In Romans, Paul devotes three chapters (9-11) to a discussion of this "remnant." After declaring his prayer for the salvation of his "countrymen according to the flesh" (9:3), as noted several times above, he makes the revolutionary assertion "they are not all Israel who are of Israel" (9:6). Let's note some teachings that follow this. Paul quotes Isaiah 10:22-23, but let's note some differences in Paul's wording and that of the Hebrew text along with some verses that come before the passage in Isaiah:

Though the number of the children of Israel be as the sand of the sea, The remnant will be saved. For He will finish the work and cut it short in righteousness, Because the LORD will make a short work upon the earth (Rom. 9:27-28).

And it shall come to pass in that day That the remnant of Israel, And such as have escaped of the house of Jacob, Will never again depend on him who defeated them, But will depend on the LORD, the Holy One of Israel, in truth. The remnant will return, the remnant of Jacob, To the Mighty God. **For though your people, O Israel, be as the sand of the sea, A remnant of them will return; The destruction decreed shall overflow with righteousness. For the Lord GOD of hosts Will make a determined end In the midst of all the land** (Isa. 10:20-23).

The wording from Isaiah shows an immediate application of this text to the captivity of the northern kingdom of Israel under Assyria. In fact, before this passage a rebuke is given to Assyria (Isa. 10:5-19) and after it the Lord declares, "Therefore thus says the Lord GOD of hosts: 'O My people, who dwell in Zion, do not be afraid of the Assyrian. He shall strike you with a rod and lift up his staff against you, in the manner of Egypt. For yet a very little while and the indignation will cease, as will My anger in their destruction'" (Isa. 10:24-25). Paul uses this to apply to the "remnant" of those who will accept the gospel to show that the focus of God's deliverance has always been upon those of His people who are willing to follow Him in truth. He explains further, "Even so then, at this present time there is a remnant according to the election of grace" (Rom. 11:5). Remember he has already described those who follow the gospel (Rom. 1:16) as being "not under law, but under grace" (Rom. 6:14-15). The "remnant" of Israel according to the flesh and those who are part of this "election of grace" are those who accept and follow the system of grace found in Christ Jesus. Will this be a *gathering* that Paul anticipated in the future? No. Paul asks further, "For if their being cast away is the reconciling of the world, what will their acceptance be but life from the dead?" (Rom. 11:15). Israel according to the flesh had been "cast away" and this had already allowed for the "reconciling of the world" (cf. Rom. 5:10-11—a present condition when Paul wrote this). Why were they "cast away"? He continues, "Because of unbelief they were broken off" (Rom. 11:19). While AD 70 would be a judgment on Israel, those who refused to believe in the Messiah were already "cast away" and "broken off." How may they be included within this remnant? He explains, "If they do not continue in unbelief, will be grafted in, for God is able to graft them in again" (Rom. 11:23). This is not a collective *grafting in*, just as belief and unbelief is not a collective measure of one's relationship to God. Individual Jews (according to the flesh) who accept Jesus as the Messiah can be included within the "remnant" that was already *gathered* upon the proclamation of the gospel. This is how, "all Israel will be saved, as it is written: 'The Deliverer will come out of Zion, and He will turn away ungodliness from Jacob; For this is My covenant with them, when I take away their sins'" (Rom. 11:26-27; quoting Isa. 59:20-21). Christ was this Deliverer, the sacrifice for sins was offered at the cross, and the true remnant of Israel that "will be saved" are those who accept and obey the gospel. This was a gathering that was already happening long before AD 70. So, the *gathering* of Jeremiah 31:10 of this "remnant" (Jer. 31:7) must be understood in the same way. It would not be a *gathering* in AD 70, it had already begun before that time.

6. "And I will bring them out from the peoples and gather them from the countries, and will bring them to their own land; I will feed them on the mountains of Israel, in the valleys and in all the inhabited places of the country" (Ezek. 34:13). Once again, we would agree that this has Messianic overtones, but it was accomplished at the cross and in the gospel of Jesus Christ. Consider Paul's words:

> Now all things are of God, who has reconciled us to Himself through Jesus Christ, and has given us the ministry of reconciliation, that is, that God was in Christ reconciling the world to Himself, not imputing their trespasses to them, and has committed to us the word of reconciliation. Now then, we are ambassadors for Christ, as though God were pleading through us: we implore you on Christ's behalf, be reconciled to God (2 Cor. 5:18-20).

If God, in Christ had already reconciled "the world to Himself," and the apostles, as His ambassadors could already make the appeal, "be reconciled to God," this *gathering* foretold by the prophets had already occurred.

7. "Thus says the Lord GOD: 'Surely I will take the children of Israel from among the nations, wherever they have gone, and will gather them from every side and bring them into their own land; and I will make them one nation in the land, on the mountains of Israel; and one king shall be king over them all; they shall no longer be two nations, nor shall they ever be divided into two kingdoms again'" (Ezek. 37:21-22). This text comes in a prophecy the Lord revealed to Ezekiel of two sticks—one representing Judah and the other representing Ephraim (the son of Joseph) often used to refer to the northern kingdom of Israel (Ezek. 37:16). The Lord promises a reunion of the two kingdoms (37:17-20). This foreshadows a reunion under the Messiah. Ezekiel is told, "David My servant shall be king over them, and they shall all have one shepherd; they shall also walk in My judgments and observe My statutes, and do them" (Ezek. 37:24). This would not be David reincarnated, but Jesus (a descendent of David) who would reign on David's throne. Before Mary's conception, the angel announced to her, "He will be great, and will be called the Son of the Highest; and the Lord God will give Him the throne of His father David" (Luke 1:32).

Ezekiel's prophecy helps us determine some things about when this *gathering* would happen. Ezekiel is told, "I will make them one nation" and "one king shall be king over them all." When did the Messiah have a "nation" and when did Jesus reign as "king over them all"? Peter told Christians (before AD 70) "But you are a chosen generation, a royal priesthood, A HOLY NATION, His own special people, that you may proclaim the praises of Him who called you out of darkness into His marvelous light" (1 Pet. 2:9, emphasis mine). Ezekiel was told these reunited peoples would be "one nation," yet Peter says it was already *gathered* before AD 70. Before His ascension, Jesus proclaimed that He had "all authority" both "in heaven and on earth" (Matt. 28:18). We have used this for years to show premillennialists that Jesus already reigns over His kingdom. The preterist must see the same thing. Jesus was already the "one king" reigning over the promised "one nation" that was gathered of both Jews and Gentiles through the gospel long before AD 70.

8. **"Yet the number of the children of Israel Shall be as the sand of the sea, Which cannot be measured or numbered. And it shall come to pass In the place where it was said to them, 'You are not My people,' There it shall be said to them, 'You are sons of the living God.' Then the children of Judah and the children of Israel Shall be gathered together, And appoint for themselves one head; And they shall come up out of the land, For great will be the day of Jezreel!"** (Hosea 1:10-11). Hosea, of course, was the prophet called to take a wife of harlotry to illustrate by his own life God's patience with Israel and Judah in the face of their continued unfaithfulness. These words are quoted by Paul in the discussion mentioned above on the "remnant" in Romans. Paul first quotes from Hosea 2:23, "As He says also in Hosea: 'I will call them My people, who were not My people, and her beloved, who was not beloved'" (Rom. 9:25), and then quotes Hosea 1:10, "And it shall come to pass in the place where it was said to them, 'You are not My people,' There they shall be called sons of the living God" (Rom. 9:26). In the context, the prophet is called to proclaim judgment upon the sinful northern kingdom of Israel. In her judgment, God will consider her, "Lo, Ammi" (meaning "not My people"), the Lord says, "For you are not My people" (Hosea 1:9). The promise of Hosea 1:10-11 promises God's willingness to receive her people back after this judgment—a promise fulfilled in part when Jews scattered throughout the world returned throughout the years and ultimately through the call of the gospel. Paul's use in Romans is interesting. He applies it not only to the dispersed Jews, but to Gentiles (Rom. 9:24). Like Israel of old, although they were not the people of God, they would be allowed to be considered "sons of the living God." When did God extend this acceptance? Paul taught, "you are all sons of God through faith in Christ Jesus. For as many of you as were baptized into Christ have put on Christ" (Gal. 3:26-27). Jesus sent out His apostles to make disciples by teaching and baptizing them before His ascension (Matt. 28:19-20). Not only does this show us that souls were considered "sons of the living God" well before AD 70, but Paul's use of this text once again demonstrates the redefinition of the true Israel as those who obey God in truth.

9. "I will surely assemble all of you, O Jacob, I will surely gather the remnant of Israel; I will put them together like sheep of the fold, Like a flock in the midst of their pasture; They shall make a loud noise because of so many people" (Micah 2:12). Agreed, this is Messianic, but the *flock,* the *remnant,* and the *gathering* of both happened in the cross and the gospel.

10. "Now it shall come to pass in the latter days that the mountain of the LORD'S house shall be established on the top of the mountains, and shall be exalted above the hills; and peoples shall flow to it. Many nations shall come and say, 'Come, and let us go up to the mountain of the LORD, to the house of the God of Jacob; He will teach us His ways, and we shall walk in His paths.' For out of Zion the law shall go forth, and the word of the LORD from Jerusalem. He shall judge between many peoples, and rebuke strong nations afar off; they shall beat their swords into plowshares, and their spears into pruning hooks; nation shall not lift up sword against nation, neither shall they learn war any more. But everyone shall sit under his vine and under his fig tree, and no one shall make them afraid; For the mouth of the LORD of hosts has spoken. For all people walk each in the name of his god, but we will walk in the name of the LORD our God forever and ever. 'In that day,' says the LORD, 'I will assemble the lame, I will gather the outcast and those whom I have afflicted; I will make the lame a remnant, and the outcast a strong nation; So the LORD will reign over them in Mount Zion from now on, even forever" (Micah 4:1-7). As we noticed in our study on the Song of Moses, Isaiah 2:2-4 parallels Micah 4:1-3. However, beginning in verse 4 ("But everyone shall sit under his vine . . .") the text of Micah diverges from the text of Isaiah. We should note several points from this text:

- It will happen "in the latter days."—Jesus offered His life as a sacrifice for sins "at the end of the ages" (Heb. 9:26).
- "Many nations" shall come "to the house of the God of Jacob."—Christ, "abolished in His flesh the enmity, that is, the law of commandments contained in ordinances, so as to create in Himself one new man from the two, thus making peace, and that He might reconcile them both to God in one body through the cross, thereby putting to death the enmity" (Eph. 2:15-16). In Christ, "there is neither Greek nor Jew, circumcised nor uncircumcised, barbarian, Scythian, slave nor free, but Christ is all and in all" (Col. 3:11).

- **"Nation shall not lift up sword against nation, neither shall they learn war any more."**—"He Himself is our peace, who has made both one, and has broken down the middle wall of separation" (Eph. 2:14). "And He came and preached peace to you who were afar off and to those who were near. For through Him we both have access by one Spirit to the Father" (Eph. 2:17-19).
- **At this time "out of Zion the law shall go forth, and the word of the LORD from Jerusalem."**—The apostles were told, "you shall be witnesses to Me in Jerusalem, and in all Judea and Samaria, and to the end of the earth" (Acts 1:8).
- **"The LORD will reign over them in Mount Zion from now on, even forever."**—"He has delivered us from the power of darkness and conveyed us into the kingdom of the Son of His love" (Col. 1:13). The kingdom of the Messiah, "shall stand forever" (Dan. 2:44).

All of these characteristics apply to what Christ accomplished by the cross, in the gospel, and the establishment of His kingdom, the church. This was not a *gathering* awaiting the destruction of Jerusalem.

Summary

There are many other similar Scriptures we could consider, but these all demonstrate the same basic principles. In her book, after considering the texts above, Collins drew the following conclusion, "All of these gatherings refer to the same event. That event is the 'gathering together in one all things in Christ' (Eph. 1:10)" (13). We have seen that some of these texts have nothing to do with a gathering under the Messiah and those that do apply to what was accomplished at the cross and in the establishment of the Lord's church. Her citation of Ephesians 1:10 is interesting. She seems to imagine that this was something that was not accomplished until AD 70. Is that what the text teaches?

The full text reads, "That in the dispensation of the fullness of the times He might gather together in one all things in Christ, both which are in heaven and which are on earth—in Him" (Eph. 1:10). We note that Christ is said to "gather together in one all things" in a time referred to as "the dispensation" (or "administration" NASB, GLT, LO) "of the fullness of the times." When was this? Before and after this Paul speaks of this as a condition that has been accomplished. He says, "In Him we have redemption" (1:7), His grace, "He made to abound toward us" (1:8), "having made known to us the mystery of His will" (1:9), and "In Him also we have obtained an inheritance" (1:11). If

Collins applies these gathering passages to Ephesians 1:10 she is unwittingly applying them to a condition that applied before AD 70. We are in full agreement with that. This is not a *gathering* at AD 70.

The Application of Hebrews 10:25

So how should this impact our understanding of Hebrews 10:25? If these gathering passages prophesied in the Old Testament pointed to the cross and the church—if such a gathering under the Messiah had already occurred—is the Hebrew writer urging the reader not to turn away from this? Perhaps. To return to the Mosaic Law would be turning away from the reconciliation of all "things on earth or things in heaven, having made peace through the blood of His cross" (Col. 1:20). It would restore the separation between Jew and Gentile and leave these Jewish Christians in a condition in which "there no longer remains a sacrifice for sins" (Heb. 10:27). Yet, that interpretation treats the book of Hebrews as if it is the book of Galatians. The churches in Galatia were "turning away so soon from Him who called you in the grace of Christ, to a different gospel" (Gal. 1:6). They struggled with separating themselves from Gentile believers (Gal. 2:11-21) and seeking to return to the Law for justification (Gal. 5:4). The writer of the book of Hebrews, on the other hand, rebukes his readers for their immaturity (Heb. 5:12-6:3), which he tells them prevents him from being able to explain meatier things to them (Heb. 5:11). His focus is on helping them understand how the Mosaic Covenant pointed to the New Covenant. That is not the same as turning back to Mosaic Law.

Let's look closer at Hebrews 10:25 and consider it within its context:

23 **Let us hold fast the confession of our hope without wavering, for He who promised is faithful.**—He wants them to be faithful, in the recognition that God is faithful.

24 **And let us consider one another in order to stir up love and good works**—This faithfulness has a collective aspect to it. Consideration of "one another" allows one believer to "stir up" within another believer "love and good works." This is personal, but it contributes to the collective good.

25 **not forsaking the assembling of ourselves together, as is the manner of some, but exhorting one another, and so much the more as you see the Day approaching.**—Certainly a failure to recognize the important nature of what it means to be a part of this gathering together of God's people would not lead believers to exhort one another, but again, there is a very personal element here that calls each Christian to see his or her duty to strengthen the collective. This

reminds us of Paul's instructions regarding church discipline—"In the name of our Lord Jesus Christ, when you are gathered together, along with my spirit, with the power of our Lord Jesus Christ" (1 Cor. 5:4). They were to collectively act for the benefit of each individual soul.

26 For if we sin willfully after we have received the knowledge of the truth, there no longer remains a sacrifice for sins, but a certain fearful expectation of judgment, and fiery indignation which will devour the adversaries (Heb. 10:23-26). Yes, this could carry a sense of turning away from Christ's sacrifice in turning back to Mosaic Law, yet in the context of the book as a whole this more likely describes what can result when faithfulness is not maintained (10:23) and members do not exhort one another (10:27). Neglect of the grandeur of the gathering of souls in submission to the Messiah could result in that, but even it would be seen only in how it was manifested in the Christian's relationships toward other Christians (i.e., their assembling together in local churches).

Collins argues that, "The gathering which some were forsaking by turning back to Judaism, was coming soon (the Hebrews could see the day of the gathering approaching); Hebrews 10:37 states that it would arrive in a very, very little while and "The Coming One" (WEY) would not tarry" (9). This ignores what we have already observed, that the *gathering* of the remnant of Israel together with the Gentiles under the Messiah had already taken place. It assumes that the readers would have read the word "Day" and interpret it as the preterist does to refer to AD 70. Can the context of Hebrews support that assumption?

In the book, we believe we can identify at least two *days* to which the author has previously alluded that could be the "Day" he says they could *see* "approaching." In the previous chapter he wrote, "as it is appointed for men to die once, but after this the judgment, so Christ was offered once to bear the sins of many. To those who eagerly wait for Him He will appear a second time, apart from sin, for salvation" (Heb. 9:27-28). Although he does not use the word "Day," it seems very likely that the reader would immediately recall this foreboding promise of Christ's "second" coming "for salvation." Jesus spoke often of the "last day" (John 6:39, 40, 44, 54; 11:24; 12:48).

A second, yet very similar possibility comes even earlier in the book. He writes, "There remains therefore a rest for the people of God. For he who has entered His rest has himself also ceased from his works as God did from His. Let us therefore be diligent to enter that rest, lest anyone fall according to the same example of disobedience" (Heb. 4:9-11). Now, in one sense the writer had declared that as Christians, "we who have believed do enter that rest" (Heb. 4:3), in 4:9 he makes it clear that something still awaits the believer— "There remains therefore a rest for the people of God." This is not to suggest that the "rest" described here is different from the "salvation" described in 9:28, but in the context it stands as another possible antecedent of the term "Day approaching."

Collins points out that the word translated "the assembling" is the Greek word *episunagōgē* (ἐπισυναγωγή), defined as "(1) a gathering together in one place, (2) the (religious) assembly (of Christians)" (Thayer), and points out the only other passage where it is used in 2 Thessalonians 2:1. We should first note that (with the omission prefix *epi*, which merely intensifies the noun) this is the word used throughout Scripture usually translated "synagogue"— applied to congregations of Jewish worshippers each Sabbath. James used the Greek word *sunagōgē* in reference to a Christian assembly of a local church in James 2:2. So, the most natural application in Hebrews 10:25 would carry the same meaning—don't stop *synagoging* yourselves together (so to speak). But, let's look at its other usage. 2 Thessalonians 2:1-2 reads, "Now, brethren, concerning the coming of our Lord Jesus Christ and our gathering together (*episunagōgē*) to Him, we ask you, not to be soon shaken in mind or troubled, either by spirit or by word or by letter, as if from us, as though the day of Christ had come." The preterist would understand this to refer to the Lord's coming in judgment on Jerusalem in AD 70, and at that time gathering together His people as the "New Jerusalem" promised in Revelation 21-22. If we go back to Hebrews, however, two chapters after 10:25, the writer declares

> . . . You have come to Mount Zion and to the city of the living God, the heavenly Jerusalem, to an innumerable company of angels, to the general assembly and church of the firstborn who are registered in heaven, to God the Judge of all, to the spirits of just men made perfect, to Jesus the Mediator of the new covenant, and to the blood of sprinkling that speaks better things than that of Abel (Heb. 12:22-24).

If the writer says his readers already had come to the "heavenly Jerusalem," which he equates with the *church* and those *registered in heaven*, that can hardly be the sense in which "the New Jerusalem" is being described in Revelation, nor a "Day approaching" in AD 70 as preterists imagine it.

So what is the sense of *episunagōgē* in 2 Thessalonians 2:1? While it is conceivable that Paul is urging them, in light of either Jesus's first coming (or future second coming), not to allow false claims that it had already happened to lead them to neglect their responsibility to the local assemblies of the church—that is probably not the sense of Paul's use. It may be that it is used of the *gathering* under the Messiah, yet the fact that this gathering under the Messiah had already occurred before AD 70 precludes us from taking it to refer to an AD 70 *gathering* (as preterists conceive it).

More likely, is the sense used in the Olivet Discourse (which we shall discuss in depth later in these studies). Jesus declares that the Son of Man, "will send His angels with a great sound of a trumpet, and they will gather together His elect from the four winds, from one end of heaven to the other" (Matt. 24:31). Now, we recognize that the full-preterist (and even some partial-preterists) apply this to AD 70, but consider some things. If, as we have already shown, a type of *gathering* had already occurred well before AD 70, we would have to conclude that this *gathering together of the elect*, must be a different kind of gathering. Both preterists and non-preterists must admit that! So, if we can agree that this is a different *gathering* the only question is "when would it occur?"

If this is the sense of 2 Thessalonians 2:1, Paul is talking to those who may have heard false claims that "the Day of Christ" had already occurred. This would easily lead them to be "shaken in mind or troubled" imagining that they had missed out on Christ's calling together of His elect. That seems to me to be a reasonable interpretation of the text.

Conclusion

We have demonstrated that the Law of Moses as a binding standard before God ended at the cross. We have also shown that the *gathering* foretold in the Old Testament Scriptures was accomplished in the proclamation of the gospel and establishment of the church. A question that we must ask if it is true that Jews were still *under* Mosaic Law is how was sin determined? As Paul taught Jews and Gentiles, to what could he appeal in order to define those sins from which they should repent? If two laws were then in force, would it not result in confusion? This is much like the view that some have embraced that the alien sinner is not "amenable to law toward Christ." If today, two laws are in force what determines and defines sin? If two laws were in force from the cross to AD 70, what determined and defined sin during that period? "God is not the author of confusion" (1 Cor. 14:33). After the cross, it is the Law of Christ to which all souls are now accountable.

THE RESURRECTION OF THE DEAD

A fundamental doctrine espoused by many preterists concerns their understanding of biblical promises regarding the resurrection of the dead. Full-preterists do not believe that there will be a future bodily resurrection of all human souls who have ever lived upon the earth, but contend that most passages referring to resurrection must be interpreted as spiritual, figurative, or even collective descriptions of the revival of a cause or a condition of fellowship with God. In this, preterism dramatically departs from what has been taught for the last 2000 years by virtually all who have held a belief in Jesus as the Messiah.

Spiritual Resurrections

Clearly, there are times in which Scripture speaks of resurrection in spiritual or figurative terms. Ezekiel's vision of a valley filled with dry bones is an example of this (Ezek. 37:1-14). At a time when the Jewish exiles felt as if they were hopeless dry bones, Ezekiel was shown a restoration back to life of a valley full of bones, whom God identifies as "the whole house of Israel" (Ezek. 37:11). They were not literally dead, nor literally in their graves, but God promised a time when they would be restored back to life in their "own land" (Ezek. 37:14). In a similar way, in John's visions in Revelation, after the fall of Babylon—identified as Rome in Revelation 17:9 and 17:18—souls who had died for their testimony of Jesus are said to live again a reign with Christ for one thousand years (Rev. 20:4). Although this is called "the first resurrection" (Rev. 20:5b-6), nothing is ever said about it being a bodily resurrection upon the earth. It is the resurrection of the cause for which they died, not an inferred *second* resurrection that will one day involve "the rest of the dead" (Rev. 20:5a). So, just because Scripture speaks of spiritual or figurative types of resurrection doesn't mean there will never be a literal bodily resurrection.

Jesus and Peter's Exposition of Resurrection Passages

It is often asserted that bodily resurrection was not taught in the Old Testament. It is interesting, however, to note two subtle passages that Jesus and Peter appeal to in defense of the resurrection. When Jesus was questioned by the Sadducees, "who say there is no resurrection" (Matt. 22:23; Mark 12:18; cf. Acts 23:8; Luke 20:27), Jesus appealed to Exodus 3:6—"I am the God of Abraham, the God of Isaac, and the God of Jacob"—declaring that it proves "concerning the dead, that they rise" (Mark 12:26; cf. Matt. 22:31; Luke 20:37). We should note, although no explicit statement about resurrection is found in Exodus 3:6, Jesus argued that it was the necessary inference of the text in the fact that God, "is not the God of the dead, but the God of the living" (Mark 12:27; cf. Matt 22:32; Luke 20:37). This is a remarkable interpretation! Jesus doesn't merely say this proves these patriarchs are still alive, but that "they rise" (Mark 12:26) or "are raised" (Luke 20:37). Here Jesus uses the present tense, so does that mean this is spiritual and collective resurrection? Does it mean they have already risen? No. Jesus also said, one day "all who are in the graves WILL hear His voice and come forth" (John 5:28-29, emphasis mine). If Exodus 3:6 means Abraham, Isaac, and Jacob have already experienced a spiritual resurrection Jesus could not say they (with all in the graves) "will" one day "come forth" from their graves. Instead, He declares that the personal, living condition of these patriarchs proves that the dead (generally) will one day rise.

Peter draws a similar inference from David's words, "For You will not leave my soul in Hades, Nor will You allow Your Holy One to see corruption" (Acts 2:27; Ps. 16:10). Peter explained:

> Therefore, being a prophet, and knowing that God had sworn with an oath to him that of the fruit of his body, according to the flesh, He would raise up the Christ to sit on his throne, he, foreseeing this, spoke concerning the resurrection of the Christ, that His soul was not left in Hades, nor did His flesh see corruption (Acts 2:30-31).

Peter, through the Holy Spirit argued that David's words necessarily inferred that Christ would be resurrected. If these subtle passages infer the reality of the resurrection of Christ and the dead generally, how many other passages in the Old Testament affirm similar principles?

The Resurrection in Daniel

One of the most explicit Old Testament Scriptures that addresses the resurrection is Daniel 12:2—"many of those who sleep in the dust of the earth shall awake, Some to everlasting life, some to shame and everlasting contempt." Preterists deny that this is promising a literal bodily resurrection, and appeal to Daniel 12:7 in defense of their contention. It reads, "when the power of the holy people has been completely shattered, all these things shall be finished." Their argument is that however Daniel 12:2 is understood, it must be interpreted in light of Daniel 12:7. In Don Preston's 2015 debate with

Jason Wallace on preterism, Daniel 12:7 was one of the major texts he introduced to defend his conclusion that it points to the AD 70 destruction of Jerusalem. Preston argued that in AD 70 there was a spiritual, collective resurrection, and judgment of the just and unjust that ushered in a new age that he argues will never end. Although Preston believes that judgment happens to each individual at the point of death, and the righteous will live with God in heaven, he does not believe in a literal bodily resurrection of the dead, or a final day of judgment at which time the present universe will be destroyed, and the resurrected assigned to heaven or hell.[1]

Since this interpretation figures so prominently in preterist teaching, we would like to begin our study of what the Bible teaches on the resurrection of the dead by looking in depth at what Daniel 12 is teaching on this subject. As one of the most explicit passages in the Old Testament on the subject of the resurrection of the dead, it stands to reason that whatever it teaches has a bearing on how we should understand any later teachings on the subject in the New Testament.

Analysis of Daniel 12:2 and 7

These verses come at the end of a vision given to Daniel by an unnamed angel who speaks to Daniel, in answer to his prayer of collective repentance in the third year of Cyrus (Dan. 10:1). The vision spans 10:1-12:13. It is described as revealing to Daniel, "what will happen to your people in the latter days," explaining further that it "refers to many days yet to come" (Dan. 10:14). For our purposes, let's focus on chapters 11 and 12. This section begins with the angel declaring, "in the first year of Darius the Mede, I, even I, stood up to confirm and strengthen him" (Dan. 11:1). He then declares:

> And now I will tell you the truth: Behold, three more kings will arise in Persia, and the fourth shall be far richer than them all; by his strength, through his riches, he shall stir up all against the realm of Greece. Then a mighty king shall arise, who shall rule with great dominion, and do according to his will. And when he has arisen, his kingdom shall be broken up and divided toward the four winds of heaven, but not among his posterity nor according to his dominion with which he ruled; for his kingdom shall be uprooted, even for others besides these. (Dan. 11:2-4)

This appears to describe the campaigns of Darius I and his son Xerxes I against the Greek city states, that served to "stir up all against the realm of Greece." This ultimately led to the rise of Alexander the Great, who conquered Darius III, taking his kingdom in 330 BC. Upon his death, Alexan-

---

[1] "Don K Preston Debates Jason Wallace on the Validity of Preterism," September 12, 2015, https://www.youtube.com/watch?v=PjOMCLbPhvc.

der's kingdom was divided among his generals. The dynasty that began from his commander Ptolemy appears to be what is referred to in the vision as the "king of the south" (11:5, 6, 9, 11, 14, 15, 25, 29, 40), while the dynasty that began from his commander Seleucus appears to be what is referred to in the vision as the "king of the north" (11:6, 7, 8, 9, 11, 13, 15, 40, 44). Palestine became a continual battleground between these two kingdoms, with each controlling the region during different periods of time. The climax of the vision describes the horrible events of the reign of Antiochus IV, called Epiphanes (215 BC – 164 BC), who persecuted the Jews during his control of Palestine. His action to set up idol worship in the temple of Jerusalem was identified by Jews as the "abomination of desolation" foretold in the vision (1 Maccabees 1:54; cf. Babylonian Talmud, *Ta'anith* 28b).

As the vision continues we should note several references to "the end." The context allows us to determine what *end* is being considered. The angel declares, "And at the end of some years"—referring to the end of this series of particular events—"they shall join forces, for the daughter of the king of the South shall go to the king of the North to make an agreement; but she shall not retain the power of her authority, and neither he nor his authority shall stand; but she shall be given up, with those who brought her, and with him who begot her, and with him who strengthened her in those times" (Dan. 11:6). Later, he relates, "For the king of the North will return and muster a multitude greater than the former, and shall certainly come at the end of some years with a great army and much equipment" (Dan. 11:13). This is not the same "end" as in 11:6. It is the "end" of this series of particular events. Five verses later, he continues, "After this he shall turn his face to the coastlands, and shall take many. But a ruler shall bring the reproach against them to an end"—referring to the end of the reproach—"and with the reproach removed, he shall turn back on him" (Dan. 11:18). This is not "the end" of 11:6 or of 11:13, but the end of "reproach against them."

It is not until verse 27 that an *end* is mentioned that is more than just the completion of events that are being described. The angel continues, "Both these kings' hearts shall be bent on evil, and they shall speak lies at the same table; but it shall not prosper, for the end will still be at the appointed time" (Dan. 11:27). What end does this describe? Is it the end of their efforts? Is it the end of their power? Twice after this the text speaks of "the appointed time." Two verses later it speaks of a change in the plans of one of these kings "at the appointed time" (11:29) when "ships from Cyprus [Heb. *Kittim*] shall come against him" (11:30a). *Kittim* is the usual Hebrew name for the island of Cyprus, which was already controlled by Rome at the time of Antiochus IV. In Qumran texts of the Dead Sea Scrolls *Kittim* is the standard designation used to refer to Rome. If that is the sense, some believe that this refers to an event when Roman forces blocked Antiochus' efforts against Cyprus and compelled him to withdraw from Egypt (Polybius, *The Histories* 29.27.4; Livy, *The History of Rome* 45.12.4ff.). Does that identify the "end" of 11:27 with the "appointed time" of 11:29-30a when Antiochus power would be curtailed? If so, while it was the beginning of the end of Antiochus' power, it was not the end of his persecution of the Jews.

The angel tells Daniel that when this happens, "he shall be grieved, and return in rage against the holy covenant, and do damage. So he shall return and show regard for those who forsake the holy covenant" (11:30b). We should note that his rage is against "the holy covenant," yet that doesn't seem to mean he was angry at God's word or His covenant with Israel. He was angry with those who *kept* the "holy covenant," and showed favor towards those who would "forsake the holy covenant." Does this have any bearing on those referred to in 12:7 as the "holy people"? What do we know about the events prophesied here?

The historical book of 1 Maccabees (included by Roman Catholics and Eastern Orthodox churches in their Bibles) describes events during the reign of Antiochus Epiphanes that parallel what Daniel prophesies. While we do not believe this is an inspired text, we can appreciate it as a historical witness to the events that took place in the period between the Old and New Testaments. Let's note the prophecies of Daniel 11 and their fulfillment as recorded in 1 Maccabees:

31 And forces shall be mustered by him, and they shall defile the sanctuary fortress; then they shall take away the daily sacrifices, and place there the abomination of desolation.—1 Maccabees records that during the reign of Antiochus Epiphanes, many Jews, "abandoned the holy covenant. They joined with the Gentiles and sold themselves to do evil" (1 Macc. 1:15, RSV; cf. Dan. 11:30b). Antiochus first looted the temple (1 Macc. 1:21-23), then later sent a great force to Jerusalem (1 Macc. 1:29), that "plundered the city, burned it with fire, and tore down its houses and its surrounding walls. And they took captive the women and children, and seized the cattle" (1 Macc. 1:31-32). Antiochus gave the command that all under his rule should serve the Greek gods and "forget the law" of Moses (1 Macc. 1:49) which included the end of temple sacrifice, sabbaths, and feasts (1 Macc. 1:45), circumcision of children (1 Macc. 1:48), and began the worship of idols (1 Macc. 1:47). Daniel's reference to "the abomination of desolation" is significant. 1 Maccabees uses this exact wording, recording, "Now the fifteenth day of the month Casleu, in the hundred forty and fifth year, they set up the abomination of desolation upon the altar, and builded [sic] idol altars throughout the cities of Judah on every side" (1:54, KJV; cf. Dan. 11:31; 12:11).

32 Those who do wickedly against the covenant he shall corrupt with flattery; but the people who know their God shall be strong, and carry out great exploits.—1 Maccabees records that failure to follow the command of Antiochus was a capital offense. The command included the warning, "And whoever does not obey the command of the king shall die" (1 Macc. 1:50, RSV). Sadly, "Many of the people, every one who forsook the law, joined them, and they did evil in the land" (1 Macc. 1:52).

33 And those of the people who understand shall instruct many; yet for many days they shall fall by sword and flame, by captivity and plundering.—We should note that the text speaks here of those who "shall fall by the sword and flame." We must remember this in the next two verses that further describe this "fall." While a fall by "captivity and plunder" might not involve death, a "fall by the sword and flame" most certainly would (cf. Ps. 78:64; Ezek. 39:23). 1 Maccabees records that during this time books of Old Testament Scriptures were burned (1 Macc. 1:56) and those who followed the Mosaic Law were killed (1 Macc. 1:57). During this chilling time, the text records: "According to the decree, they put to death the women who had their children circumcised, and their families and those who circumcised them; and they hung the infants from their mothers' necks" (1 Macc. 1:60-61).

34-35 Now when they fall, they shall be aided with a little help; but many shall join with them by intrigue. And some of those of understanding shall fall, to refine them, purify them, and make them white, until the time of the end; because it is still for the appointed time.—1 Maccabees records, "But many in Israel stood firm and were resolved in their hearts not to eat unclean food. They chose to die rather than to be defiled by food or to profane the holy covenant; and they did die" (1 Macc. 1:62-63). We should note that the angel tells Daniel "those of understanding SHALL FALL" (emphasis mine), in other words they will "fall by the sword and flame" (Dan. 11:33), that is they will die. And yet, they will fall, "to refine them, purify them, and make them white." We must remember this as we consider the meaning of 12:2 on resurrection. Notice what Daniel is told and how it parallels this text.

Daniel 12:3	Daniel 11:35
Those who are wise	And some of those of understanding
shall shine like the brightness of the firmament,	shall fall, to refine them, purify them, and make them white,
And those who turn many to righteousness	[those of the people who understand shall instruct many—Dan. 11:34]
like the stars forever and ever	until the time of the end; because it is still for the appointed time

We must ask here, when are these people said to be *purified, refined,* and *made white?* It is *after* they have fallen (i.e., after they died). We must also note that the time this will happen is at "the time of the end," which is also said to be, "for the appointed time." This "end" cannot be the same as 11:6, 11:13, or even 11:27. Remember, although 11:27 may correspond to "the appointed time" of 11:29 that would speak of the end of Antiochus' power. This looks to an "end" and "appointed time" beyond the time when his persecution comes to an end. So that means we have at least the fifth distinct use of "end" in the same vision with a distinct meaning.

As the vision draws to a close, the angel tells more details about this tumultuous time, but let's note a few specifics. He tells Daniel, "At the time of the end the king of the South shall attack him; and the king of the North shall come against him like a whirlwind, with chariots, horsemen, and with many ships; and he shall enter the countries, overwhelm them, and pass through" (Dan. 11:40). This appear to refer to the "end" of Antiochus' dominion, as is echoed in the final verse of the chapter—"And he shall plant the tents of his palace between the seas and the glorious holy mountain; yet he shall come to his end, and no one will help him" (Dan. 11:45). If this refers to the "end" of Antiochus' reign, we could say that this it is the same as the end of 11:40 and 11:27-29, which also speak of the "end" of Antiochus' reign (and thus the wicked persecution of the Jews).

We should note that preterists do not share this understanding of the end of chapter eleven. A website called *A Preterist Bible Commentary* operated by Daniel Morris argues that a transition occurs in the vision at verse 35 that shifts to prophecies that concern Rome's deeds in Palestine rather than the end of the reign of Antiochus.[2] Don K. Preston also believes in a transition to Rome, but in his debate he expressed a belief that it takes place in verse 45.

---

2 https://revelationrevolution.org/daniel-chapter-11-35-45-commentary-every-prophecy-miraculously-fulfilled/

Identifying such a transition is necessary to the preterist interpretation if the reader is going to associate 12:7 with the events of AD 70, but we find nothing in the text to support that conclusion. After speaking of the fallen in 11:35, note all of the subjects of the verbs that follow:

- **Then the king shall do . . . he shall exalt and magnify himself . . .** (11:36). Note: the antecedent of the pronoun "he" comes in 11:32— "he shall corrupt with flattery." All of the references to "he," or "him,," or "his" that follow must reasonably apply to the same subject unless we can grammatically identify a different subject.
- **He shall regard neither . . . he shall exalt himself . . .** (11:37).
- **He shall honor . . . he shall honor with gold . . .** (11:38).
- **Thus he shall act against . . . which he shall acknowledge . . .**(11:39).
- **At the time of the end the king of the South shall attack him; and the king of the North shall come against him . . . he shall enter the countries, overwhelm them, and pass through** (11:40). Note: In this verse it is unclear whether the final pronoun "he" refers to the "king of the North" or shifts back to the "he" of all of the previous verses. If it is the "king of the North" we could argue that he continues to be the subject of all the following references to "he" or "his."
- **He shall also enter the Glorious Land . . .** (11:41).
- **He shall stretch out his hand against the countries . . .** (11:42).
- **He shall have power over . . .** (11:43).
- **But news from the east and the north shall trouble him; therefore he shall go out with great fury to destroy and annihilate many** (11:44).
- **And he shall plant the tents of his palace . . . yet he shall come to his end, and no one will help him** (11:45).

Grammatically the only possibility for a shift in subjects comes in verse 40, but if so it leaves the account of Antiochus hanging. It seems much more reasonable to understand the final verses as a prophetic description of the end of the reign of this wicked leader.

That brings us to the final chapter, where our questions rest. It begins, "At that time Michael shall stand up, the great prince who stands watch over the sons of your people" (Dan. 12:1a). From the New Testament we understand that "Michael" is an archangel (Jude 9) who has charge of other angels (Rev. 12:7). Although in Daniel he is called "your prince," a "great prince," or "one of the chief princes," this is the third time he is mentioned in the vision. In Daniel 10:13 the unnamed angel says Michael came to his aid in fighting against the "prince of Persia" (presumably an evil angel aiding Persia against God's people). In Daniel 10:21, he echoes the same idea, speaking of the "prince of Persia" and "the prince of Greece" in 10:20, explaining, "no one upholds me against these, except Michael your prince" (Dan. 10:21). This makes it clear that Michael works in the unseen spiritual realm to aid God's people in some ways against the forces of evil.

The text continues, "And there shall be a time of trouble, such as never was since there was a nation, even to that time" (Dan. 12:1b). Preterists fittingly notice the similarity between this statement and Jesus's words in the Olivet Discourse. In a text that we would agree, clearly describes the events leading to the AD 70 destruction of Jerusalem, Jesus declares, "For then there will be great tribulation, such as has not been since the beginning of the world until this time, no, nor ever shall be" (Matt. 24:21). We should note a significant difference in wording. Jesus adds the phrase "nor ever shall be." Does that suggest that Jesus was distinguishing if from this horrible period that had already occurred in Israel's history? As we shall note later in our studies in the Olivet Discourse, Jesus told that generation that they would "see the 'abomination of desolation,' spoken of by Daniel" (Matt. 24:15). If He was saying Daniel's reference is what they would see, we have a problem from our studies above. Even preterists don't generally argue that Daniel 11:31 has transitioned to Rome. Where can we imagine any transition that would justify that view? On the other hand, if Jesus is saying they would see something *like* the "abomination of desolation" Daniel had described, it would make sense to understand the relationship of Daniel 12:1b and Matthew 24:21 in the same way. The tribulation of Matthew 24:21 would be *like* Daniel's prophesied tribulation, but it would actually be worse—"no, nor ever shall be."

The text continues, "and at that time your people shall be delivered, every one who is found written in the book" (Dan. 12:1c). We should remember that those who fell "by sword and flame" were said to fall "to refine them, purify them, and make them white" (Dan. 11:35). What deliverance is being described here? We note that those delivered are those "found written in the book." This seems to describe their spiritual state. Michael won't prevent them from dying.

Immediately after this promise of deliverance, the angel promises, "And many of those who sleep in the dust of the earth shall awake, some to everlasting life, some to shame and everlasting contempt" (Dan. 12:2). We should note, while Michael's standing is said to come "at that time" (12:1a) the text speaks of the great "time of trouble" (12:1b) in connection with the ongoing trouble and his deliverance "at that time." That doesn't necessarily mean that the time they "awake" is the same time as their deliverance (as we shall consider below). Let's also note that the text describes "those who sleep in the dust of the earth." *Sleep* in the *dust* is clearly a way of describing death. Nahum declares, "Your shepherds slumber, O king of Assyria; your nobles rest in the dust. Your people are scattered on the mountains, and no one gathers them" (Nahum 3:18). It can also be used as a synonym for Sheol (or Hades). Job 17:16 asks, "Will they go down to the gates of Sheol? Shall we have rest together in the dust?" Yet, the wording here is curious. The preterist argues that Daniel 12:2 describes a spiritual resurrection of God's people. They equate it with the time when "The sea gave up the dead who were in it, and Death and Hades delivered up the dead who were in them" (Rev. 20:13). If there will be no literal bodily resurrection why speak of the place where their bodies lie? Why speak of "the sea" and the "dust" if this is an unseen, spiritual deliverance from Hades that will never have any relationship again to the earth, the dust, or the sea? Is it not more reasonable to consider that this describes the place where the bodies lie because it will have a relationship to where those bodies will "awake"?

Immediately after this resurrection passage is the declaration we considered above—"Those who are wise shall shine like the brightness of the firmament, and those who turn many to righteousness like the stars forever and ever" (Dan. 12:3). Remember the parallel:

Daniel 12:3	Daniel 11:35
Those who are wise	And some of those of understanding
shall shine like the brightness of the firmament,	shall fall, to refine them, purify them, and make them white,
And those who turn many to righteousness	[those of the people who understand shall instruct many—Dan. 11:34]
like the stars forever and ever	until the time of the end; because it is still for the appointed time

Are these the same people? We believe the context suggests that they are. This leads to another *end* reference. The text reads, "But you, Daniel, shut up the words, and seal the book until the time of the end; many shall run to and fro, and knowledge shall increase" (Dan. 12:4). What "end" is addressed here? Is this the end of the things just prophesied? If so, how could Daniel "seal the book until" that time? Daniel would not live into the time of Antiochus Epiphanes (or for that matter into the Roman period or the AD 70 destruction of Jerusalem). It is possible that Daniel is being told to *seal* it up, in the fact that it will not be completely understood until it happens, but if so, it is still not something that "you, Daniel" could actually accomplish. On the other hand, could this be talking about Daniel's "end"? Perhaps. That *end* is certainly mentioned at the end of the book. He is told, "But you, go your way till the end; for you shall rest" (Dan. 12:13a). If so, we would see another distinct "end" that does not point to AD 70, but is used in the context to apply to the termination of the things being discussed—in this case, Daniel's life.

This formally ends the angel's message, but Daniel looks and sees "two others" on either side of the riverbank, with the angel "clothed in linen" (who has been speaking to him) "above the waters of the river" (Dan. 12:5-6a; cf. 10:5-6). One then asks the angel "How long shall the fulfillment of these wonders be?" (Dan. 12:6b). Almost all translations dynamically translate this question, but he literally asks, "Until when is the end of the wonders?" (GLT) or "Till when is the end of these wonders?" (YLT). To what "wonders" does the question refer? Jeremiah used the same Hebrew word describing the disaster of Jerusalem's destruction. At "her end" he mourns "her fall has been a WONDER" (Lam. 1:9, BBE, emphasis mine). The angel may be asking when these "astonishing things" (NIV) will end. If so, this is similar to what was said earlier in Daniel—God "would accomplish seventy years in the desolations of Jerusalem" (Dan. 9:2). He would *finish* the wonder of Jerusalem's punishment. Daniel is told of a future hardship on Jerusalem. The question asks when it will be "finished" (cf. Gen. 15:16; of another hardship in AD 70, Luke 21:24). This would not require that we understand the answer that follows to refer to *everything* that has been said before this, only the "wonders" or "astonishing" and horrible things concerning the persecution. It is after this that the angel offers the crucial answer:

> Then I heard the man clothed in linen, who was above the waters of the river, when he held up his right hand and his left hand to heaven, and swore by Him who lives forever, that it shall be for a time, times, and half a time; and when the power of the holy people has been completely shattered, all these things shall be finished (Dan. 12:7).

Many writers have devoted a great deal of time to trying to identify the significance of the phrase "a time, times, and half a time." Dan King, in *Truth Commentaries: The Book of Daniel* (Athens, AL: Guardian of Truth Foundation, 2012), observes that the phrase is literally "three and a half" and may correspond to the days specified later which both are around 3½ years (Dan. 12:11-12), or it may simply symbolize half of the number seven, associated with Divine perfection (762). If it is to be understood literally the date of the persecution of Antiochus Epiphanes was 168 or 167 BC. Antiochus died in 164 BC, around 3½ years later.

The part of this passage that is the focus of our questions reads, "when the power of the holy people has been completely shattered, all these things shall be finished" (Dan. 12:7b). Let's first look at the specific wording of the passage as seen in the chart below.

וּכְכַלּוֹת	נַפֵּץ	יַד־עַם־קֹדֶשׁ	תִּכְלֶינָה	כָּל־אֵלֶּה
Interlinear Text of Daniel 12:7b		← **Right to Left**		
vu-kᵉ-kallioth ←	napets ←	yad-'am-qodesh ←	ti-kᵉleynah ←	kal-'alleh
And—so-as—to- completely-end	to-dash-to -pieces	(the)-hand—of-(the)-people—holy	they-will-complete	all—these-(things)
And so as to completely end (inf.), to dash to pieces (inf.) the hand of the holy people, they will complete all these things.				
And as soon as (NASB) the completion of the shattering (YLT) the power of the holy people, they will complete all these things (KP)				
When the shattering of the holy people has finally come to an end, all these things will have happened (NLT)				

The above chart shows the Hebrew text, with a transliteration, a literal translation below each phrase, my translation putting it all together, a composite translation, and a good dynamic equivalence translation that expresses the sense.

Let's note a few things about the grammar and vocabulary here. First, the word "when" is not actually in the Hebrew text. After the word for "and," the particle *kᵉ* meaning "like, as" is used. It can have the sense of "when," but that is not its basic meaning. Translations that render this "they have made an end" are putting the verb at the end of the passage at the beginning (and probably with the wrong subject). There are two infinitives used at the beginning of this text, and both are in the Piel stem, which in Hebrew intensifies a verb. So literally it is, "And as to completely end to dash to pieces . . ." The closest translations we could find that bring these elements out are the NASB, which begins, "and as soon as," and Young's Literal Translation, which treats the two infinitives as nouns, "the completion of the shattering." The word for "power" is *yad,* which means literally "hand," although it is often used of one's power. We should not define it so narrowly as political power, or national identity. It is *strength, force,* or *power* of self-determination. The plural "they" properly applies to the final phrase "all these." The word "things" is inferred, but not actually in the text. The verb properly expresses the sense "all these, they are completed." The New Living Translation is dynamic in its translation, but it may well express the sense the best.

Interpretation of Daniel 12:2 and 7
Preterist Interpretation

The preterist interpretation of these passages concludes that "when the power of the holy people has been completely shattered, all these things shall be finished"—describes AD 70 as the time when the power of Israel was shattered. It then concludes that the promise, "And many of those who sleep in the dust of the earth shall awake, some to everlasting life, some to shame and everlasting contempt"—must fall within those things included in the phrase "all these things." The conclusion is then made that the resurrection of 12:2 was not a literal bodily resurrection, but a spiritual, collective resurrection of God's people unto an eternal heavenly relationship with God.

It is clear to me that this view demands a number of assumptions. First, one must assume that the phrase "holy people" must refer to Israel as a collective whole and the phrase "power . . . completely shattered" is AD 70. The inconsistency of this assumption is that preterists argue that first-century Judaism was the ultimate "perverse generation" of the Song of Moses (see chapter 2), yet they assume the Lord would speak of them here as His "holy people." That is unlikely. Second, to sustain this assumption one must conclude that a transition occurs in the text at 11:45 (or earlier) from a discussion of the Greek period of Antiochus Epiphanes to the Roman period. If this is true, are we to believe that the vision jumps from 164 BC (when Antiochus died) to AD 70 in one verse?

Third, it assumes that "all these things shall be finished" must mean everything mentioned before this in the text would happen by the time the "power" of the "holy people" is "completely shattered." Clearly, some things said before it could not be "finished"—he was told "the wise" would shine "like the stars for ever and ever" (12:3). There are other times in Scripture when "all things" doesn't mean *every single thing* mentioned. Jesus told the twelve, "Behold, we are going up to Jerusalem, and all things that are written by the prophets concerning the Son of Man will be accomplished" (Luke 18:31). Was *every single thing* mentioned in Scripture accomplished in Jerusalem at Jesus's death? After His resurrection, He told them, "These are the words which I spoke to you while I was still with you, that all things must be fulfilled which were written in the Law of Moses and the Prophets and the Psalms concerning Me" (Luke 24:44). Had *every single thing* mentioned in Scripture been accomplished by this time? Near the end of the conquest of Canaan, Joshua said, "Not a word failed of any good thing which the LORD had spoken to the house of Israel. All came to pass" (Josh. 21:45). Had *every single thing* mentioned in the Law of Moses happened at that time? Why must we assume that 12:2 had to be finished?

Finally, the preterist interpretation assumes that the "end" (of 12:9) and "end of the days" (of 12:13) are the same. Let's consider these issues and see if there is a better interpretation.

A Better Interpretation

After the angel gives the answer of Daniel 12:7, Daniel comments, "Although I heard, I did not understand. Then I said, 'My lord, what shall be the end of these things?' And he said, 'Go your way, Daniel, for the words are closed up and sealed till the time of the end'" (Dan. 12:8-9). Perhaps we should draw some comfort in our own discussions of this text to hear that when the prophet himself first heard this, he confesses that he "did not understand." His question seems to repeat the question just answered, and so the angel will give him an answer (12:10-12) that likely parallels the answer of 12:7. To this parallel we must add 12:10, "Many shall be purified, made white, and refined, but the wicked shall do wickedly; and none of the wicked shall understand, but the wise shall understand." This verse also corresponds to the two passages we compared earlier:

Daniel 12:10	Daniel 12:3	Daniel 11:35
...but the wise shall understand (12:10c)	Those who are wise	And some of those of understanding
Many shall be purified, made white, and refined (12:10a)	shall shine like the brightness of the firmament,	shall fall, to refine them, purify them, and make them white,
[many shall run to and fro, and knowledge shall increase— Dan. 12:4]	And those who turn many to righteousness	[those of the people who understand shall instruct many—Dan. 11:34]
[you shall rest, and will arise to your inheritance at the end of the days—Dan. 12:13]	like the stars forever and ever	until the time of the end; because it is still for the appointed time

Does this suggest that each of these passages speak of the same souls? If so let's consider what that would mean if we consider all things in context. Let's notice two references to the "end" that have come into the texts above. Daniel asks about "the end of these things" (12:8) and he again is told of "the time of the end" (12:9). He likely wants to know as was asked earlier, when the events described will end, but as noted above, he is called to seal them to the "end" (something he could only do within his lifetime). The book ends, "But you, go your way till the end," that is the end of his life "for you shall rest," He too will "sleep in the dust of the earth" (12:2), but he is promised that he, "will arise to your inheritance at the end of the days" (12:13). While we might acknowledge that 12:7 and 8 refer to the time when the things prophesied will happen, this final "end" is different. It is not simply the "end," it is "the end of the days," a phrase unique in Scripture.

So let's tie this all together. The text has just addressed those of "the sons of your people" (12:1a) who will face a "time of trouble, such as never was since there was a nation" (12:1b), and yet Daniel is promised that they "shall be delivered" (12:1c). In Daniel 12 those who "shall be delivered" (12:1c) are delivered because in their faithfulness they are among those "found written in the book" (12:1d). They are "those who are wise" and "shall shine like the brightness of the firmament" (12:3a). These are "those who turn many to righteousness like the stars forever and ever" (12:3b). We have shown that these are likely the same people who "shall be purified, made white, and refined" (12:10a) even though "the wicked shall do wickedly" (12:10b). These are the same souls described in the previous chapter that fell "by sword and flame" (11:33), yet would "fall, to refine them, purify them, and make them white" (11:35). These are those who remained faithful to the "holy covenant" (11:30). These are the "holy people" of 12:7. Daniel frequently uses the related term "saints" (*qaddish*) in the book, not of Israel as a whole, but of those who are faithful to God (Dan. 7:18, 21, 25, 27). It should not surprise us if he used the term "holy people" (*'am-qodesh*) in the same sense of those faithful to the "holy covenant." Daniel is told exactly how they "shall be delivered" (12:1c). Although this time of trouble might even lead to death—Daniel is assured "many of those who sleep in the dust of the earth shall awake, some to everlasting life, some to shame and everlasting contempt" (Dan. 12:2). Those who stood firm were truly "holy people" whose "power (lit. "hand")" was "completely shattered" by the horrible persecution imposed upon them. The great comfort that Daniel is given is that those courageous souls would not die in vain—"many of those who sleep in the dust of the earth shall awake, some to everlasting life, some to shame and everlasting contempt" (12:2).

We believe Daniel 12:1-2 is promising a deliverance to those who would face a "time of trouble, such as never was since there was a nation," even if it led to death, in the comfort that one day "many of those who sleep in the dust of the earth shall awake, some to everlasting life." If this is the sense, Daniel is not being told that the *waking* would happen when the *deliverance* comes, but that its inevitability is offered as a comfort although they must face such a difficult time. If so, it is similar to Revelation 2:10—"Be faithful until death, and I will give you the crown of life." Those in Daniel who have faced such difficult times are the wise. Though they may die in such persecution, they ultimately "shall shine like the brightness of the firmament, and those who turn many to righteousness like the stars forever and ever" (Dan. 12:3).

The wording to Daniel at the end of the book is compelling! "But you, go your way till the end; for you shall rest, and will arise to your inheritance at the end of the days" (Dan. 12:13). This isn't saying that Daniel would live until the time that these things would be fulfilled. He would not live to the time of Antiochus Epiphanes (or AD 70). So, "the end" here seems to be speaking of the end of Daniel's life, after which he is said to "rest" (i.e., die, cf. "sleep in the dust of the earth"). He then is told that he too will "arise to" his "inheritance at the end of the days." This leads us to ask, what is Daniel's "inheritance," and when is "the end of the days" when he will receive this inheritance?

A post-death "inheritance" must describe some provision God grants to Daniel after this life. The fact that he is said to "arise" to his "inheritance" suggests that this is not the resurrection of a cause, or some unseen spiritual vindication of the faithful dead. This is something that will grant an "inheritance" to him personally. This suggests a literal (not a figurative or collective) resurrection. The timing of this is also compelling. It is not simply "the end" (towards which Daniel is told to *go his way*). Rather, it is at "the end of the days." This is a contrast between other references to "the end" in the vision that are given a specific event connected with them. This is the end of *all* the days (i.e., the end of time). What other end of days can be described *post-mortem* and at a *rising* to one's *inheritance*?

Resurrection in the New Testament

Having examined Daniel 12 in depth, let's now consider how this foundational doctrine expressed in Daniel is expanded in the New Testament. Imagine one of two things. First, imagine you open the New Testament for the first time with no knowledge of the Christian faith or what came before it. Consider how you would naturally understand New Testament passages that address the resurrection. Second, imagine that you were a Jew who came to the New Testament for the first time with the knowledge of Daniel 12 as your background. What would you find? How would you naturally understand the passages you encounter?

First, as noted above, you would learn about a Jewish sect called the Sadducees who, "say there is no resurrection" (Matt. 22:23). They test Jesus with a question set "in the resurrection," which they offer in an effort to prove their position (Matt. 22:28). In answer, Jesus declared that the Old Testament words, "I am the God of Abraham, the God of Isaac, and the God of Jacob" (Exod. 3:6) concerned the "resurrection of the dead" (Matt. 22:31). Would you assume, "One day they will experience an unseen spiritual resurrection?" Probably not. Jesus further explained, "But those who are counted worthy to attain that age, and the resurrection from the dead, neither marry nor are given in marriage; nor can they die anymore, for they are equal to the angels and are sons of God, being sons of the resurrection" (Luke 20:35-36). Don Preston in his debate with Wallace argued that Jesus is only talking about Mosaic Laws of marriage to a childless brother's widowed wife.[3] Reading this for the first time would you conclude that? He even tells the Sadducees, "You are therefore greatly mistaken" (Mark 12:27). Wouldn't you conclude that Jesus affirmed the reality of a bodily resurrection?

Later you read about Paul before the Jewish council, "But when Paul perceived that one part were Sadducees and the other Pharisees, he cried out in the council, 'Men *and* brethren, I am a Pharisee, the son of a Pharisee; concerning the hope and resurrection of the dead I am being judged!'" (Acts 23:6). The sources confirm that Pharisees believed in a literal bodily resurrection (Josephus, *Wars of the Jews* 2.8.14). Preston, in the same debate, argued they mistakenly borrowed this from the Greeks, but earlier you read that Greeks mocked Paul when he taught "the resurrection from the dead" (Acts 17:32). Before the council Paul says, "I am a Pharisee," and they believe in a bodily resurrection (cf. Acts 23:8). He restates this same belief later, saying, "I have hope in God, which they themselves also accept, that there will be a resurrection of the dead, both of the just and the unjust" (Acts 24:15), confessing that as the reason he is being judged (Acts 24:21). Is he lying? Was he being deceptive? Did he know it was only spiritual, collective, and not bodily, but try to make them think he believed as they did? That wouldn't be honest. Since Paul is an honest man you would conclude that Paul believed in the reality of a bodily resurrection.

Back in the gospels, you remember reading an account of some at Jesus's death, "coming out of the graves after His resurrection, they went into the holy city and appeared to many" (Matt. 27:53). This was not unseen and spiritual, they came out of "the graves" and "appeared" to those in Jerusalem. Then your read in John this profound declaration by Jesus:

> Most assuredly, I say to you, the hour is coming, and now is, when the dead will hear the voice of the Son of God; and those who hear will live. For as the Father has life in Himself, so He has granted the Son to have life in Himself, and has given Him authority to execute judgment also, because He is the Son of Man. Do not marvel at this; for the hour is coming in which all who are in the graves will hear His voice and come forth—those who have

---

[3] https://www.youtube.com/watch?v=PjOMCLbPhvc.

done good, to the resurrection of life, and those who have done evil, to the resurrection of condemnation (John 5:25-29).

If you were new to all concepts in Scripture can we honestly imagine that you would read that those "in the graves will hear His voice and come forth" and not instantly call to mind the "graves" opened at the crucifixion and not equate one with the other? If you were familiar with Daniel 12 would you not immediately recall the words—"Some to everlasting life, Some to shame and everlasting contempt," as you read Jesus's promise of "those who have done good, to the resurrection of life, and those who have done evil, to the resurrection of condemnation"? You would also see in Jesus's claim to have "authority to execute judgment" a connection between resurrection and judgment. When would you expect this judgment? "When the dead will hear the voice of the Son of God."

As you read the Scriptures further, you repeatedly see the connections between "judgment" and "resurrection." Those who give to those in need, "shall be repaid at the resurrection of the just" (Luke 14:14). The long dead "men of Nineveh," "the queen of the South," and "this generation" are promised to "rise up in the judgment" (Matt. 12:41-42). Will you not expect, one day to do the same?

As you study the gospel of John, you learn about Jesus's friendship with Mary, Martha, and their brother Lazarus. He died, and as Jesus approaches where he was buried, He says to Martha, "Your brother will rise again" (John 11:23). She is not surprised by this statement. She affirms, "I know that he will rise again in the resurrection at the last day" (John 11:24). Perhaps she remembers the promise to Daniel—he would "rise at the end of the days." How else would she know of a "last day"? Jesus doesn't tell her, "You know, the world is never really going to end." He reinforces her initial conviction. He says to her, "I am the resurrection and the life. He who believes in Me, though he may die, he shall live" (John 11:25). Jesus raises her brother, which prefigures what He has just described. Would this lead you to imagine that Jesus meant that He will spiritually raise those who believe in Him—not a bodily resurrection? Not likely. You remember that others in the past, like Lazarus, "received their dead raised to life again," but hoped to "obtain a better resurrection" (Heb. 11:35). Is it better because those who attain it can no longer die (Luke 20:35-36)? You consider as Paul discussed the "bondage to corruption" this creation endures, as we "groan within ourselves" longing for the "redemption of our body" (Rom. 8:21, 23). Would you not long within for such *redemption*? How could you not associate it with all that you have read about resurrection?

As noted above, you read the first gospel sermon, which records that David foretold Christ's resurrection, "foreseeing this, spoke concerning the resurrection of the Christ, that His soul was not left in Hades, nor did His flesh see corruption" (Acts 2:31). That reminds you of the promise of Revelation 20:13-14—"The sea gave up the dead who were in it, and Death and Hades delivered up the dead who were in them. And they were judged, each one according to his works. Then Death and Hades were cast into the lake of fire. This is the second death." Jesus's escape from Hades involved a resurrection. You remember Jesus promising judgment to those who rise from the graves upon hearing His voice (John 5:25-29). Would you imagine that your soul would go directly to God without resurrection? Not likely.

You remember Paul's description of our bodies as a *tent*, writing:

> For we know that if our earthly house, this tent, is destroyed, we have a building from God, a house not made with hands, eternal in the heavens. For in this we groan, earnestly desiring to be clothed with our habitation which is from heaven, if indeed, having been clothed, we shall not be found naked. For we who are in this tent groan, being burdened, not because we want to be unclothed, but further clothed, that mortality may be swallowed up by life (2 Cor. 5:1-4).

This does not describe disembodied souls returning to God. That would be a condition in which we are "found naked." You would long to be clothed with an incorruptible body!

Having read many things now about the resurrection you come to two unusual texts. One speaks of some, "who have strayed concerning the truth, saying that the resurrection is already past; and they overthrow the faith of some" (2 Tim. 2:18). Another tells of those who, like the Sadducees "say that there is no resurrection of the dead" (1 Cor. 15:12). The second comes in a 58-verse chapter devoted to the subject. To argue the point, Paul appeals to Christ's resurrection (1 Cor. 15:12-17), describing His resurrection as the "firstfruits of those who have fallen asleep" (1 Cor. 15:20). You would assume that there is some similarity between Christ's bodily resurrection, and that which will one day happen in the future. In that chapter you read Paul's words, "If in this life only we have hope in Christ, we are of all men the most pitiable" (1 Cor. 15:19). You would assume that the Christian's hope is not "in this life," but in a life after the resurrection. You remember the words Luke recorded in Acts 26:23—"that the Christ would suffer, that He would be the first to rise from the dead, and would proclaim light to the Jewish people and to the Gentiles." If Christ is the "first to rise from the dead," our resurrection must resemble His. His was a bodily resurrection. You remember Paul declared his hope, "that I may know Him and the power of His resurrection, and the fellowship of His sufferings, being conformed to His death, if, by any means, I may attain to the resurrection from the dead" (Phil. 3:10-11). Why share in His sufferings, or be "conformed to His death" and hope for the "power of His resurrection" if ours is not to be like His?

As you think further about those who say the "resurrection is already past" or say "there is no resurrection," you suspect that any doctrine that denies this is like those Paul rebuked as *straying from the truth*. You remember the Hebrew writer counting doctrines "of resurrection of the dead, and of eternal judgment" as elementary principles the babe in Christ must accept, but move beyond unto maturity (Heb. 6:2).

You read of Paul's effort to comfort the Thessalonians' fears regarding those who had "fallen asleep" (1 Thess. 4:13). He assures them that when Christ returns, "the dead in Christ will rise first" (1 Thess. 4:16). If you were familiar with Daniel 12, again you are reminded that Daniel was said to "rest" and then "rise" to his inheritance (Dan. 12:13). You think of those said to "sleep in the dust of the earth" who "shall awake, some to everlasting life, some to shame and everlasting contempt" (Dan. 12:2). Would you honestly consider Christ as the "firstfruits of those who have fallen asleep" (1 Cor. 15:20), but imagine that we will not rise as He did? You then read that, "flesh and blood cannot inherit the kingdom of God" (1 Cor. 15:50), but then notice that in "the resurrection of the dead"—"The body is sown in corruption, it is raised in incorruption" (1 Cor. 15:42). You envision a body free of corruption that will rise from the grave upon hearing Jesus's voice.

When all of these things are considered together it becomes clear that the concept that preterists try to brand as "tradition" with "no foundation in Scripture," in fact runs throughout Scripture. It is a theme built upon all Scripture that has gone before it, and is a fundamental truth of the gospel, as confirmed by the Law and the Prophets.

"That's Not How They Would Have Understood It"

Finally, it's not uncommon to hear preterists make the assertion, "That's not how Jews in the first century would have understood it." As we have stated earlier, we must ask again, *how can we know that?* When I was preaching in Birmingham my wife and I had just purchased a "new to us" used mini-van, when an uninsured motorist drove through a red light and hit it. I tried to work with the owner to get him to pay for the damage, but when he was unwilling, my insurance company took him to court. When the court date came, the owner didn't show up. When the judge began to reschedule, I made the rather foolish statement, "I doubt he will show up even if we reschedule." The judge rather sternly replied, "Mr. Pope, do you have the ability to read other people's minds? If not, let's not assume to know what he will do!" I have appreciated his rebuke ever since then, and I believe it has application to the issues we are discussing.

How can we know that Jews in the first century would not have looked for a literal bodily resurrection? How can we know they would have understood *all* cosmological eschatological language figuratively? How do we know that they did not see in these words a present application to the judgment being described with a future promise of a more literal fulfillment? What evidence do we find to support these assumptions?

Evidence of Jewish Concepts

Certainly there is much more evidence for a belief in the resurrection and a literal expectation of cosmological eschatological events found in early Christian writing than is found in Jewish sources, but there are, nonetheless, some compelling pieces of evidence.

Among the Dead Sea Scrolls from Qumran there is a non-Biblical text identified as 4Q521, sometimes called *On the Resurrection*. It reads, "And the Lord will perform marvelous acts such as have not existed, just as he sa[id,] 12 [for] he will heal the badly wounded and will make the dead live, he will proclaim good news to the poor" (Frag. 2, Col. 2, 11). We may notice immediately the wording borrowed from Isaiah, which reads, "The Spirit of the Lord GOD is upon Me, because the LORD has anointed Me to preach good tidings to the poor; He has sent Me to heal the brokenhearted, to proclaim liberty to the captives, and the opening of the prison to those who are bound; to proclaim the acceptable year of the LORD, and the day of vengeance of our God; to comfort all who mourn" (Isa. 61:1-2). Jesus read this Scripture in the synagogue in Nazareth, as Luke records, "The Spirit of the LORD is upon Me, because He has anointed Me to preach the gospel to the poor; He has sent Me to heal the brokenhearted, to proclaim liberty to the captives and recovery of sight to the blind, to set at liberty those who are oppressed; to proclaim the acceptable year of the LORD" (Luke 4:18-19). Concerning which He proclaimed, "Today this Scripture is fulfilled in your hearing" (Luke 4:21). While the Qumran text does not specify that the "dead" who "live" experience bodily resurrection, the association with healing the bodies of the sick (as Jesus carried out in His early ministry) suggests the writer of 4Q521 anticipated a bodily resurrection.

The first century historian Josephus, in his work entitled *Wars of the Jews* discusses the beliefs of the Pharisees. He writes, "They say that all souls are incorruptible, but that the souls of good men only are removed into other bodies, but that the souls of bad men are subject to eternal punishment" (2.8.14). This reference to "other bodies" is significant. Their hope was not in an unseen spiritual resurrection, but a removal into another body. Here we have a first century Jew telling us what other first century Jews believed. We must remember that Paul, without qualification, even after his conversion confessed himself to be "a Pharisee, the son of a Pharisee" who was being judged "concerning the hope and resurrection of the dead" (Acts 23:6).

In the second century, a Christian named Justin wrote a work entitled *Dialogue with Trypho*. Justin was from Flavia Neapolis, the modern city of Nablus in what was identified as Samaria in the New Testament. Justin was martyred for his faith in Christ in AD 165, earning himself the epithet by which he is usually known "Justin Martyr." The *Dialogue with Trypho* is a conversation between Justin and a Jew named Trypho, set in Ephesus. Trypho had fled from the Jewish wars in Palestine, and Justin had recently left Platonism to convert to faith in Christ. Like similar dialogues written by Plato, it is unclear whether the *Dialogue* was meant to represent an actual historical discussion, or if it is simply a literary device used by Justin to explain his understanding of the gospel's relationship to Judaism.

In the *Dialogue*, Justin quotes Daniel 7:9-28 to argue, "if so great a power is shown to have followed and to be still following the dispensation of His [i.e., Christ's] suffering, how great shall that be which shall follow His glorious advent! For He shall come on the clouds as the Son of man, so Daniel foretold, and His angels shall come with Him" (31.1). From this, we at the very least see that Justin did not take these things figuratively, but let's notice how his Jewish counterpart responds. Trypho replies, "These and such like Scriptures, sir, compel us to wait for Him who, as Son of man, receives from the Ancient of days the everlasting kingdom" (32.1). If this was an actual discussion, we have a second century Jewish critic of faith in Christ applying cosmological eschatological language to future literal events. Wouldn't this have been the perfect time for Trypho to tell Justin that the text should have been interpreted figuratively? Instead, he claims such texts lead Jews to continue to look for a Messiah. If this is merely a literary device, we have Justin record his own understanding of how Jews viewed such things. At any rate, this does not support the assertion that Jews "would not have seen it this way."

Since the ninth century AD, in a work known as the *Bibliotheca* of Photius (the Patriarch of Constantinople) a text known as the *Discourse to the Greeks Concerning Hades* has been attributed to Josephus, the first century Jewish historian. Its similarity to a section of a work by Hippolytus, a third century church theologian, known as *Against Plato, on the Cause of the Universe,* has led many modern scholars to attribute it to him. However, the fact that part of the discourse not found in Hippolytus' text parallels a section found in Justin's *Dialogue with Trypho,* which occasionally cites Josephus directly, leaves the possibility that both were drawing from an original work, in fact written by Josephus. If so, we should note what it reflects about Jewish concepts of eschatology.

First, the text describes an understanding of Hades that parallels Luke 16:19-31. Speaking of Hades he writes:

> In this region there is a certain place set apart, as a lake of unquenchable fire, whereinto we suppose no one hath hitherto been cast; but it is prepared for a day afore-determined by God, in which one righteous sentence shall deservedly be passed upon all men; when the unjust, and those that have been disobedient to God, and have given honor to such idols as have been the vain operations of the hands of men as to God himself, shall be adjudged to this everlasting punishment, as having been the causes of defilement; while the just shall obtain an incorruptible and never-fading kingdom. These are now indeed confined in Hades, but not in the same place wherein the unjust are confined (2).

He further expresses an explicit understanding of resurrection as a personal bodily resurrection. Notice his claims:

> This is the discourse concerning Hades, wherein the souls of all men are confined until a proper season, which God hath determined, when he will make a resurrection of all men from the dead, not procuring a transmigration of souls from one body to another, but raising again those very bodies, which you Greeks, seeing to be dissolved, do not believe [their resurrection]. But learn not to disbelieve it; for while you believe that the soul is created, and yet is made immortal by God, according to the doctrine of Plato, and this in time, be not incredulous; but believe that God is able, when he hath raised to life that body which was made as a compound of the same elements, to make it immortal; for it must never be said of God, that he is able to do some things, and unable to do others. We have therefore believed that the body will be raised again; for although it be dissolved, it is not perished; for the earth receives its remains, and preserves them; and while they are like seed, and are mixed among the more fruitful soil, they flourish, and what is sown is indeed sown bare grain, but at the mighty sound of God the Creator, it will sprout up, and be raised in a clothed and glorious condition, though not before it has been dissolved, and mixed [with the earth]. So that we have not rashly believed the resurrection of the body; for although it be dissolved for a time on account of the original transgression, it exists still, and is cast into the earth as into a potter's furnace, in order to be

formed again, not in order to rise again such as it was before, but in a state of purity, and so as never to he destroyed any more. And to every body shall its own soul be restored. And when it hath clothed itself with that body, it will not be subject to misery, but, being itself pure, it will continue with its pure body, and rejoice with it, with which it having walked righteously now in this world, and never having had it as a snare, it will receive it again with great gladness. But as for the unjust, they will receive their bodies not changed, not freed from diseases or distempers, nor made glorious, but with the same diseases wherein they died; and such as they were in their unbelief, the same shall they be when they shall be faithfully judged (5).

If the attribution to Josephus is accurate, this is a phenomenal example of concepts of Hades, final judgment, and a bodily resurrection from a first century Jewish source. If instead, it should be attributed to a later Christian source, it still demonstrates how early Christians understood biblical teachings.

Evidence of Early Christian Concepts

A serious weakness of preterism concerns its place in religious history. Many critics claim that it is not until the 19th century that we see examples of preterist views being taught. Others try to push it back to the 16th or 17th centuries. The problem is, if preterism is the sound and scriptural method of interpreting biblical eschatology how can we explain its absence in early church history?

As one who is committed to the restoration of New Testament Christianity, we recognize that such a view must often reject doctrines adopted by the majority throughout history. However, in such cases we can often see within early church history, the point at which early Christians first turned to accept apostate beliefs. For example, although early works such as *First Clement* speak only of "elders and deacons," the works of Ignatius are the first to distinguish a "bishop" from the "elders." In baptism, the earliest sources describe baptism as immersion for the forgiveness of sins, but we see within a work known as the *Didache* the first time men began to substitute sprinkling or pouring for immersion.

Consider the overwhelming evidence we find in early Christian writings. In the late first, or early second century, Clement cites examples from nature that he argues demonstrate that, "there shall be a future resurrection, of which He has rendered the Lord Jesus Christ the first-fruits by raising Him from the dead" (*First Clement*, 24). In the second century the *Didache* quotes Matthew 24:49 and applies it to Christ's second coming, interpreting it as literally describing Him coming on the clouds, with a literal trumpet sound, and a literal bodily resurrection (16)

In the second century Justin (ca. AD 150) wrote, "…We expect to receive again our own bodies, though they be dead and cast into the earth, for we maintain that with God nothing is impossible" (Justin, *First Apology* 18). This statement comes in a text written to the emperor in defense of the Christian faith. In the same work he continues, ". . . Judge ye that it is not impossible that the bodies of men, after they have been dissolved, and like seeds resolved into earth, should in God's appointed time rise again and put on incorruption" (Ibid., 19). He writes further:

> For the prophets have proclaimed two advents of His: the one, that which is already past, when He came as a dishonoured and suffering Man; but the second, when, according to prophecy, He shall come from heaven with glory, accompanied by His angelic host, when also He shall raise the bodies of all men who have lived, and shall clothe those of the worthy with immortality, and shall send those of the wicked, endued with eternal sensibility, into everlasting fire with the wicked devils. And that these things also have been foretold as yet to be, we will prove. By Ezekiel the prophet it was said: "Joint shall be joined to joint, and bone to bone, and flesh shall grow again; and every knee shall bow to the Lord, and every tongue shall confess Him" (Ibid., 52).

He quotes here Ezekiel 37 and the vision of the dry bones we discussed above. We would not agree with Justin that Ezekiel 37 speaks of a future, literal, bodily resurrection—the vision to Ezekiel is a figure of the nation's return from exile (see Appendix). Even so, it may be that Justin saw in that text such similarity to the doctrine of the resurrection so universally accepted among Christians (and some Jews) that he believed it prefigured the doctrines revealed in Christ.

Tertullian (ca. AD 160-220), in a work called *Prescription Against the Heretics* writes, ". . . He preached the new law and the new promise of the kingdom of heaven, worked miracles; having been crucified, He rose again the third day; (then) having ascended into the heavens, He sat at the right hand of the Father; sent instead of Himself the Power of the Holy Ghost to lead such as believe; will come with glory to take the saints to the enjoyment of everlasting life and of the heavenly promises, and to condemn the wicked to everlasting fire, after the resurrection of both these classes shall have happened, together with the restoration of their flesh" (13). Irenaeus (ca. 125-202) understood Revelation 20-22 literally not spiritually (*Against Heresies* 5.35) and expected an actual resurrection (5.36).

Summary

This is not to say that there were no voices in early church history that denied a literal, bodily resurrection. This was, in fact, a major view adopted by some Gnostic sects. In their belief that Christ had not literally come in the flesh, they extended it to imagine that in their secret knowledge they had discovered that there would be no literal, bodily resurrection of those who possessed such knowledge, but a spiritual elevation to some other reality. Many early Christian writers passionately rebuked these false doctrines. Tertullian, for example wrote that one who would deny a resurrection of the flesh, "will not be a Christian who shall deny this doctrine which is confessed by Christians" (*On the Resurrection of the Flesh* 3).

Obviously all such sources do not compare with the inspired word of God. Scripture is the basis upon which we must base all of our doctrines and practices. At the same time, the gospel was not proclaimed in a vacuum. It is reasonable to assume that doctrines so fundamental to faith in Christ would leave a footprint of some sort on the path of church history. Can we truly believe that a figurative, spiritual interpretation of biblical eschatology that did not involve a bodily resurrection, the end of the universe, and a literal final day of judgment was the true doctrine of Christ and yet it left no evidence for centuries? That seems unlikely for a kingdom that "shall never be destroyed; and the kingdom shall not be left to other people; it shall break in pieces and consume all these kingdoms, and it shall stand forever" (Dan. 2:44).

THE MOUNT OF OLIVES DISCOURSE

We now come to what is perhaps the most pivotal text in determining how to interpret New Testament eschatology—Jesus's discourse with His disciples on the Mount of Olives. How we understand its focus and symbolism will lead us in one direction or the other. Certainly, we must approach this taking into consideration the Old Testament promises and prophecies that came before it, but we must also be careful not to bring to it assumptions about the meaning of figures used in different contexts, if it cannot be proven conclusively that these same figures are employed in this discourse. We must also avoid presuming that we can know how Christ's disciples in the first century understood the things that were said, if the text gives us no indication of what was in their hearts and minds.

I have become convinced that what shapes the concepts of how many preterists interpret the Olivet Discourse are the concepts they bring to the text, not the text itself. If so, they are allowing their preconceptions to direct their understanding of the passage, rather than the Scripture itself. Now, they might hear that and say, "We bring to the text what is taught in Moses and the Prophets. Our only preconceptions rest on the things taught in Scripture." Fair enough, but what if those conclusions about what was taught in Moses and the Prophets are flawed? Would that not bring to the text erroneous preconceptions that could distort the true meaning of the passage?

Please understand, I am not saying, "They have preconceptions—I do not!" All of us are the product of our experience and understanding. All of us bring to any study of a biblical text our past study of Scripture. That inevitably influences how we read any biblical passage. The challenge must be to make certain that we don't allow that to subconsciously influence the conclusions we draw if the Scriptures will not sustain them.

What We Bring to the Text

So how could this be a factor in looking at the Olivet Discourse? We hope that in the studies we have gone through so far we have sufficiently demonstrated that there are valid reasons to question the conclusions preterists have drawn. If so, as we come to the Mount of Olives Discourse what impact should that have on our expectations?

- We have seen that the Song of Moses was a general warning that served as a witness to Israel throughout its history, not a specific prophecy pointing exclusively to AD 70.

  > That means that we cannot conclude that every time we see the word *end* in the Olivet Discourse it is describing AD 70—unless we can prove that from the text.

- We have seen that the terms *heaven* and *earth* are not used universally (if ever) to apply to the Jews and the Mosaic System.

  > That prohibits us from concluding that references to *heaven* and *earth* in the Olivet Discourse automatically refer to the Mosaic System—unless we can prove from the text that it is the focus.

- We have seen that, while the Law and the Prophets set the backdrop of all New Testament teaching, the gospel system is intended to replace and fulfill the intent of the Old Law.

- We have seen that Old Testament promises of a gathering of God's people under the Messiah found their fulfillment in the gathering of the remnant of Israel and the inclusion of the Gentiles under the Messiah.

  > We cannot, therefore, conclude that references to a gathering in the Olivet Discourse automatically point to an AD 70 spiritual gathering, or a continuation of the binding force of Mosaic Law—unless we can prove otherwise from the text.

- We have seen that references to the *end* in Daniel 10-12 do not always (if ever) point to an end in AD 70, and that Daniel's references to a resurrection in Daniel 12:2 and 13 cannot be dismissed as purely figurative or spiritual.

- We have also seen that assuming that Jews in the first century would have automatically interpreted references to eschatological cosmological prophetic events and the resurrection as figurative and spiritual cannot be proven from Scripture, nor from extra-biblical sources that demonstrate Jewish and Christian concepts.

That means as we encounter such wording in the Olivet Discourse we cannot automatically dismiss it as figurative or spiritual—if the text itself doesn't lead us to that conclusion.

So, the challenge we face is to approach our study of this account with a mind as open as possible to consider the text for what it says, avoiding assumptions that cannot be conclusively demonstrated.

Accounts of the Mount of Olives Discourse

From Matthew's account of the events of Jesus's final week we can determine that this discourse took place on the Tuesday before Jesus's crucifixion.[1] It happened after Jesus left the temple following a variety of teachings (Matt. 21:23-23:39). Although John does not record this discourse, it is recorded in each of the synoptic gospels: Matthew (24:1-25:46); Mark (13:1-37); Luke (21:5-38) with some parallel teachings preserved outside of the context of the Olivet Discourse (Luke 12:35-46; 17:20-37; 19:11-27; John 16:2). The specific content can be seen in the chart we shall see below, but it all starts when Jesus foretells the destruction of the temple as He departs from it (Matt. 24:1-2; Mark 13:1-3; Luke 21:5-6). When He and His disciples reach the Mount of Olives, which overlooked the temple, His disciples (specifically Peter, Andrew, James, and John – Mark 13:3) ask Him privately a question that sets the stage for the focus of the discourse.

As we see in the chart below, the question is essentially the same in all the gospels—"when will these things be? And what will be the sign when all these things will be fulfilled?" (Mark 13:4) or "when will these things be? And what sign will there be when these things are about to take place?" (Luke 21:5-6). The challenge comes in the wording offered in Matthew, who puts it, "when will these things be? And what will be the sign of Your coming, and of the end of the age?" (Matt. 24:3b). How can we explain or understand the difference in wording?

---

[1] In my commentary on Matthew, at the beginning of my comments on chapter 21, I trace all of the time indicators in the gospel accounts that allow us to track the chronology of Jesus's final week (*Truth Commentaries: Matthew.* Athens, AL: Guardian of Truth Foundation, 2013, 692-694). I recognize that there are alternative chronologies that are put forth that differ from mine, but I am confident in the conclusions I have drawn on this and would welcome consideration of the data I used to draw these conclusions.

The Disciples' Question		
Matthew	**Mark**	**Luke**
"Tell us, when will these things be? And what will be the sign of Your coming, and of the end of the age?" (24:3b)	"Tell us, when will these things be? And what will be the sign when all these things will be fulfilled?" (13:4)	"Teacher, but when will these things be? And what sign will there be when these things are about to take place?" (21:5-6)

Two explanations are generally offered: (1) These must be understood as strictly synonymous (i.e., two ways of asking the same thing), or (2) Matthew records an element of the question that is not addressed as directly in the other accounts.

Preterists (and some partial-preterists) accept this first explanation and build their interpretation of the entire discourse based on that explanation. In so doing, they must interpret the words "Your coming" and "the end of the age" as terms that can apply to the destruction of Jerusalem (and the temple) which we know was fulfilled in AD 70. Is that interpretation valid? Does the use of these terms in Matthew (and elsewhere in Scripture) support this interpretation? We will consider this below.

If the second explanation is valid, Matthew is recording a second element of the disciples' question not recorded in the other gospels. In my commentary on Matthew, I offered the possibility that the disciples may have concluded that when the temple was destroyed it would be at the end of the world. Preterists generally reject that possibility. Preston, for example, argues that, the world didn't end when Nebuchadnezzar destroyed the temple—why would they assume it would end if it was destroyed again?[2] Fair enough. As we have cautioned previously in this study—the only way we can know the thoughts of another person is by the things he has chosen to reveal about those thoughts. So, although I still see that as a possibility, let's look at it a different way. Regardless of what they may have thought, is it possible that Matthew records a distinct aspect of the question that is not recorded in Mark and Luke? If so, do we ever see other times when that happened? If so, can we see in Mark and Luke hints that this element of the question was also addressed even though they do not record that part of the question?

Another Incident in Matthew and Mark

There is another incident recorded in Matthew and Mark that does this very thing. Both Matthew and Mark record an incident when the Pharisees came to Jesus and questioned Him about divorce. Over the years many have puzzled over a key difference in the accounts. As seen in the chart below:

---

[2] Don K. Preston, "Testimony Regarding Full Preterism," March 31, 2014, https://youtu.be/tGI3gGDCj7g

Pharisee's Question on Divorce	
Matthew	**Mark**
The Pharisees also came to Him, testing Him, and saying to Him, "Is it lawful for a man to divorce his wife . . ." (19:3)	The Pharisees came and asked Him, "Is it lawful for a man to divorce his wife?" testing Him (10:2)
". . . for just any reason?" (19:3b)	
And He answered and said to them, "Have you not read that He who made them at the beginning 'made them male and female'" (19:4) "and said, 'For this reason a man shall leave his father and mother and be joined to his wife, and the two shall become one flesh'? So then, they are no longer two but one flesh" (19:5-6a) Therefore what God has joined together, let not man separate." (19:6b) They said to Him, "Why then did Moses command to give a certificate of divorce, and to put her away?" (19:7) He said to them, "Moses, because of the hardness of your hearts, permitted you to divorce your wives, but from the beginning it was not so" (19:8)	And He answered and said to them, "What did Moses command you?" (10:3) They said, "Moses permitted a man to write a certificate of divorce, and to dismiss her" (10:4) And Jesus answered and said to them, "Because of the hardness of your heart he wrote you this precept" (10:5) "But from the beginning of the creation, God 'made them male and female'" (10:6) "'For this reason a man shall leave his father and mother and be joined to his wife, and the two shall become one flesh'; so then they are no longer two, but one flesh" (10:7-8) "Therefore what God has joined together, let not man separate" (10:9)
"And I say to you, whoever divorces his wife, except for sexual immorality, and marries another, commits adultery; and whoever marries her who is divorced commits adultery" (19:9)	
His disciples said to Him, "If such is the case of the man with his wife, it is better not to marry." (19:10)	
	In the house His disciples also asked Him again about the same matter (10:10)
	So He said to them, "Whoever divorces his wife and marries another commits adultery against her. And if a woman divorces her husband and marries another, she commits adultery" (10:11-12)

Mark records them asking the more general question, "Is it lawful for a man to divorce his wife?" (Mark 10:2). After discussing God's original intent for marriage, as Mark records it, Jesus answered simply, "what God has joined together, let not man separate" (Mark 10:9). Even when He later discusses the issue further with His disciples, "in the house" (Mark 10:10), nothing is said about any exception for fornication. He simply tells them, "Whoever divorces his wife and marries another commits adultery against her. And if a woman divorces her husband and marries another, she commits adultery" (Mark 10:11-12). As we know, Matthew records an exception for fornication (Matthew 19:9). Is this a contradiction? No. Matthew recorded a portion of the question that Mark did not. While Mark records the basic question focusing on the permanence of marriage, Matthew reveals that the full question was, "Is it lawful for a man to divorce his wife for just any reason?" (Matt. 19:3). This is why Matthew also records the full portion of Jesus's answer that specifically answers that part of the question—"whoever divorces his wife, except for sexual immorality, and marries another, commits adultery; and whoever marries her who is divorced commits adultery" (Matt. 19:9). This is the same account, but the Holy Spirit led one writer to bring out an element of the discussion that the other did not. In this incident, we would not imagine that the questions are strictly synonymous, but the fact that one writer brings out another element of the question explains why another part of the answer is given in one gospel and not the other.

We must consider the possibility that the same thing is happening in the gospel accounts of the Olivet Discourse. While all three gospels record the same incident, it is clear from the chart on the next page that Matthew gives the fullest version of this incident. We should note that not only is Matthew the only gospel writer to record the element of the question that asks about "the end of the age" (24:3b), but he is also the only gospel writer to record Jesus's *sheep* and *goats* judgment scene (25:31-46). Is it possible, as in Matthew's account of the Pharisee's questions on divorce, the reason he records an element of the answer other gospels do not is because he records an element of the question the other gospels do not? We would not look at the differences between Matthew and Mark on divorce and conclude, since they are the same incident, they must be strictly synonymous in everything and thus dismiss Jesus's teaching on the exception for fornication. Why would we conclude that Matthew, Mark, and Luke's account of the Olivet Discourse must be seen as strictly synonymous and dismiss the possibility that the judgment scene at the end of the account addresses a specific element of the question that Matthew records?

"The End of the Age"

Before we can consider that possibility, we must first examine the two elements of Matthew's wording that preterists assume are synonymous with the questions of Mark and Luke. Let's begin with the final phrase "the end of the age."

As we begin we face some challenges. We have seen from our earlier studies that we cannot assume that "the end" in the Song of Moses necessarily points to the end of Israel. We saw it was a general witness applicable to the *after-times* of Israel throughout its history. Nor can we assume that "the

The Mount of Olives Discourse

Matthew	Mark	Luke	John
Foretelling Destruction of the Temple (24:1-2)	Foretelling Destruction of the Temple (13:1-2)	Foretelling Destruction of the Temple (21:5-6)	
Disciples' Question (24:3)	Disciples' Question (13:3-4)	Disciples' Question (21:7)	
The Beginning of Birthpangs (24:4-8)	The Beginning of Birthpangs (13:5-8)	The Beginning of Birthpangs (21:8-11)	
Coming Persecutions (24:9-14)	Coming Persecutions (13:9-13)	Coming Persecutions (21:12-19)	[Put out of synagogues – John 16:2]
Abomination of Desolation (24:15-22)	Abomination of Desolation (13:14-20)	Surrounded by Armies (21:20-24)	
False Christ's and False Prophets (24:23-28)	False Christ's and False Prophets (13:21-23)	[Lightning and Eagles Gathering – 17:23-24; 37]	
Coming of the Son of Man (24:29-31)	Coming of the Son of Man (13:24-27)	Coming of the Son of Man (21:25-28)	
Parable of the Fig Tree (24:32-36)	Parable of the Fig Tree (13:28-32)	Parable of the Fig Tree (21:29-33)	
[Watch, man on journey, unknown day and hour – 25:13-15; 24:40]	Watch, man on journey, unknown day and hour (13:33-37)	Watch, unknown hour, "all on the face of the earth" (21:34-36)	
As the Days of Noah (24:37-44)		[As the Days of Noah – 17:26-36]	
Parable of Faithful Servant (24:45-51)		[Parable of Faithful Servant – 12:41-46]	
Parable of the Ten Virgins (25:1-13)		[Lamps burning and knocking – 12:35-38]	
Parable of the Talents (25:14-30)		[Parable of the Minas –19:11-27]	
Judgment Scene (25:31-46)			

end of the days" of Daniel 12:13 points to the end of Israel. That phrase is distinct from "the end" of Daniel 12:4, which either refers to the end of Daniel's life or the end of the persecution of Antiochus Epiphanes. We can only apply it to Rome if we assume a jump in the text to describe Roman events. Even if we draw that conclusion, the "end" of Daniel 12:4 is never conclusively called "the end of the days." So, we must avoid bringing that assumption to the term, unless it can be proven from the text. In the same way, we must not automatically assume that it means *the end of the world,* unless we can demonstrate it from the text.

The phrase "end of the age" translates the phrase *tēs sunteleias tou aiōnos* (τῆς συντελείας τοῦ αἰῶνος). Most modern translations have rejected the KJV rendering "end of the world," because the Greek word *aiōn* carries a basic conceptual idea of time. Thayer defines it, "(1) for ever, an unbroken age, perpetuity of time, eternity; (2) the worlds, universe; (3) period of time, age." We should note, however, from Thayer's second definition that it can refer to the *world,* as is reflected at times in Scripture. For example, God through Christ, "made the worlds (*aiōn*)" (Heb. 1:2). The "worlds (*aiōn*) were framed by the word of God" (Heb. 11:3). With that said, we agree that "age" is the preferable sense in the phrase *tēs sunteleias tou aiōnos.*

Six times in Scripture we find this phrase and five of them are in Matthew. This helps us see the scope of its use in the book. Three instances are found in parables in chapter 13. In the Parable of the Wheat and Tares, as Jesus offered the explanation He declared, "The enemy who sowed them is the devil, the harvest is THE END OF THE AGE, and the reapers are the angels. Therefore as the tares are gathered and burned in the fire, so it will be at THE END OF THE AGE" (Matt. 13:39-40, emphasis mine). In the Parable of the Dragnet, He offers a similar explanation, "So it will be at THE END OF THE AGE. The angels will come forth, separate the wicked from among the just, and cast them into the furnace of fire. There will be wailing and gnashing of teeth" (Matt. 13:49-50, emphasis mine). In each of these examples of its use we see it as a time that involves angels, separation of the just from the wicked, and the assignment of punishment. The preterist would seek to identify this with AD 70, but it must be acknowledged that if so any separation of the just and the wicked could only be seen in spiritual terms. Sin, wickedness, and evil still continue to function. That hardly seems like it would fit a description of separating "the wicked from among the just."

The final example in Matthew poses the greatest challenge to the preterist position. At the close of the Great Commission, Jesus promised, "lo, I am with you always, even to THE END OF THE AGE" (Matt. 28:20, emphasis mine). If the "end of the age" is the end of the Jewish Age, how can we understand this promise? The world continued after AD 70. Preterists argue that Christ dwells with His people in the church, applying the promise of Revelation 21:3 to the age of Christ. Yet, was Jesus only promising to be with His people until the end of the Jewish Age? No. He was promising to be with them "always." Now, the preterist might argue, "if this means the end of the universe, could we argue that to mean He won't be with Christians after that?" The difference has to do with the view we take of Christ living with His people. If "age to come" means end of the world, the Christian is promised a literal, rather than spiritual presence of God with His people. If the preterist view is correct, the problem remains the same—how can they hope for His continued presence with them? How is it any different from His dwelling with us now in the church?

The final example is equally challenging to the preterist position. The Hebrew writer speaks of Christ's sacrifice of Himself, "now, once at THE END OF THE AGES, He has appeared to put away sin by the sacrifice of Himself" (Heb. 9:26, emphasis mine). We have discussed this passage earlier in our studies, noting that Christ's sacrifice was said to come "at the end of the ages," so, within the first century, before AD 70 the Holy Spirit described the time of Jesus's death as at "the end of the ages." We should note, unlike the phrases in Matthew this is in the plural. If Jesus died in the Jewish Age, and (as preterists argue) the age of Christ begins at AD 70, what "ages" are being described here?

An oft repeated statement used by preterists to defend their position is—"the Christian age has no end." We assume that argument is drawn from promises regarding the kingdom, that it, "shall stand forever" (Dan. 2:44). Their assertion, however, assumes that the conditions of the kingdom once established, cannot continue on into a changed new and heavenly existence. The assertion also fails to explain how Paul could speak of showing the riches of His grace" in the "AGES [plural] to come" (Eph. 2:7, emphasis mine). Their argument is that the Christian age came after AD 70 and "has no end." Like the Hebrew writer, Paul said of the accounts in the Old Testament, "Now all these things happened to them as examples, and they were written for our admonition, upon whom THE ENDS OF THE AGES have come" (1 Cor. 10:11, emphasis mine). Here, not only is "ages" plural, but "ends." How can they explain multiple "ends of the ages" if their limited concept of the "Christian age" has no end? This preterist argument doesn't work.

We can also, learn the sense of "the end of the age" by looking at some texts that speak of the "age to come." As Jesus speaks of those who sacrifice to serve Him, He contrasts, "this present time" with the "age to come" (Luke

18:30). In Mark's account He promises they shall, "receive a hundredfold now in this time—houses and brothers and sisters and mothers and children and lands, with persecutions—and in the age to come, eternal life" (Mark 10:30). Preterists argue that after AD 70 Christians now have eternal life, but notice the contrast here infers that the "persecutions" in "this time" (which they would identify as the Jewish Age) do not carry over into the "age to come." Have persecutions ended? No.

So, what can we conclude about Matthew's use of the phrase in Matthew 24:3b? Its use in Matthew 28:20 as a promise of Christ's presence "always" with His people, and its use earlier in the gospel in connection with angels, separation of the wicked, and punishment make it certain it is looking beyond the judgment that would come on Jerusalem in AD 70 to a more universal judgment at the end of the present universe.

"Your Coming"

The second phrase we must consider to determine if Matthew 24:3b is synonymous with the question of Mark and Luke or a distinct element is reference to "Your coming." The word translated "coming" is the Greek word *parousia* (παρουσία). We must confess that the study of the meaning and use of this word, perhaps more than anything else, has influenced my understanding of the focus of this discourse.

Preterists have also considered this word important to their concepts. In 1878, J. Stuart Russell wrote a book entitled *The Parousia: A Critical Inquiry into the New Testament Doctrine of Our Lord's Second Coming* (London: Daldy, Isbister & Co., 1878). Although not a full-preterist, this book, originally published anonymously, laid the foundation for preterist thought in modern times. In 1987, Max King, another former evangelist among churches of Christ who adopted full-preterism, authored *The Cross and the Parousia: The Two Dimensions of One Age-Changing Eschaton* (Warren, OH: Parkman Road Church of Christ, 1987). King's work was very influential in persuading some members of churches of Christ (especially in the Ohio area) to leave the church and adopt full-preterism.

My study of *parousia* led me in a much different direction. After its use in Matthew 24:3b, it is used three other times in the same chapter (24:27, 37, 39). The word is formed from *ousia* (the present participle of the verb *eimi*) meaning "being"—to which is added the prefix *para* meaning "by" or "beside." The word literally means "being beside" and always carries a very direct sense of one's actual, not figurative, emotional, spiritual, or mental presence. This is illustrated in the numerous times it is used in Scripture in its most basic sense. For example, Paul praised the Philippians for their obedience "not as in my presence (*parousia*) only, but now much more in my absence" (Phil. 2:12). Paul quoted his critics who claimed, "his bodily presence (*parousia*) is weak, and his speech is contemptible" (2 Cor. 10:10). This sense is frequently applied to those who have traveled somewhere and are finally present, whether it is Paul's companions (1 Cor. 16:17; 2 Cor. 7:6-7), Paul himself (Phil. 1:26), or even the "man of sin" of whom he warns the Thessalonians (2 Thess. 2:9).

To this basic sense, we must add a very distinct and specialized application of this word that has great bearing on its use in our text. Adolf Deissman, in his book *Light from the Ancient East* (New York: Hodder and Stoughton, 1910) writes, "From the Ptolemaic Period down into the second century AD we are able to trace the word in the East as a technical expression for the arrival or visit of the king or the emperor" (372). He explains further, that *parousia* came to be a time reference, explaining that in the second century, "in Greece a new era was reckoned from the *parousia* of the Emperor Hadrian" and "all over the world advent-coins were struck after a *parousia* of the emperor" (Ibid.). This technical sense is undoubtedly how *parousia* is used in the majority of instances in the New Testament. Christ's coming to earth in the first place was His *parousia*. Peter wrote, "For we did not follow cunningly devised fables when we made known to you the power and coming (*parousia*) of our Lord Jesus Christ, but were eyewitnesses of His majesty" (2 Pet. 1:16). Peter also speaks, however, of a future judgment as Christ's *parousia* (2 Pet. 3:4, 12). On that day he says the heavens will "be dissolved" and "the elements will melt with fervent heat" (2 Pet. 3:12). Remember, we saw that the text does not support interpreting this to mean *elements of the Mosaic System*. Paul tells us, this will be a day Christ will raise His people from the dead "at His coming (*parousia*)" (1 Cor. 15:23), so as not to be preceded by those "who are alive and remain until the coming (*parousia*) of the Lord" (1 Thess. 4:15). The "man of sin" will be consumed "with the brightness of His," that is Christ's, "coming (*parousia*)" (2 Thess. 2:8), but His people will be "preserved blameless unto the coming (*parousia*) of our Lord Jesus Christ" (1 Thess. 5:23; cf. 1 Thess. 3:13). Christians must be "patient unto the coming (*parousia*) of the Lord" (Jas. 5:7), that we may "not be ashamed before Him at His coming (*parousia*)" (1 John 2:28). This inevitability must call the disciple to "establish" his heart (Jas. 5:8) and not be "shaken in mind" or "troubled" (2 Thess. 2:1-2).

Now, we recognize that preterists might look at many of these examples and argue, "These are talking about AD 70, not final judgment." But, let's go back to Deissman's point. When I was a child, I remember Richard

Nixon's historic trip to China. It was a monumental thing for a strongly anti-communist US president to travel to this country that had, for so long been closed-off to the West. It too, became a type of time reference. A friend of mine from India loved Nixon, because when he came to China he also went to India. My friend measured his own personal timeline looking back to the time of *Nixon's Coming* (so to speak). If Deissman is correct that *parousia* carried this significance in connection with an actual coming and literal presence of someone, it must influence how we interpret its use in Scripture.

It is my contention that all references to Christ's *parousia* refer to an actual presence of Christ in connection with His *parousia* or "coming." Paul even indicates that the Thessalonians would, themselves be in "the presence (*emprosthen*) of our Lord Jesus Christ at his coming (*parousia*)" (1 Thess. 2:19). In consideration of the New Testament usage of *parousia*, Harold W. Mare concludes, "This summary of the testimony to the *parousia* certainly points to a widespread belief in the future advent of Christ, a hope that no doubt came from the Savior Himself (Matt. 24-25, etc.)."[3]

All of this tells us that in the first century the term *parousia* would not be applied to something short of an actual *visit* or *coming* of Christ. Mare writes further, "He does not use *parousia* simply to describe a *presence*. Rather, His usage of the word has a dynamic force—Jesus will come and be present in resurrection power and glory (cf. 1 Cor. 15:23)" (338).[4] The second century apologist Justin Martyr, is one of the first to speak of Christ's life on earth as His "first coming (*proten parousian*)" (*Dialogue* 14). Justin explicitly explains his understanding that Christ's first *parousia* was when He walked on earth, His second will be "according to prophecy, when He shall come from heaven with glory, accompanied by His angelic host, when also He shall raise the bodies of all men" (*First Apology* 52). Deissman, noting Justin's application of this word, comments, "There is something peculiarly touching in the fact that towards the end of the second century, at the very time when the Christians were beginning to distinguish the 'first *parousia*' of Christ from the 'second,' an inscription at Tegea was dated: 'in the year 69 of the first *parousia* of the god Hadrian in Greece'" (*Light from the Ancient East*, 376-377). Clearly,

---

[3] "A Study of the New Testament Concept of the *Parousia*." *Current Issues of Biblical and Patristic Interpretation: Studies in Honor of Merrill C. Tenney.* Ed. Gerald F. Hawthorne. Grand Rapids: William B. Eerdmans Pub. Co., 1975, 339.

[4] Josephus used *parousia* of God's presence at Sinai (*Antiquities* 3.5.2) and in the tabernacle (*Antiquities* 3.8.5), but this is consistent with its application of an actual *presence* of the one to whom it is being applied. God was actually *present* in the Israelite camp, He did not accomplish this through the agency of another.

Hadrian was not a "god," but Jesus Christ was God in His first *parousia* just as He will continue to be in His second *parousia* or "coming."

Some argue that the disciples would not have understood a promise of a future "second coming." Robertson L. Whiteside, in his book *Doctrinal Discourses* (Denton, TX: Miss Inys Whiteside, 1955) asked the question, "How could the disciples have asked about His second coming when they did not believe He would be killed?" (295). We must remember, immediately before leaving the temple Jesus warned the Jewish leaders, "for I say to you, you shall see Me no more till you say, 'Blessed is he who comes in the name of the Lord!'" (Matt. 23:39). These are the very words the disciples heard shouted upon Jesus's entry into the city only a few days before (Matt. 21:9). Matthew would cite this as fulfillment of Zechariah 9:9 —"Your King is coming to you" (Matt. 21:5). Deissman, in light of the application of *parousia* to kings and emperors, explains, "We now may say that the best interpretation of the primitive Christian hope of the *parousia* is the old advent text 'Behold thy *King* cometh unto thee'" (372). The disciples had seen His entry into Jerusalem, but there had been no conquest. He had made His *parousia* into Jerusalem, but no kingdom was yet established. Although the disciples may not have understood all that would later be revealed to them about a future coming, they certainly would have wanted to understand when the *coming* was of which He had just warned the Jewish leaders (23:39).

So what can we conclude about the phrase "Your coming" in Matthew 24:3b? Its specialized meaning of the actual presence of the one to whom the word is being applied would preclude interpreting its use in a figurative, spiritual, or metaphorical sense. As a result we cannot understand the phrases "Your coming" and "the end of the age" as strictly synonymous with the questions of Mark and Luke. We must conclude, therefore that Matthew's inclusion of these elements anticipates aspects of Jesus's answer in the discourse that will address these parts of the question.

The Content of the Discourse

I hope that the arguments offered above have been persuasive to convince the reader of the two-pronged focus of the discourse. I recognize, however, that many preterists might not be convinced by my reasoning. When I started work on this section of Matthew for my commentary I saw very quickly that this is a passage that has inspired mountains of literature and a plethora of diverse opinions and explanations of its meaning. What I decided to do, rather than trying to pick a view that someone else had advocated, was to sit down with a Bible and pen and paper and track what I could see in the text. The charts that follow were the result of this process.

Having determined the two elements that Jesus set out to address I listed all of the points from 24:4-14. Jesus starts by telling them all of the things that will happen that do not signal "the end of the age" or the destruction of Jerusalem. While I recognized that the phrase "the end" could refer to either of these in the context of the things Jesus set out to answer, it seemed most likely that its use would point to "the end of the age" unless otherwise indicated by the text. Remarkably, I began to see that much of the text explains different things that will happen that will *not* be signs that either of these things is about to happen. These things are compared to "the beginning of birth pangs" (NASB). Jesus tells His disciples that in spite of all the ominous things that will happen "the end is not yet" (Matt. 24: 6).

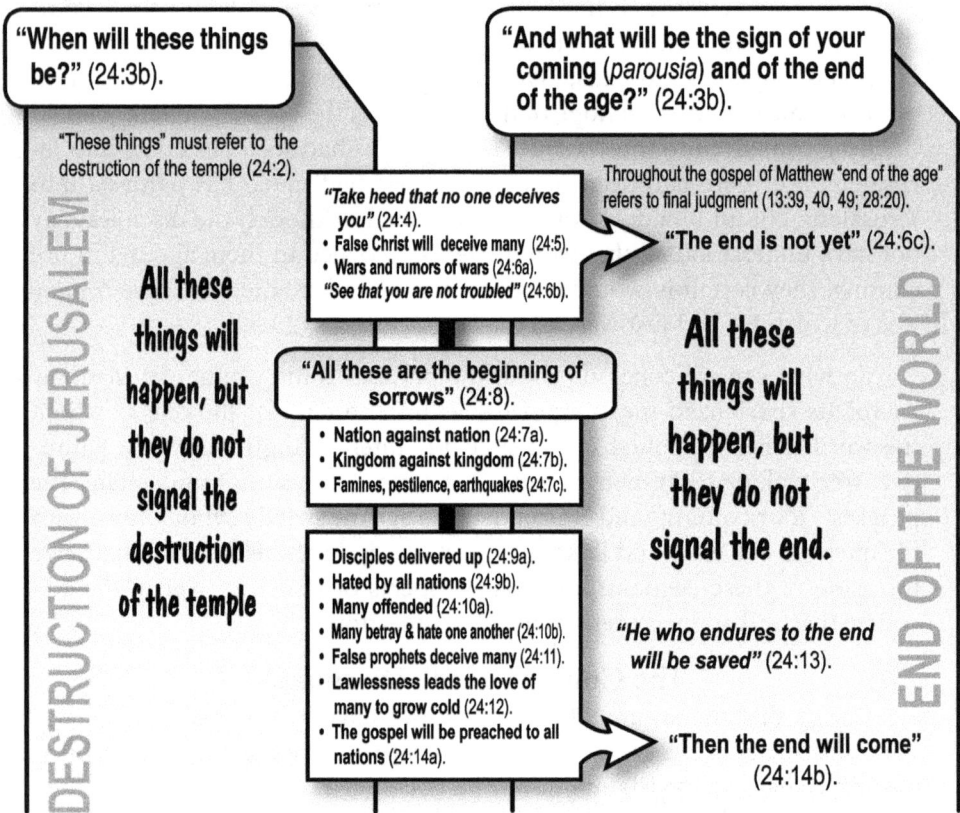

"When will these things be?" (24:3b).

"And what will be the sign of your coming (*parousia*) and of the end of the age?" (24:3b).

"These things" must refer to the destruction of the temple (24:2).

Throughout the gospel of Matthew "end of the age" refers to final judgment (13:39, 40, 49; 28:20).

"Take heed that no one deceives you" (24:4).
• False Christ will deceive many (24:5).
• Wars and rumors of wars (24:6a).
"See that you are not troubled" (24:6b).

"The end is not yet" (24:6c).

DESTRUCTION OF JERUSALEM

All these things will happen, but they do not signal the destruction of the temple

"All these are the beginning of sorrows" (24:8).
• Nation against nation (24:7a).
• Kingdom against kingdom (24:7b).
• Famines, pestilence, earthquakes (24:7c).

END OF THE WORLD

All these things will happen, but they do not signal the end.

• Disciples delivered up (24:9a).
• Hated by all nations (24:9b).
• Many offended (24:10a).
• Many betray & hate one another (24:10b).
• False prophets deceive many (24:11).
• Lawlessness leads the love of many to grow cold (24:12).
• The gospel will be preached to all nations (24:14a).

"He who endures to the end will be saved" (24:13).

"Then the end will come" (24:14b).

The first things that Jesus began to address which He told His disciples they would "see" come in Matthew 24:15-17. Both Matthew and Mark call it the "Abomination of Desolation" (Matt. 24:15; Mark 13:14), which He says was "spoken of by the prophet Daniel." We observed in our study of Daniel 11-12 that our understanding of Jesus's meaning in the Olivet Discourse influences how we must interpret that text. If Jesus meant this is *exactly* what Daniel was pointing to, it forces us to see a shift in Daniel's focus away from events related to Antiochus Epiphanes and towards Roman involvement in Palestine much earlier in the text than even most preterists generally argue. We should remember that Jews since the time of Antiochus consistently identified his institution of idol worship in the temple with the "abomination of desolation" (1 Maccabees 1:54; cf. Babylonian Talmud, *Ta'anith* 28b). On the other hand, if Jesus is saying that this will be *like* the thing spoken of by Daniel we do not have to force a transition to Rome upon the text of Daniel where the content does not allow for it.

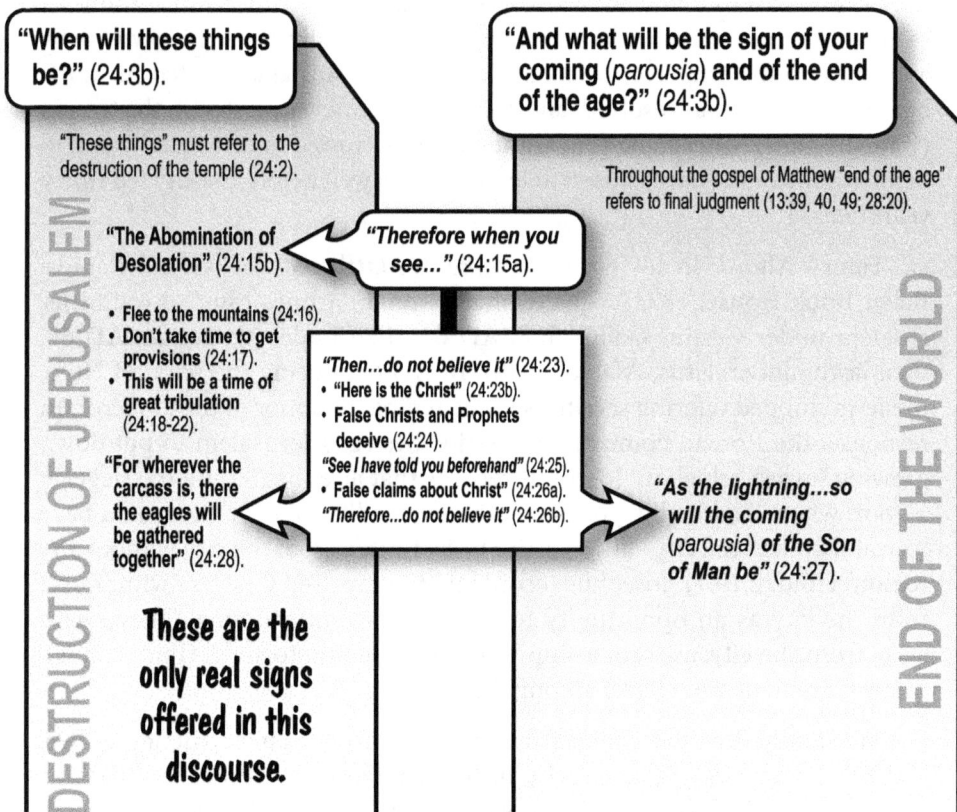

"When will these things be?" (24:3b).

"And what will be the sign of your coming (*parousia*) and of the end of the age?" (24:3b).

"These things" must refer to the destruction of the temple (24:2).

Throughout the gospel of Matthew "end of the age" refers to final judgment (13:39, 40, 49; 28:20).

DESTRUCTION OF JERUSALEM

END OF THE WORLD

"The Abomination of Desolation" (24:15b).

"Therefore when you see..." (24:15a).

- Flee to the mountains (24:16).
- Don't take time to get provisions (24:17).
- This will be a time of great tribulation (24:18-22).

"Then...do not believe it" (24:23).
- "Here is the Christ" (24:23b).
- False Christs and Prophets deceive (24:24).
"See I have told you beforehand" (24:25).
- False claims about Christ (24:26a).
"Therefore...do not believe it" (24:26b).

"For wherever the carcass is, there the eagles will be gathered together" (24:28).

"As the lightning...so will the coming (*parousia*) of the Son of Man be" (24:27).

These are the only real signs offered in this discourse.

As Luke addresses this section of the discourse he does not use the phrase "Abomination of Desolation," which should not surprise us, since Luke is generally believed to be aimed at a Gentile audience who might not recognize as readily the wording of Daniel. He put it, "But when you see Jerusalem surrounded by armies, then know that its desolation is near" (Luke 21:20).

That may suggest that what Jesus says they will "see" is the growing Roman presence in the city that would eventually lead to its destruction.

Several things happened in the years before the fall of Jerusalem that could have matched Jesus's description. For example, Jesus told them they would see this abomination "stand in the holy place," or as Mark puts it "standing where it ought not" (Mark 13:14). Around AD 40 the Roman emperor Gaius (better known by his nickname Caligula) in his arrogance commanded that a statue of himself be set up in the temple (Philo, *Embassy to Gaius* 188, 198-348 cf. Josephus, *Antiquities* 18.8.1-19.1.2). Josephus records that in order to "take himself to be a god," he sent the Roman commander Petronius with orders to kill or take into captivity any who opposed his plan (*Wars* 2.10.1). The Jews in great numbers appealed to Petronius, who eventually risked his own life by appealing to the emperor to reconsider. Caligula was assassinated in Rome before the matter was resolved, and the statue was never erected in the temple (Ibid. 2.10.2-5). Christians who witnessed how close this command came to being fulfilled may have chosen to leave the city well before the city fell thirty years later.

Henry Alford, in his *Greek Testament: Matthew–John* (Grand Rapids: Baker Book House, 1874) explains that, "Roman armies camped round Jerusalem under Cestius Gallus first, AD 66, then under Vespasian, AD 68, then lastly under Titus, AD 70" (238). In AD 66, during the reign of Nero, the Jews stopped offering sacrifices in the temple in honor of the emperor. In response, the Roman commander Cestius besieged Jerusalem to put down growing Jewish rebellion. Josephus records that after beginning the siege, at a point when "had he but continued the siege a little longer" he would have "certainly taken the city" (*Wars* 2.19.6), "he retired from the city without any reason" (Ibid. 2.19.7). Josephus records that many used Cestius's withdrawal from the city as an opportunity to leave Jerusalem, claiming, "they swam away from the city, as from a ship when it was going to sink" (Ibid. 2.20.1). Many Christians were likely among this number.

We should note two things from Jesus's words: (1) an instruction to flee, and (2) a warning of the severity of this tribulation. Although Christians had been taught, "do not resist an evil person" (Matt. 5:39), Jesus makes it clear, there is no shame in avoiding persecution when possible. The church historian Eusebius records that before Jerusalem fell, Christians left the city. Describing "one of the cities of Perea, named Pella," he records:

> To it those who believed on Christ migrated from Jerusalem, that when holy men had altogether deserted the royal capital of the Jews and the whole

land of Judea, the judgment of God might at last overtake them for all their crimes against the Christ and his Apostles . . . (*Ecclesiastical History* 3.5.3).

Understanding that many hardships would come as the natural course of life in this age (24:4-14), distinguishing these from the abomination of desolation that Jesus warned them they would see, was intended to lead the believer to prudence in avoiding unnecessary exposure to persecution. Disciples were not called to stand their ground in the face of the Roman assault on Jerusalem. They were to flee to the mountains to be spared the horror of Jerusalem's destruction.

We observed in our study of Daniel, the similar, but distinct wording that both apply to the times of hardship being foretold. Daniel reads, "And there shall be a time of trouble, such as never was since there was a nation, even to that time" (Dan. 12:1b). Jesus declares, "For then there will be great tribulation, such as has not been since the beginning of the world until this time, no, nor ever shall be" (Matt. 24:21). His addition of the words "no, nor ever shall be" make it likely He was distinguishing the hardships under Antiochus Epiphanes from the Roman destruction of Jerusalem.

The question sometimes arises, were either of these events truly the most horrible times of tribulation that ever were or shall be? We should note that both are addressing what would happen to God's people, and specifically Israel as a nation. Its final destruction as a people would end all that could be imposed upon it. We might look at the Holocaust of World War II and wonder if it was not more oppressive upon those who endured it, but that simply illustrates that the modern day Jews who suffered through that horror were no longer considered a nation or in covenant with God.

History has recorded just how horrible the Roman destruction of Jerusalem truly was and how accurately the Lord's words were fulfilled. Josephus records that the siege of the Roman commander Titus lasted from April to September during which 1,100,000 died and 97,000 were taken away captive (*Wars* 6.9.3). 600,000 dead bodies were thrown from the gates, and within the city the bodies of the dead lay in heaps (Ibid. 5.13.7). During this horrible time the lack of food led to fighting over every morsel of food, with the hungry forced to gnaw on leather straps and sandals for some sustenance (Ibid. 6.3.3). Some even killed nursing infants and cooked them for food (Ibid. 6.3.4). Josephus wrote that one cannot "imagine anything either greater or more terrible than this noise" as the fire from the burning temple roared, the Roman legions shouted, and the defeated Jewish citizens groaned in anguish watching the most important symbol of their faith go up in flames (Ibid.

6.5.1). Indeed this was an event of agony and horror "such as has not been since the beginning of the world until this time, no, nor ever shall be."

In Matthew 24:23-26 Jesus restates some of the same warning from the beginning of the discourse against being deceived by false Christs. He then makes two statements we believe are likely intended to distinguish "the end of the age" (i.e., the end of the world) from the events of the destruction of Jerusalem. He declares, "For as the lightning comes from the east and flashes to the west, so also will the coming of the Son of Man be. For wherever the carcass is, there the eagles will be gathered together" (Matt. 24:27-28). Preterists have argued that it would not make sense for Jesus to shift back and forth to address different subjects in the same discourse. Yet, consider the possibility that, in answer to the initial question regarding His "coming" (or *presence*), for the first time in the discourse He returns to address specifically the issue of His "coming (*parousia*)." We realize that preterists (and some partial-preterists) want to take these concepts together, and thus conclude that the destruction of Jerusalem was the "coming of the Son of Man," being discussed. However, if it is correct that *parousia* always carries with it the sense of one's *actual presence* what would that indicate in Jesus's use of it here? We believe Jesus is saying when the actual presence (the "coming" or *parousia*) of the "Son of Man" occurs there will be no question, no doubt, no confusion with false messiahs. Everyone will see it, like lightning that "comes from the east and flashes to the west." By contrast, the destruction of Jerusalem (i.e., where "the carcass is") will be where "the eagles will be gathered together."

Neither Mark nor Luke includes this statement in their accounts of this discourse. Luke includes a similar statement, however, in Jesus's answer to the Pharisees' question regarding "when the kingdom of God would come" (Luke 17:20b). After a similar warning not to follow those who claim "Look here" or "Look there" for the kingdom (Luke 17:23), He proclaimed, "For as the lightning that flashes out of one part under heaven shines to the other part under heaven, so also the Son of Man will be in his day" (Luke 17:24). Jesus may do the same thing in Luke He does in Matthew's account of the Olivet Discourse. After declaring that "the kingdom of heaven does not come with observation" (Luke 17:20c), He warned them not to be deceived by those who would claim it was "here" or "there" (Luke 17:21a). Jesus does not say the coming of the kingdom is "as the lightning"—rather, "the Son of Man will be in His day" (Luke 17:24). Jesus has affirmed that, "the kingdom of God is within you" (Luke 17:21b). He does not contradict what He has just said. Instead, just as in the Olivet Discourse, Jesus distinguishes false claims from true by the evident nature of His true *parousia*. The "Son of Man . . . in

His day" cannot refer to the establishment of the kingdom, but it must refer to final judgment.

Some brethren argue that this verse (and the discourse as a whole) apply to the destruction of Jerusalem and not final judgment. Arthur Ogden, for example in his commentary on Revelation entitled *The Avenging of the Apostles and Prophets: A Commentary on Revelation* (Pinson, AL: Ogden Publications, 1985), compares Jesus's words in the Olivet Discourse with Matthew 16:28 and Mark 9:1 when Jesus promised His disciples they would not "taste death until they see the Son of Man coming in His kingdom" writing, "there are no indications that anyone saw Him personally with the human eye, yet they did see evidence of His presence in the power of His comforter, the Holy Spirit" (65). Fair enough, but we should note that Matthew 16:28 and Mark 9:1 do not use the term *parousia* of Christ's "coming (*erchomenon*) in his kingdom" (16:28) as it would be accomplished on Pentecost. Christ's "coming in His kingdom" cannot be equated with His *parousia*. Kenneth Chumbley, in his commentary on Matthew, also takes this as a reference to the destruction of Jerusalem, writing "Christ's coming in judgment on Israel would not be done in secret; it would be unmistakable and obvious as a bolt of lightning (Isa. 30:30-31; Zech. 9:14)" (427).[5] Certainly all in Palestine in the first century would have seen the destruction of Jerusalem as a significant military conquest, however, the very fact that today we still debate whether it was the Lord's "coming" or not shows that it was not.

If it is correct that Matthew 24:27 describes Jesus's final "coming" or *parousia*, how are we to understand this reference to "the eagles" gathered together around the carcass? Some have suggested that Jesus is alluding to the description of eagles given in Job 39:27-30. Speaking of God's power over various creatures within nature, the Hebrew text puts it "where the slain are there it is." The Greek Old Testament which was translated prior to the New Testament reads very similar to our text, "wherever the carcasses may be, immediately they are found" (Brenton). If this is the sense, Jesus may offer a paraphrase of Job 39:30, to illustrate how evident His final coming will be. If this is the case, then the word "for" connects this verse to the previous verse comparing Jesus's *parousia* to "lightning."

While this may be the sense, there is good reason to conclude that Jesus's reference to "eagles" is a reference to the standards carried by Roman legions. On the top of the military standards carried by Roman legions there was usually an image of the emperor just below the image of an eagle. Unlike the decorative and symbolic use we see in the United States, the Ro-

---

[5] Chumbley, Kenneth L. *The Gospel of Matthew*. Nashville: Selfpublished, 1999.

man eagle had religious and military significance within Roman culture. F. F. Bruce explains, "it is a fact that the 'eagles' and other standards of the Roman army were regarded as sacred objects. The 'eagle' the standard of the legion, was kept in a special shrine in the military camp and regarded as affording sanctuary" (13).[6] The Greek historian Appian, speaking of the Roman standards seized by Pompey called "the eagle (*ton aieton*)" something that was "the most lordly (*kuriotaton*) thing among the Romans" (*Civil Wars* 2.9). In describing the procession of a Roman army, Josephus wrote:

> Then came the ensigns encompassing the eagle (*ton aeton*), which is at the head of every Roman legion, the king and strongest of the birds, which seems to them a signal of dominion, and an omen that they shall conquer all against whom they march; these sacred ensigns are followed by trumpeters (*Wars* 3.6.2; 5.2.1).

Would Jesus have referred to "eagles" here as an allusion to Roman power? Would this have been understood by His Jewish disciples? There is evidence that in the time of Jesus the Roman use of these images had already come into conflict with Jewish opposition to idolatry. Pilate, for example, was the first procurator to bring into Jerusalem standards with the image of the emperor. This caused such a stir, that some Jews who petitioned for their removal were even willing to lay down their lives rather than see what they viewed as idols set up in Jerusalem. Pilate eventually had the standards moved back to Caesarea (Josephus, *Antiquities* 18.3.1). Near the close of the reign of Tiberius, the Roman commander Vitellius planned to march through Judea to go to battle against the Nabataean king Aretas. When Jewish leaders learned of his plans, they persuaded him not to because "the laws of their country would not permit them to overlook those images that were brought into it" on the standards of the Roman legions (Josephus, *Antiquities* 18.5.3). The Qumran Habakkuk Commentary (1QpHab), discovered among the Dead Sea Scrolls, refers to a people it calls the *Kittim*, believed (as discussed earlier) by many scholars to refer to the Romans. Daniel 11:30 prophetically used this designation of Rome. The Qumran text not only speaks of them as devouring nations "like an eagle" (3.8-11), but also "sacrificing to their standards" (6.4). Josephus records that after the Romans had burned the temple, they set their standards against the eastern gate and offered sacrifices to them there (*Wars* 6.6.1). If this is the sense, Jesus is alluding prophetically to what would happen when the Roman armies would surround the spiritual carcass of Jerusalem. If this is the focus, the word "for" must be understood to refer back to the previous subject in verses 15-22 of the "Abomination of Desolation" as seen in God's punishment of Jerusalem.

---

[6] F. F. Bruce, "The Dead Sea Habakkuk Scroll." *The Annual Leeds University Oriental Society* I (1958/59) 5-24.

Luke records that Jesus had previously made this same statement in a discussion prompted by a question from the Pharisees about when the kingdom would come (Luke 17:20-37). In that discourse, He also offered a similar declaration regarding the Son of Man's coming like lightning (Luke 17:24), and offered the parallel to our text after a description of some who are taken and some left (Luke 17:31-36). After being asked "where, Lord?" Jesus declared, "Wherever the body is, there the eagles will be gathered together" (Luke 17:37). The context in Luke doesn't help us determine if Jesus's reference to "eagles" applies to Roman power, or something like lightning that is clearly seen.

Matthew 24:29a introduces a time transition with the words "Immediately after the tribulation of those days," followed by cosmological apocalyptic language (24:29b). Notice the transition in the chart below:

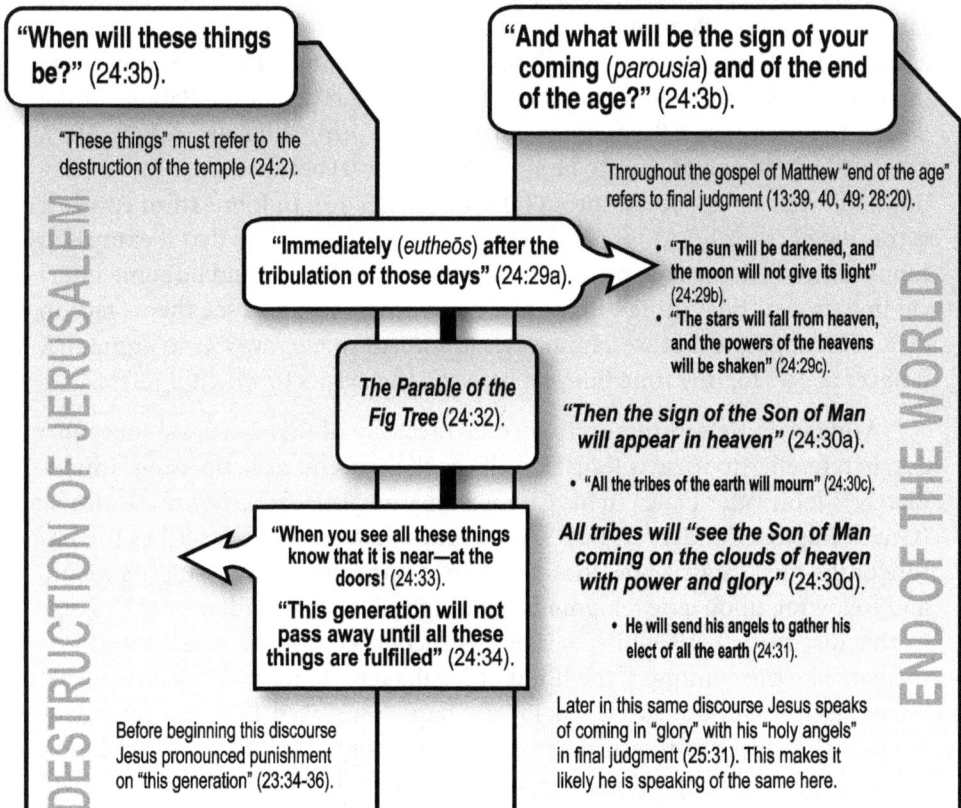

Many brethren would not make the same application we do to these words, concluding that it is not until after 24:34 that Jesus shifts to a discussion of final judgment. In my judgment that conclusion is drawn from a perceived need to oppose false claims made by premillennialists and is not demanded within the text itself. To address this we must consider two questions: (1) What timeframe is indicated by the phrase "immediately after"? and (2) Should the heavenly signs that follow be understood literally or as figurative eschatological language?

It is clear that the events described are said to happen "after (*meta*)" the tribulation surrounding the destruction of Jerusalem. What is more difficult to determine is the timeframe indicated by the word translated "immediately (*eutheōs*)." Many understand *eutheōs* to indicate a thing that happens in consecutive order after something else with no time interval in between. Certainly *eutheōs* often has that sense. In the New Testament it is used of miraculous healings that took place "immediately" (Matt. 8:3; 20:34; Mark 1:31; 2:12), or of actions that happened directly in response to something else (Matt. 4:20, 22; 27:48; Mark 1:10). The word, however, literally refers to the *straightness* of something and is often translated "straightway" in the KJV (Matt. 14:22; 21:2; Mark 2:2). Although that generally involves something with little or no time interval in between, that is not always true. For example, in the Parable of the Sower, the seed that fell on stony soil sprang up "immediately" (Matt. 13:5). Obviously there would have to be some time interval between the time of sowing, and when a plant could sprout (cf. Matt. 25:15-16). In John's third epistle it is translated "shortly" (3 John 14). The context makes it clear that it expressed John's desire to come as soon as possible, although there would be some interval in between the writing of his epistle and when he could see them "face to face." This suggests that we cannot define *eutheōs* so narrowly as to argue that it never allows for any time interval between the events to which it refers.

Aside from determining the specific meaning of this word, we must also ask, in reference to *what* is Jesus describing these events as happening "immediately"? John Peter Lange in his *Commentary on the Holy Scriptures: Matthew* (Grand Rapids: Zondervan Pub. Co.), argues that, "*eutheōs* describes the nature of the final catastrophe, that it will be at once swift, surpassingly sudden, and following upon a development seemingly slow and gradual" (427). Later in this discourse Jesus will speak of His second coming as sudden and immediate like the coming of the flood of Noah's day (Matt. 24:37-39) or a thief breaking into a house (Matt. 24:43). Perhaps Jesus used this term consecutively with respect to the subjects under discussion. That is, the destruction of Jerusalem will happen first, but His *parousia* and "the end of the age" will come next (*straightway*) in the order of things with no time actually specified.

Clearly, with God, great periods of time can be viewed as taking place "shortly" or "immediately." We might compare Jesus's words in our text with the phrase He used later in the gospel when standing before the High Priest.

He declared, "hereafter (ap' arti) you will see the Son of Man sitting at the right hand of the Power, and coming on the clouds of heaven" (26:64, NKJV). The term translated "hereafter" comes from the Greek words *apo* meaning "from" and *arti* meaning "just now, this moment" (Thayer). Jesus used the same phrase when telling Nathanael, "hereafter (ap' arti) you shall see heaven open, and the angels of God ascending and descending upon the Son of Man" (John 1:51). Neither Nathanael nor the high priest saw the things promised "just now" or at "this moment" when Jesus spoke these things, but with these words Jesus expressed the pending immediacy of the things they would see in the future. This may be the same way that Jesus used the term "immediately (*eutheōs*)" in Matthew 24:29a.

The question of the timeframe indicated by the term "immediately" becomes significant in light of how we understand the heavenly signs described. Jesus said, "the sun will be darkened, and the moon will not give its light; the stars will fall from heaven, and the powers of the heavens will be shaken." (Matt. 24:29b). Obviously, in literal terms the sun was not "darkened" nor did the moon fail to "give her light" in the days right after the destruction of Jerusalem. Josephus claimed that there were various "stars" and "comets" in the sky that were seen before the Jewish rebellion took place that some interpreted as good omens (*Wars* 6.5.3), but even if such things happened it would not match all of the events described in our text, which are said to happen "after the tribulation of those days." This leads many to conclude that Jesus was not speaking literally, but using *eschatological* (or "end times") language in reference to a significant act of Divine judgment.

There is no question that throughout Scripture such language is used of significant acts of divine judgment when no literal fulfillment is involved. Isaiah was led by the Holy Spirit to use similar language regarding the sun, moon, and stars in prophesying the destruction of Babylon (Isa. 13:1-11). As we noticed earlier in our studies, Isaiah spoke of the heavens being "dissolved" and "rolled back as a scroll" in punishment of Edom (Isa. 34:4-5). Ezekiel used similar language in prophecies concerning Egypt (Ezek. 32:1-8). In the New Testament, Joel 2:30-31 is quoted as being fulfilled in Acts 2:19-20 on the day of Pentecost. It described wonders in the heavens taking place, but connects them with what happened in the outpouring of the Holy Spirit on Pentecost. The book of Revelation speaks of the sun and moon being darkened and the stars falling in connection with "the great day of his wrath" as the sixth seal is opened. It is unclear if this points to a Divine judgment before the final judgment or to one of the many cycles of hardship followed by deliverance described throughout the book (Rev. 6:12-17).

While we acknowledge that end times language is common in Scripture in a figurative sense, it raises an issue that must be addressed. Does such language foreshadow future realities, or is it simply poetic hyperbole? Preterists must interpret every use of eschatological language as hyperbole, symbolic, or figurative. Which means the heavens and earth will never literally be destroyed by fire. The stars will never *fall*, and there will not be a literal "new heaven" or "new earth." As we noticed earlier, this presumes that Jews who read the Old Testament had no concept of a final destruction of the universe—which we have already demonstrated is a presumption that the Scriptures disprove (e.g., Gen. 8:22; Ps. 102:26; Dan. 12:13, et al.). Even so, preterists argue that all eschatological language is simply a way of expressing significant changes in the present order of things that, in reality (so they argue), will continue indefinitely.

If that is true would it not compromise the very nature of God? The Hebrew writer said, "it is impossible for God to lie" (Heb. 6:18). Paul, spoke of things, "God, who cannot lie, promised" (Titus 1:2). If God says He will do things that He will never actually carry out, He has lied. This would be like parents who repeatedly threaten to punish a disobedient child, yet never follow through on their threat. This is not the God of the Bible! God told Ezekiel, "For I am the LORD. I speak, and the word which I speak will come to pass" (Ezek. 12:25).

On the other hand, if cosmological apocalyptic language has an immediate application and a future literal application there is no compromise of God's honesty. As God told Jeremiah, "I am watching over My word to perform it" (Jer. 1:12, NASB). Eschatological language is not unrealized threat. It foreshadows events that one day will actually happen (see chapter 3). So, before we are too quick to dismiss a text of Scripture as simply *end times* prophetic language, we must ask ourselves if the text offers clues that point beyond the immediate application of the imagery and connect it with literal promises of future events.

In Luke's account of the Olivet Discourse, he records that Jesus may have used some eschatological language in application to the destruction of Jerusalem (Luke 21:25-26a). However, if so, he simply speaks of "signs in the sun and moon and stars" (Luke 21:25) then quickly shifts to language that looks ahead to final judgment (Luke 21:26b-28). Matthew, however, records more direct language that we believe clearly points to final judgment. For example, only a few verses after this Jesus declared, "heaven and earth will pass away, but My words will by no means pass away" (Matt. 24:35). We have seen that we cannot assume this means the *Mosaic System*. So there is no contextual reason to see this as speaking of anything other than the literal heaven and earth—otherwise the comparison fails. So, would Jesus speak figuratively of the "sun" and "moon," the two great lights that rule the heavens failing in their function, then literally of their *passing away* in the same discourse without explanation or clear distinction? Reference to *shaking* "heaven and earth" was used in the Old Testament of the overthrowing of political powers (Hag. 2:21-23), but in the same context allusion was made to a future time when God would "shake heaven and earth" and "all nations" (Hag. 2:6-7). The Hebrew writer applies this to the final destruction of heaven and earth at a time when "the things that are made" will be removed, so that the "things which cannot be shaken may remain" (Heb. 12:25-27). That cannot refer to the Mosaic System—now under Christ "things that are made" still exist. All of this must suggest that Jesus's statement that, the "powers of the heavens shall be shaken" parallels His declaration "heaven and earth will pass away."

After reference to these heavenly signs, Jesus then declared:

> Then the sign of the Son of Man will appear in heaven, and then all the tribes of the earth will mourn, and they will see the Son of Man coming on the clouds of heaven with power and great glory. And He will send His angels with a great sound of a trumpet, and they will gather together His elect from the four winds, from one end of heaven to the other (Matt. 24:30-31).

Preterists and some partial-preterists seek to apply this to the destruction of Jerusalem, but let's see if that explanation is valid. The disciples had asked what would be "the sign" of His coming (Matt. 24:3), yet so far, Jesus had only given one identifiable event that could warn them of the impending destruction of Jerusalem (Matt. 24:15). All other hardships, disasters, and persecutions were identified as "the beginning of sorrows" (Matt. 24:8), that must not to be taken as signs of His *parousia* or "coming" (Matt. 24:6). Now, after warning them that His coming would be something about which no one would need to inform them (Matt. 24:5, 23-26), because it would be evident to all (Matt. 24:27), He tells them "the sign of the Son of man" will not be something that precedes His coming, it will be His *parousia* itself! We must remember that Jesus said this will "appear" after the tribulation "of those days"—i.e., after the destruction of Jerusalem (Matt. 24:29). Mark also places the sign of the Son of Man "after" the tribulation of Jerusalem (Mark 13:24). This negates any conclusion that equates Jesus's *parousia* with the destruction of Jerusalem. We cannot equate the "tribulation of those days" with a divine act of *coming* in judgment if the text says it would happen "after" the very act considered by some to be Christ's *parousia* or "coming."

As mentioned above, some brethren feel compelled to conclude that Jesus is using eschatological language here and in the previous verse in reference to the fall of Jerusalem because of the misapplications premillennialists have made to these Scriptures. Premillennialists argue that the "Abomination of Desolation" (Matt. 24:15) is some future desecration of a rebuilt temple, and the "great tribulation" (Matt. 24:21) is global in nature, preceding Jesus's coming to establish an earthly millennial reign. We can reject these false conclusions, but still acknowledge when Jesus addresses things that point to final judgment. We should note that this is something at which "all the tribes of the earth will mourn." This is language that is global in nature. This is restated when John is told in Revelation 1:7, "Behold, he is coming with clouds, and every eye will see him, even they who pierced him. And all the tribes of the earth will mourn because of Him." We noted at the beginning of this study that Mark and Luke do not record the element of the disciples' question directly addressing final judgment. In this case, the wording in Luke demonstrates that Jesus was addressing both subjects. He speaks of the impact that will affect "all those who dwell on the face of the whole earth" (Luke 21:35). That would not be true of the destruction of Jerusalem, but it will be true of final judgment. All the tribes of the earth did not mourn because of the tribulation connected with the destruction of Jerusalem, but they will on the Day of Judgment.

Not only will "all the tribes of the earth" weep, but "they shall see the Son of man coming in the clouds" (Matt. 24:30b). Jesus does not use *parousia* here (as in 24:3 and 27), but, all of the synoptic gospels say "they will see the Son of Man coming in the cloud" (Luke 21:27) or "clouds" (Mark 13:26). The text in Revelation noted above begins, "Behold, He is coming with clouds, and every eye will see Him, even they who pierced Him" (Rev. 1:7; cf. Zech. 12:10). This wording is first introduced in Daniel when the prophet sees "one like the Son of Man coming with the clouds of heaven" (Dan. 7:13). Daniel sees this One given "dominion, glory, and a kingdom" (Dan. 7:14; cf. Matt. 28:18-20). That reference to "coming with the clouds" describes Christ's rule and power, but not necessarily His coming in final judgment.

To understand Jesus's meaning in our text we must also compare it with other statements Jesus made in Matthew (and even in this same discourse). Earlier in the gospel Jesus spoke of the time when He would come in glory "with His angels" to "reward each according to His works" (Matt.16:27). In the same context He promised that those who heard Him would, "see the Son of Man coming in His kingdom" (Matt. 16:28). This distinguishes the final judgment when men receive their *reward* from Pentecost, when the kingdom came. Later, in this same discourse Jesus spoke of a time "when the Son of man comes in His glory and all the holy angels with Him" (Matt. 25:31). The context of this statement clearly addressed final judgment on the last day. It is reasonable to assume that, since the same wording is used within the same discourse (with no explanation of a change in application), it must apply to the same event. Only a short time after this, Jesus would declare to the high priest, "I say to you, hereafter you will see the Son of Man sitting at the right hand of the Power, and coming on the clouds of heaven" (Matt. 26:64, NKJV).[7] There is no indication this was figurative. These factors make it likely that Jesus was not simply talking about *coming* in His kingdom, or in power, but in final judgment.

We noticed earlier in our studies that preterists try to bring to Matthew 24:31 their concept of a *gathering* of the remnant of Israel together with the Gentiles under the Messiah. We saw in that study that the New Testament makes it clear that such promises pointed to all that was accomplished at the cross and in the preaching of the gospel. As we consider this text we should note that Matthew has already recorded earlier in the gospel Jesus's promise that He would one day come in glory "with His angels" on the Day of Judgment (Matt. 16:27). In Matthew chapter 25, Jesus uses the same imagery as He continues the Olivet Discourse once again of final judgment, "when the Son of man comes in His glory and all the holy angels with Him" (Matt. 25:31). It is unlikely that Jesus would speak in figurative language of *sending* angels (when talking about the destruction of Jerusalem) and then in the same discourse later speak literally of their role in final judgment without some explanation or distinction.

Jesus's teachings here establish the clear fact that on the Day of Judgment Jesus will be accompanied by His angels. Paul reasserts this, declaring that, on the Day of Judgment, Christ will come with "His mighty angels" (2 Thess. 1:7). They will come, "with a great sound of a trumpet." Few images are so closely associated with final judgment as this. Paul says there will be a "last trumpet" at the sounding of which "the dead will be raised incorruptible" (1 Cor. 15:52). On the Day of Judgment, "the Lord himself shall descend from heaven, with a shout, with the voice of the archangel, and with the trump of

---

[7] Samuel G. Dawson, yet another former evangelist among churches of Christ, but now a full-preterist, in his book *Essays on Eschatology: An Introductory Overview of the Study of Last Things* (Amarillo, TX: SGD Press, 2009), tries to argue that Jesus's words to Caiaphas were fulfilled in the destruction of Jerusalem (57), but Jesus said to the high priest, "you will see the Son of Man" (Matt. 26:64), just as in Matthew 24:30 He promises all the tribes of the earth (cf. "every eye" Rev. 1:7) shall see the Son of man. This was not fulfilled in AD 70, but it will be on the Day of Judgment.

God: and the dead in Christ shall rise first" (1 Thess. 4:16, ASV). As an inspired writer, this may have been revealed to him directly, or Paul may have drawn this imagery from our Lord's very words in this discourse.

Jesus's description that the angels "shall gather together His elect" is significant. Some argue this refers to a spiritual re-gathering of His people unto faithfulness to Him at AD 70. The Law of Moses had promised a scattering of the Israelites as punishment for sin and a re-gathering of them in their repentance (Deut. 30:1-6; Zech. 2:6-9). However, earlier in Matthew in the Parable of the Wheat and Tares, Jesus described final judgment, calling it also "the end of the age" (Matt.13:40), when He will "send out His angels" to gather out of His kingdom those who practice lawlessness (Matt. 13:41). If this is talking about AD 70 it would mean a few things: (1) This angelic gathering was spiritual and unseen—yet Jesus said He would be *seen* (Matt. 24:30); (2) The angels are to gather out of His kingdom those who practice lawlessness (Matt. 13:41). Can those in the kingdom today still practice lawlessness? Yes. That shows this gathering cannot be an AD 70 judgment.

This role of angels in *gathering* and identifying those faithful and unfaithful to God runs throughout the New Testament. The one who is "ashamed" of Christ and His words, will find Christ "ashamed" of him, "when he cometh in his own glory, and the glory of the Father, and of the holy angels" (Luke 9:26, ASV). Christ will confess or deny "before the angels of God" those who confess or deny Him (Luke 12:8-9). Although it does not refer to final judgment, upon death we learn that angels take the souls of the faithful dead to "Abraham's bosom" (Luke 16:22). Why would Jesus speak figuratively in our text of a fact treated literally throughout Scripture? Jesus is clearly shifting to discuss final judgment in answer to the last element of the disciples' question (Matt. 24:3).

The final passage we must consider directly, which pertains to the focus of the discourse is Matthew 24:34. It reads, "Assuredly, I say to you, this generation will by no means pass away till all these things take place." Since the battles within the church over premillennialism in the early 20th century, most brethren have seen this passage as a transitional verse. Among those who see the two-pronged approach dealing with both the destruction of Jerusalem and final judgment, the rationale has been, "everything before this must describe events that happened within the time of the generation then living." We should note, however, that the preceding verse says, "So you also, when you see all these things, know that it is near—at the doors!" (Matt. 24:33). We should note that so far in the discourse the only specific observable event Jesus identified was "when you see the abomination of desolation"

(Matt. 24:15). Other occurrences, which do not signal "the end," may be observable, but are not distinguishable from the ordinary events of life in this age—they are "the beginning of sorrows" or "birth pangs" (Matt. 24:8). The heavenly signs that have been cited (Matt. 24:29-31) may only be *seen* if they are understood literally. If they are literal they have not yet taken place, and must therefore apply to Christ's final coming at "the end of the age." If they constitute figurative eschatological language they are not things they could see. This suggests that what Jesus meant by the phrase "all these things," are the things He has told them to look for, not everything that was mentioned before it. They could see the "Abomination of Desolation" leading to the destruction of Jerusalem. That generation living at the time would see all those things Jesus said would be visible to them.[8]

Summary

The remainder of the discourse, as Matthew preserves it involves: A comparison to the Days of Noah (Matt. 24:37-44); the Parable of the Faithful Servant (Matt. 24:45-51); the Parable of the Ten Virgins (Matt. 25:1-13); Parable of the Talents (Matt. 25:14-30), and the Final Judgment Scene (Matt. 25:31-46). Mark and Luke do not include these elements within their account of the discourse, although Luke records similar teachings in different contexts (e.g., Comparison to the Days of Noah – Luke 17:26-36; Parable of Faithful Servant – Luke 12:41-46; Lamps burning and knocking – Luke 12:35-38, and the Parable of the Minas – Luke 19:11-27).

Most who take the two-pronged view of the discourse generally see all that follows as addressing final judgment. Preterists understand all that follows, even the final judgment scene, as applying to the destruction of Jerusalem. We fail to see how Jesus's words at the beginning of the judgment scene— "All the nations will be gathered before Him, and He will separate them one from another, as a shepherd divides his sheep from the goats" (Matt. 25:32)— could by any stretch of the imagination apply to the destruction of Jerusalem without completely robbing them of their force. "All the nations" were not *gathered* or *separated* in the destruction of Jerusalem. They will be on the Day of Judgment. Regarding the application of the end of the discourse, I personally believe that all of it has some application to both in the sense that all of the closing teachings stress the idea of being watchful and prepared before God.

---

[8] A similar issue arises in Daniel 12:7, which also uses the phrase "all these things." Like Matthew 24:34, the context discusses things that could be seen and things beyond the timeframe being discussed (and thus unobservable). Both phrases must be understood to apply the "things" that could be observed, not to every single thing discussed in the words that come before them.

That theme would explain why Mark and Luke do not emphasize as distinctly the application to one over the other.

So how can we tie all of this together? I believe we must conclude that Matthew addresses an element of the disciples' question not emphasized in Mark and Luke. This explains why Matthew includes the judgment scene at the end, and reference to "the end of the age" and the beginning. While much of the focus of the discourse is on the AD 70 destruction of Jerusalem, the use of *parousia* precludes understanding it as a reference to a spiritual, figurative, or metaphorical coming in judgment. We must conclude, therefore, that this discourse addresses both final judgment and the events of AD 70. Regarding the latter it reveals itself to be one of the most profound demonstrations of Divine foreknowledge in all of Scripture—that Jesus would predict, nearly forty years before it happened the destruction of such a monumental structure only recently completed.

Parousia in Paul's Letters to Thessalonica

Before we conclude our study of the Olivet Discourse we must also consider some texts outside of this discourse that make extensive use of the word *parousia* in order to test whether the conclusions we have drawn are valid. Preterists often appeal to these texts to argue that only if they offered immediate relief to the Jews in Thessalonica would they prove to be a source of any comfort whatsoever.[9] Paul uses the word *parousia* six times in these epistles, so let's see what they can teach us about its meaning.

The first two come in a context that is not strictly eschatological. As Paul expresses his desire to come to them, he asks, "For what is our hope, or joy, or crown of rejoicing? Is it not even you in the presence of our Lord Jesus Christ at His coming (*parousia*)?" (1 Thess. 2:19). This doesn't tell us much that can help us determine if Paul means AD 70 or final judgment. He simply expresses his hope that they will be right with God at "His coming." We might note, however, that Paul speaks of them as being "in the presence" of the Lord at His coming. Certainly, in one sense all men are always in God's presence, but how would those in Thessalonica be "in the presence" of Christ in a coming upon Jerusalem?

---

[9] In 2017, in a two-night debate that Don Preston did with David Hester, a professor at Faulkner University associated with institutional brethren on preterism, Preston repeatedly stressed this point. Unfortunately the tone of this debate became very aggressive at times, which became a distraction to what could have been a productive discussion. Night one (https://www.youtube.com/watch?v=iHQMbD22gM&t). Night two (https://www.youtube.com/watch?v=hjvu83xYrNc).

In a similar text in the next chapter, Paul writes:

> Now may our God and Father Himself, and our Lord Jesus Christ, direct our way to you. And may the Lord make you increase and abound in love to one another and to all, just as we do to you, so that He may establish your hearts blameless in holiness before our God and Father at the coming (*parousia*) of our Lord Jesus Christ with all His saints (1 Thess. 3:11-13).

Like the previous text, Paul wants to see them and prays they will be right with God at the Lord's "coming," but here he qualifies that when He comes it will be "with all His saints." Now preterists might argue that this means a spiritual resurrection of the faithful dead, but we should note, while that might involve *His saints,* it would not involve "all His saints." If this phrase can be understood absolutely, only at the final judgment will all those in fellowship with God in Christ be said to come "with" Him.

The last two chapters of 1 Thessalonians focus on eschatology. Paul is concerned that some may misunderstand some things he seeks to clarify. He writes, "But I do not want you to be ignorant, brethren, concerning those who have fallen asleep, lest you sorrow as others who have no hope" (1 Thess. 4:13). He, like Daniel 12:2 speaks of those who have died physically as those who have "fallen asleep." He wants them not to feel sorrow because their brethren have died, like those in the world who have "no hope." That suggests that the hope the Christian possesses has some relation to comfort in the face of physical death.

He continues:

> For if we believe that Jesus died and rose again, even so God will bring with Him those who sleep in Jesus. For this we say to you by the word of the Lord, that we who are alive and remain until the coming (*parousia*) of the Lord will by no means precede those who are asleep (1 Thess. 4:14-15).

As we saw in our study on the resurrection, Christ's resurrection is offered as a token to prove that those who have died have a similar hope. We must note here that a contrast is drawn between those who "are alive" at the Lord's coming and those who "are asleep" (i.e., those who are dead). Let's notice what this says in relation to what will happen at the Lord's *parousia*. He continues:

> For the Lord Himself will descend from heaven with a shout, with the voice of an archangel, and with the trumpet of God. And the dead in Christ will rise first. Then we who are alive and remain shall be caught up together with them in the clouds to meet the Lord in the air. And thus we shall always be with the Lord (1 Thess. 4:16-17).

Let's think through this and consider what it would be saying if this applies to AD 70. The preterist argues that in a spiritual sense, the trumpet sounded at that time, the Lord came spiritually in judgment and when this happened there was a spiritual resurrection of God's saints. We must notice, however, what is said about those who "are alive and remain." We saw earlier that *sleep* described physical death. There is nothing in the text that would indicate that we should shift here and apply those "alive" to mean some spiritual *raising up*. In spiritual terms, Paul taught that Christians have already been raised up to sit with Christ (cf. Eph. 2:6). Yet, Paul says here those physically alive at Christ's *parousia* "shall be caught up together with them" (i.e., the saints who were dead). How was a meeting of those physically alive with those who have been physically dead accomplished in AD 70? It was not! This must be talking about a final judgment. That helps us understand the earlier phrase "with all His saints" (1 Thess. 3:13). Paul explains that this assurance should give them *comfort*. He writes further, "therefore comfort one another with these words" (1 Thess. 4:18). Let's keep that in mind when we look at 2 Thessalonians—the assurance of a reunion of living saints with departed saints at the Lord's *parousia* was intended to offer them comfort.

This leads him to continue a further discussion of this in the next chapter. He writes:

> But concerning the times and the seasons, brethren, you have no need that I should write to you. For you yourselves know perfectly that the day of the Lord so comes as a thief in the night. For when they say, "Peace and safety!" then sudden destruction comes upon them, as labor pains upon a pregnant woman. And they shall not escape. But you, brethren, are not in darkness, so that this Day should overtake you as a thief (1 Thess. 5:1-4).

Now we recognize that Scripture can use the term "day of the Lord" in reference to judgments that are not the final judgment. However, in this context, remember he has just described a *parousia* of Christ that will involve a reunion of the living saints with saints who have died—something that did not happen in AD 70.

Don K. Preston, in many of his writings, puts great emphasis on what he calls "time statements."[10] He and others appeal to texts like James 5:7—"be patient, brethren, until the coming (*parousia*) of the Lord," or James 5:8—"Establish your hearts, for the coming (*parousia*) of the Lord is at hand," arguing that the phrase "has drawn near" (GLT) means it was just about to happen. We should note how this differs from Paul's words to Thessalonica. It was a

---

[10]   See for example "Can God Tell Time," *Bible Prophecy,* April 10, 2018, https:// donkpreston.com/can-god-tell-time/.

church in the heat of persecution. Why doesn't he tell them *"the parousia is just about to happen"*? Instead he draws upon Jesus's own words from the Olivet Discourse and tells them it will come like a thief (cf. Matt. 24:43).

We have already seen that the context of 1 Thessalonians 5 makes it clear that Paul is talking about the final judgment. Should we consider the words of James any differently? No. Paul urges the saints to live so that Jesus's *parousia* (i.e., His actual presence) will not overtake them like a thief. James does the same thing. A recognition that it could be near would lead them to the same sense of watchfulness. To argue that James is talking about AD 70 ignores the clear and consistent application of *parousia* to a literal presence of the one whose "coming" is being described.

Near the close of the chapter Paul expresses again his hope for their faithfulness at the Lord's "coming." He writes, "Now may the God of peace Himself sanctify you completely; and may your whole spirit, soul, and body be preserved blameless at the coming (*parousia*) of our Lord Jesus Christ" (1 Thess. 5:23). We have already demonstrated that the context supports the interpretation that the *parousia* is Jesus's final coming in judgment, but what would this text be saying if we interpreted it as AD 70? Thessalonica was over 1000 miles from Jerusalem. If AD 70 was the Lord's coming, why would it matter for the brethren in Thessalonica to be found "blameless" in "spirit, soul, and body" at that time? Certainly, God's people should be faithful to Him at all times, but Paul speaks of this as if it will have a bearing on their fate at the time of the *parousia*. If this is AD 70 is makes no sense. If it is final judgment it is perfectly fitting.

Finally, Paul is believed to have written 2 Thessalonians very soon after his first letter. This can be seen clearly from the fact that Paul continues in the first chapter with some further teachings on eschatology. He writes:

> We are bound to thank God always for you, brethren, as it is fitting, because your faith grows exceedingly, and the love of every one of you all abounds toward each other, so that we ourselves boast of you among the churches of God for your patience and faith in all your persecutions and tribulations that you endure, which is manifest evidence of the righteous judgment of God, that you may be counted worthy of the kingdom of God, for which you also suffer; since it is a righteous thing with God to repay with tribulation those who trouble you, and to give you who are troubled rest with us when the Lord Jesus is revealed from heaven with His mighty angels, in flaming fire taking vengeance on those who do not know God, and on those who do not obey the gospel of our Lord Jesus Christ. These shall be punished with everlasting destruction from the presence of the Lord and from the glory of His power, when He comes (*erchomai*), in that Day, to be glori-

fied in His saints and to be admired among all those who believe, because our testimony among you was believed (2 Thess. 1:3-10).

This is a key text to many preterists. They argue, "What comfort would it give to those in Thessalonica to tell them that their persecutors would face punishment thousands of years in the future?"

It is clear from this text that they were enduring "persecutions and tribulations." It is true that the Lord promises to "repay with tribulation those who trouble" them and to grant them "rest with us when the Lord Jesus is revealed from heaven." But, let's consider some questions about this. First, we must ask again, would the living saints be united with the departed saints at the destruction of Jerusalem? If not, we must conclude that the *parousia* and "day of the Lord" addressed in 1 Thessalonians 4 and 5 is final judgment. Second, could we not ask the same thing about Paul's teaching here? Couldn't we ask, "What comfort would it give them to tell them that one day in their own death in the future they would be reunited with departed saints?" In reality, as the Bible teaches it, in death the righteous receive comfort (and perhaps reunion with other saints) and the dead receive punishment "awaiting judgment" (cf. 2 Pet. 2:4; Luke 16:19-31). The point is, if promises of a future reunion upon their own death were offered as comfort, why could a promise of future punishment for their persecutors not offer them similar comfort? To insist that the "rest" had to be immediate and physical forces something on the text that it does not say. Jesus asked, "shall God not avenge His own elect who cry out day and night to Him, though He bears long with them?" (Luke 18:7).

The word *parousia* is not used in 2 Thessalonians chapter 1, but it is three times in the next chapter. Its use at the beginning of that chapter likely connects it with the coming that was just being addressed. Paul writes, "Now, brethren, concerning the coming (*parousia*) of our Lord Jesus Christ and our gathering together to Him" (2:1). We considered this text in our discussion of the preterist concept of the *gathering* in AD 70. We concluded that the gathering promised in the prophets was accomplished in the cross and the gospel. This "gathering together" echoes what was discussed in 1 Thessalonians 4—the reunion of living saints with departed saints—something that did not occur at AD 70.

The final two examples come in discussions about the "lawless one." Paul writes:

And then the lawless one will be revealed, whom the Lord will consume with the breath of His mouth and destroy with the brightness of His coming (*parousia*). The coming (*parousia*) of the lawless one is according to the working of Satan, with all power, signs, and lying wonders, and with all un-righteous deception among those who perish, because they did not receive the love of the truth, that they might be saved (2 Thess. 2:8-10).

Whoever this "lawless one" may be, it seems clear that it is a literal human being who would live upon the earth at some time. Yet, in this text we see that the second instance of the use of *parousia* actually applies to the "lawless one."

We recognize that some preterist positions identify the "lawless one" with the high priest or some other Jewish leader. The argument is that Jesus's coming in the destruction of Jerusalem would "destroy with the brightness of His coming" those who had opposed God. Yet, if we compare the *parousia* of the "lawless one" with the *parousia* of Christ, what might it indicate? If we conclude that the *presence* of one is literal, actual, and not merely representative, what is there in the text to make us conclude that the other is not also literal, actual, and not representative?

Conclusion

We have seen that the Olivet Discourse deals with both the destruction of Jerusalem and the promise of a final judgment. Its use of figures and descriptions of the Lord's *parousia* set the stage for how references to His "coming" must be understood in other passages. In all examples of its use an actual, literal, and non-representative sense is carried into the text. This precludes us from interpreting such references to His "coming" as a reference to the events of AD 70.

THE DATE OF THE BOOK OF REVELATION

A final issue that is pivotal to the understanding of many who accept full-preterism is the dating of the book of Revelation. If it was written before AD 70 it is argued that the eschatological language it uses applies ultimately to Jerusalem (rather than Rome). If so, they argue the last two chapters must describe the church age rather than the end of the world, final judgment, and heaven and hell. To defend this position advocates offer the following arguments:

- John could have been on Patmos for a reason other than exile (1:9).
- Jerusalem could have been described as the city sitting on "seven mountains" (17:9) and the city which "reigns over the kings of the earth" (17:18).
- Revelation could not have been written after AD 70 because the temple is still said to be standing (11:1-2).
- Babylon refers to Jerusalem, not Rome (17:5, et al.).
- Chapters 21 and 22 can't be heaven because "nations" are said to walk "in its light" (21:24), bringing their "glory and honor" into it (21:26), and receiving "healing" (22:2).

Let's consider each of these points.

1. John on Patmos

The inspired record says this, "I, John, both your brother and companion in the tribulation and kingdom and patience of Jesus Christ, was on the island that is called Patmos for the word of God and for the testimony of Jesus Christ" (Rev. 1:9). So, what does this tell us?

First, John identifies himself as a companion with the brethren in Asia "in the tribulation and kingdom." So, he indicates that he had experienced *tribulation* and so had the brethren in the seven churches. That leads us to consider *when* did Christians in Asia face persecution? Before we seek to answer that, notice secondly, he is on Patmos, "for the word of God and for the testimony of Jesus Christ." The word twice translated "for" in this text is the

Greek preposition *dia* (διά). When used spatially, it means "through." When used causally, Thayer tells us it means, "the ground or reason by which something is or is not done; (1) by reason of; (2) on account of; (3) because of, for this reason; (4) therefore; (5) on this account." So, this either means John was on Patmos *in order to* proclaim "the word of God and the testimony of Jesus Christ," or he was on Patmos *as a result of* proclaiming "the word of God and the testimony of Jesus Christ."

To determine which of these alternatives fits the context, we should note, how John uses this language elsewhere in the book. For example, the book begins with John identifying himself as one "who bore witness to the word of God, and to the testimony of Jesus Christ" (Rev. 1:2). In the Greek, the phrase "word of God and testimony of Jesus Christ" is almost identical to its use in 1:9. This verse is clearly talking about *proclaiming* the word, but *dia* is not used here. On the other hand, elsewhere in the book when these same elements—"word of God" and "testimony"(also translated "witness")—are used with *dia* it is addressing the *cause* of the persecution. For example, "I saw under the altar the souls of those who had been slain for (*dia*) the word of God and for (*dia*) the testimony which they held" (Rev. 6:9)—"Then I saw the souls of those who had been beheaded for (*dia*) their witness to Jesus and for (*dia*) the word of God" (Rev. 20:4). This makes it likely that John, as a partner with others who faced tribulation, was speaking of himself in 1:9 the same way he spoke of the martyrs for faith in 6:9 and 20:4. He was on Patmos *as a result of* his teaching of the "word of God and the testimony of Jesus Christ."

Roman Persecution of Christians

If we may conclude that John was on Patmos as a form of punishment for teaching the gospel, what do we know about *when* this type of persecution happened in Asia Minor? Initially, of course the first persecution of Christians came from the Jews (Acts 7:59-8:1; 12:2). Even as Paul preached among the Gentiles, this continued into cites such as Thessalonica (ca. AD 49). However, outside of Palestine, such persecution was localized and Jews in these regions held little political power. It is unlikely that Jewish persecution could account for John's exile on a Roman controlled island.

By the time of Augustine (354-430), early church writers claimed there had been ten periods of Roman persecution against Christians—the first under Nero (ca. 64-68) and the second under Domitian (ca. 81/89-96) (Augustine, *City of God* 18.52; cf. Tertullian, *Apology* 5).

The Persecution of Nero

We know much about this first persecution because of writings of both Roman and Christian sources. The Roman Historian Tacitus, for example records that it began as the result of the great fire in Rome that burned in AD 64 (*Annals of Imperial Rome* 15.38-40). When Tacitus wrote, he only suspected that Nero had started the fire (Ibid., 15.38), but as time went on Roman historians seem to unanimously accept that Nero did this in order to replace what he considered to be old and unsightly buildings near his palace (Pliny, *Natural History* 17.1; Suetonius, *Nero* 38; Cassius Dio, *Roman History* 62.16). To divert attention away from the accusations made against him, Tacitus writes:

> But all human efforts, all the lavish gifts of the emperor, and the propitiations of the gods, did not banish the sinister belief that the conflagration was the result of an order. Consequently, to get rid of the report, Nero fastened the guilt and inflicted the most exquisite tortures on a class hated for their abominations, called Christians by the populace. Christus, from whom the name had its origin, suffered the extreme penalty during the reign of Tiberius at the hands of one of our procurators, Pontius Pilatus, and a most mischievous superstition, thus checked for the moment, again broke out not only in Judea, the first source of the evil, but even in Rome, where all things hideous and shameful from every part of the world find their centre and become popular. Accordingly, an arrest was first made of all who pleaded guilty; then, upon their information, an immense multitude was convicted, not so much of the crime of firing the city, as of hatred against mankind. Mockery of every sort was added to their deaths. Covered with the skins of beasts, they were torn by dogs and perished, or were nailed to crosses, or were doomed to the flames and burnt, to serve as a nightly illumination, when daylight had expired (*Annals* 15.44).

While this is an important extra-biblical attestation to the life of Jesus (called in the text "Christus"), it is also a horrifying record of the mistreatment of early Christians, all to cloak the sinfulness of this wicked monster! It is believed that both Peter and Paul died during this persecution (*First Clement* 5; cf. Eusebius, *Ecclesiastical History* 2.25.1-5). The Roman historian Suetonius doesn't connect this persecution to the fire, but also claims, "He likewise inflicted punishments on the Christians, a sort of people who held a new and impious superstition" (*Nero* 16.2).

The Persecution of Domitian

Unfortunately, less is preserved for us about the second persecution under Domitian. While one early Christian describes Domitian as "a man of Nero's type in cruelty" (Tertullian, *Apology* 5), our most extensive source for information about the persecution of Domitian comes from the early church historian Eusebius (ca. 260-341) in his *Ecclesiastical History* (3.17-29.1-11). He records that it began with the exile of a daughter of a consul who had become a Christian along with others to the Italian island of Pontia (Ibid., 3.18.5). Roman sources claim, the charge brought against them was, "atheism, a charge on which many others who drifted into Jewish ways were condemned. Some of these were put to death, and the rest were at least deprived of their property" (Cassius Dio, *Roman History* 67.14.2; cf. Suetonius, *Domitian* 15—"superstition"). We should not be surprised that Romans ignorant of gospel teaching would consider faith in Christ a form of Judaism. Christians were often accused of being "atheists" because they refused to worship pagan gods (*Martyrdom of Polycarp*). Eusebius tells us further that Domitian ordered the death of descendants of David (*Ecclesiastical History* 3.19) and interrogated the grandchildren of Jude, the brother of Jesus (Ibid., 3.20.1-11).

Some have questioned the scope of Domitian's persecution of Christians because the Roman claims are not as extensive as those about Nero. This overlooks some significant additional data. Clement, who likely lived during the persecution of Domitian, after referring back to the deaths of Peter and Paul, wrote, "To these men who spent their lives in the practice of holiness, there is to be added a great multitude of the elect, who, having through envy endured many indignities and tortures, furnished us with a most excellent example" (*First Clement* 6.1). Tertullian (ca. AD 160-220), a converted Roman lawyer, in his *Apology* directed to, "The Rulers of the Roman Empire," wrote, "Domitian, too, a man of Nero's type in cruelty, tried his hand at persecution; but as he had something of the human in him, he soon put an end to what he had begun, even restoring again those whom he had banished. Such as these have always been our persecutors,—men unjust, impious, base, of whom even you yourselves have no good to say, the sufferers under whose sentences you have been wont to restore" (*Apology* 5). While Tertullian is a little more forgiving of Domitian, these early claims make it evident that Domitian's persecution was just as cruel.

A number of years ago I was able to travel to Greece and Turkey with Ferrell Jenkins, former head of the Bible department at Florida College, who has been hosting tours of Bible Lands for years. In Delphi, brother Jenkins called our attention to an inscription bearing the name of Domitian. According to brother Jenkins, it is rare to find such inscriptions because the infamy of his persecution of Christians led many to deface inscriptions bearing his name following his death.

The Imperial Cult in Asia Minor

A final factor that must be considered in appraising the scope of Domitian's persecution is the issue of emperor worship. A common belief in pagan Roman religion was the concept that the dead became deified upon their death. Romans generally venerated their departed ancestors, but unlike Egypt, or some eastern cultures that worshipped living kings as gods, in Rome, this usually didn't happen. When living kings tried to confer deity upon themselves, it was usually met with scorn. Caligula (ca. 37–41), who reigned before Claudius, was such an emperor. He erected a temple to himself in Rome, and forced residents of Rome to worship him (Suetonius, *Caligula* 22). He even tried to put a statue of himself in the temple in Jerusalem (Josephus, *Antiquities of the Jews* 18.8.2).

Outside of Rome it was a different matter. As far back as Augustus the emperors allowed those in the provinces to worship them as gods. The first temple to the "Divine Caesar" was built in Pergamum in 29 BC (Tacitus, *Annals* 4.37). This may give special meaning to the Lord's description of the city as "where Satan dwells" (Rev. 2:13). Domitian, like Caligula, demanded that he be treated as a god within Rome. Roman historians claim that he insisted on being addressed as *Dominus et Deus* ("Lord and God") (Suetonius, *Domitian*, 13.2; Cassius Dio, *Roman History*, 67.4.7). Extensive archaeological work has been done on a temple located in Ephesus that was established for the purpose of worshipping the Flavian dynasty (i.e., Vespasian, Titus, and Domitian). Ephesus was granted the honor of being the *neokoros* or "temple-keeper" of the imperial cult. In his book *Twice Neokoros: Ephesus, Asia, and the Cult of the Flavian Imperial Family* (New York: Brill, 1993), Steven J. Friesen analyzes the evidence from inscriptions found on the remains of this temple and concludes:

> This examination of the temple inscriptions has produced several conclusions about the cult. First, the inscriptions allow us to date the cult precisely since they indicate that the temple was dedicated in 89/90 CE. This in turn leads to the conclusion that the right to establish the provincial cult in Ephesus was granted by Domitian, in the early to mid-eighties of the first century CE (49).

This dating is significant. Early in the first century the Imperial Cult in Asia Minor offered worship to the emperor as an option, but it was not bound upon all residents within the provinces. By the time of the emperor Trajan (98-117), letters written to him from the Roman governor of Bithynia, Pliny the Younger, indicate that it had become a capital offense to refuse to proclaim "Caesar is Lord," and sacrifice to him (*Letters* 10.96-97; cf. *Martyrdom of Polycarp* 8). This suggests that the later we move into the first century the more we may expect this as a binding law upon residents of Asia Minor, putting the lives of Christians in jeopardy.

According to Eusebius, Vespasian (ca. 69-79), the father of Domitian, who started the Flavian dynasty, did not persecute Christians (*Ecclesiastical History*

Temple of Domitian in Ephesus

3:17). Yet, it is clear that his son, Domitian, during his reign exiled Christians, insisted that he be honored as a god, and promoted emperor worship in Asia Minor. If John was on Patmos as a punishment for teaching the gospel, and describes himself as a partner in suffering with those in Asia Minor, it is reasonable to conclude that his exile occurred during the reign of Domitian.

Evidence for Exile under Domitian

Is there evidence to support this? Yes. One of the earliest writers to mention the time and place of the writing of the book of Revelation is Irenaeus (ca. 125-202).[1] He was born in Smyrna, one of the seven churches of Asia and later served as a bishop in Lyon, France. In his work entitled *Against Heresies,* he claimed that John wrote, "almost in our day, towards the end of Domitian's reign" (5.30.3). Domitian reigned from AD 81-96, and his persecution of Christians began about 89. So Irenaeus is placing the date of Revelation sometime during the years 89-96.

---

[1] Preterists try to discredit the claims of Irenaeus because his writings reflect that he had already begun to accept some false doctrines that would later grow into Roman Catholic doctrines, such as apostolic succession and one bishop over a church. We should note that those doctrinal errors are unrelated to any issues concerning the dating of Revelation. This treatment of Ireneaus ignores the close connection he had to people and places who were in a position to know exactly when the book was written. First, he is believed to have been from Smyrna and raised in a home of those who were already Christians. Second, he knew Polycarp (a bishop in Smyrna), who knew John (*Against Heresies* 3.3.4, cf Eusebius, *Ecclesiastical History* 5.20.5ff). This suggests that his claims likely reflect the testimony of those who were members of the church in Smyrna when the letters to the seven churches were first sent to them. This should not be casually dismissed.

A contemporary of Irenaeus, Clement of Alexandria (who died around AD 215) wrote a work entitled *On the Salvation of the Rich Man*. In it he echoes the claim that John was on Patmos as a punishment. He writes, "on the tyrant's death, he returned to Ephesus from the isle of Patmos" (42). Although he does not identify who the "tyrant" was, there would be no reason to mention his death unless it had some connection with why John was on Patmos.

Another near contemporary of Irenaeus was a Christian named Tertullian (ca. AD 160-220), who was from Carthage. We noted above his reference to Domitian as "a man of Nero's type in cruelty" (Tertullian, *Apology* 5). He quoted extensively from the book of Revelation and preserves a tradition that there was a failed attempt to kill John. He writes, "John was first plunged, unhurt, into boiling oil, and thence remitted to his island-exile" (*Prescription against Heretics* 36). Whether we accept this claim that John was delivered from boiling oil or not, his reference to Patmos is significant. Although he does not specify when John was on Patmos he speaks of it as an "island-exile." Thus, he too affirms the claim that John was on the island as punishment—not in order to preach.

Before we consider other sources, let's not miss the significance of these three early writers. We have three men from different places (Smyrna, Alexandria, and Carthage) who lived in the second century who all affirm that the reason John was on Patmos was as a punishment.

This is echoed further in the writings of Eusebius of Caesarea (ca. 260-341). He wrote one of the first extensive histories of the early church. He claimed that John, "was still living in Asia, and governing the churches of that region, having returned after the death of Domitian from his exile on the island" (*Ecclesiastical History* 3.23.1). He cited Irenaeus and Clement in support of this (Ibid. 3.18.2-7), quoting Irenaeus' additional claim, "And all the elders that associated with John the disciple of the Lord in Asia bear witness that John delivered it to them. For he remained among them until the time of Trajan" (Ibid., 3.23.3; cf. Irenaeus, *Against Heresies* 1.22.5). Eusebius wrote further:

> But after Domitian had reigned fifteen years, and Nerva had succeeded to the empire, the Roman Senate, according to the writers that record the history of those days, voted that Domitian's honors should be cancelled, and that those who had been unjustly banished should return to their homes and have their property restored to them. It was at this time that the apostle John returned from his banishment in the island and took up his abode at Ephesus, according to an ancient Christian tradition (Ibid., 3.20.10-11).

We should notice several things about this. First, he affirms that the time and reason for John's stay on Patmos was within the reign of Domitian and as a punishment. Second, it is interesting that the most extensive ancient historian of the early church identifies these facts as "an ancient Christian tradition." In other words, by his day these facts were the accepted and understood explanation of why John was on Patmos.

This understanding is further confirmed in the writings of Victorinus of Pettau (who was martyred under Diocletian around AD 303). In his commentary on Revelation, which is one of the earliest known to have survived, he writes:

> ... When John said these things he was in the island of Patmos, condemned to the labor of the mines by Caesar Domitian. There, therefore, he saw the Apocalypse; and when grown old, he thought that he should at length receive his quittance by suffering, Domitian being killed, all his judgments were discharged. And John being dismissed from the mines, thus subsequently delivered the same Apocalypse, which he had received from God (10.11).

Not only does Victorinus further affirm the view that John was on Patmos as punishment in the reign of Domitian, but adds the claim that his exile involved forced labor in the mines.

Finally, we should consider a claim by Jerome (AD 340-420), who was responsible for the first careful Latin translation of the New Testament. In his work entitled *Lives of Illustrious Men,* he wrote of John, "In the fourteenth year then after Nero, Domitian having raised a second persecution he was banished to the island of Patmos, and wrote the Apocalypse . . . . But Domitian having been put to death and his acts, on account of his excessive cruelty, having been annulled by the senate, he returned to Ephesus . . ." (9). Nero reigned from AD 54-68, so fourteen years after this would be 82. That is a little earlier than some date the persecution of Domitian, but it is well into his reign, which began in 81.

Opposing Claims

From what we can find, there are only three ancient writers that make claims contrary to this, and they are all very late. The first, is Epiphanius of Salamis (ca. 310-403), who wrote a series of works refuting heresies. He forcefully refuted those who rejected the inspiration of the book of Revelation. In addressing when the gospel of John was written, after discussing the other gospels, he wrote, "Later, therefore, though from caution and humility he had declined to be an evangelist [i.e., to write a gospel], the Holy Spirit compelled John to issue the gospel in his old age when he was past ninety, after his return from Patmos under Claudius Caesar and several years of his residence in Asia" (*Panarion* 51 "Against the sect which does not accept the gospel according to John or his Revelation," 12.2). In the same work he later spoke of John, "who prophesied before his falling asleep, during the time of Claudius Caesar and earlier, when he was on the island of Patmos" (Ibid., 33.9).

As we consider his claims, aside from presuming to know what the Holy Spirit compelled John to do—something not revealed in Scripture, it is clear that something is seriously off in his dating. For example, if he is claiming that John was ninety during the time of Claudius Caesar—Claudius reigned from AD 41-54—that would make John in his late sixties during the ministry of Jesus! Yet, he is clearly portrayed as young in the gospels (cf. John 20:4). Perhaps, he's not saying that John was ninety while on Patmos, but turned ninety some time after that when he wrote the gospel. Even so, he affirms that John's time on Patmos was in connection with his move to Asia and Ephesus, which causes some other problems. As late as the meeting in Jerusalem to discuss Gentile circumcision, the apostles were still in Jerusalem (Acts 15:2, 4; 16:4). This is thought to have been around AD 50. By that time Paul had not yet gone to Ephesus. That comes in Acts 18:19 when he is only there briefly near the end of his second journey—thought to have begun around AD 51. It is during his third journey (Acts 18:23-21:17), thought to have begun in AD 54, that Paul spent two years in Ephesus (Acts 19:10) and likely helped establish many of the seven churches of Asia. Yet, Luke says nothing about John being in Asia or Ephesus at that time.

So, if Epiphanius is correct, are we to believe that John left Jerusalem (after the meeting in Jerusalem) lived "several years in Asia" during which time he was on Patmos "under Claudius Caesar" at the very time Paul was there and Luke says nothing about his presence there? Claudius's reign ended in 54—yet Epiphanius claims he was on Patmos "under Claudius." Is he claiming he was *exiled* by Claudius? History records Claudius compelling the Jews to leave Rome (Acts 18:2), but there is nothing said about a persecution of Christians or exile of apostles. Not only is Epiphanius's writing too late to be given much weight, he rejects the overwhelming testimony of those who lived closer to the place and time of John's residence in Asia, and he offers a chronology that conflicts with the biblical record.

The second writer may actually cite Epiphanius's claim. In the sixth century Apringius of Beja, from Iberia (in modern Portugal), claimed that, "The ecclesiastical writers have taught" that "in the time of Claudius Caesar," during "the famine which the prophet Agabus had announced in the Acts of the Apostles" (cf. Acts 11:28), Claudius "instituted a persecution of the churches" and transported John "into exile" where he wrote the book of Revelation (*Tractate on the Apocalypse* 1:9). While he claims church "writers" (plural) taught this, his claim has the same problems as those of Epiphanius. We should note that (although his timing is flawed), he too claims John was exiled. It is also clear that his view was not universally accepted. In the next century, the British monk Bede (AD 673-725), the author of the monumental *Ecclesiastical History of the English People,* and widely considered one of the most educated men of his time, wrote, "History notes that John had been banished to this island by the emperor Domitian on account of the gospel" (*Explanation of the Apocalypse* 1.9).

Finally, the third writer who gives an opposing view is even later than Epiphanius. Arethas, the Greek Archbishop of Caesarea, (born around AD 860), wrote a commentary on Revelation. In discussing the 144,000 sealed in Revelation 7:4-8 he wrote:

> For there were many, yea, a countless multitude from among the Jews, who believed in Christ: as even they testify, who said to St Paul on his arrival at Jerusalem: Thou seest, brother, how many thousands of Jews there are which believe. (Acts 21.20.) And He who gave this revelation to the Evangelist, declares, that these men shall not share the destruction inflicted by the Romans. For the ruin brought by the Romans had not yet fallen upon the Jews, when this Evangelist received these prophecies: and he did not receive them at Jerusalem, but in Ionia near Ephesus. For after the suffering of the Lord he remained only fourteen years at Jerusalem, during which time the tabernacle of the mother of the Lord, which had conceived this Divine offspring, was preserved in this temporal life, after the suffering and resurrection of her incorruptible Son. For he continued with her as with a mother committed to him by the Lord. For after her death it is reported that he no longer chose to remain in Judea, but passed over to Ephesus, where, as we have said, this present Apocalypse also was composed; which is a revelation of future things, inasmuch as forty years after the ascension of the Lord this tribulation came upon the Jews (*Commentary on Revelation* 19 on 7:4-8).

Arethas claims present many of the same problems as those of Epiphanius. Fourteen years after Jesus's death would be AD 47, yet (as noted above) John was still in Jerusalem for the meeting over Gentile circumcision (ca. AD 50), and Paul had not yet preached in Ephesus and Asia (ca. 51-56). Although he doesn't try to connect John's time on Patmos to Claudius, his chronology is still in conflict with the biblical record. So, we may weigh the sources as follows:

	Late Date Sources	Early Date Sources
2nd – 3rd Century	Irenaeus (125-202) "End of Domitian's reign"	
	Clement of Alexandria (–215) On Patmos until "Tyrant's death"	
	Tertullian (160-220) "Island-exile"	
4th Century	Victorinus (–303) Domitian, labor in the mines	
	Eusebius (260-341) Domitian, exile, "ancient Christian tradition"	
5th Century	Jerome (340-420) Domitian, exile	Epiphanius (310-403) "Under Claudius Caesar"
6th Century		Apringius (ca. 500s) Claudius Caesar, exile
7th Century	Bede (673-725) Domitian, exile	
9th Century		Arethas (860—) Left Jerusalem 14 years after Jesus's death

This makes it clear that the overwhelming testimony of ancient sources closest to the time of the writing of the New Testament confirms a late date for the writing of Revelation during the reign of Domitian and John's exile. The claims of late writers who contradict this must be rejected because they stand in conflict with biblical chronology.

2. The City on Seven Hills

In the inspired record, after identifying the harlot seated on a scarlet beast of seven heads and ten horns as "Babylon the Great, the Mother of Harlots" (Rev. 17:1-5), the Holy Spirit leads John to write, "Here is the mind which has wisdom: The seven heads are seven mountains on which the woman sits" (Rev. 17:9). In my judgment this is one of the most important verses in the entire book when considering issues of dating and interpretation. How we understand this verse will determine how we interpret the entire book and how we place its date.

It begins with the unusual statement "here is the mind which has wisdom" (NKJV, NASB—"hath" KJV, ASV). Some dynamic equivalence translations put it "this calls for a mind with wisdom" (RSV, NIV, ESV), "Here there is need for a discerning mind" (TCNT), or "In this situation a wise mind is needed" (GW). This tells us John is giving the reader a clue the *wise mind* can grasp. This should not be seen as a mystery that cannot be unraveled. We can understand it and John's audience could have understood it. So, any conclusion we reach must be something Christians in first century Asia Minor could have understood as easily as we can.

The text identifies the seven heads as "seven mountains on which the woman sits" and the last verse of the chapter identifies the woman as a "great city" (Rev. 17:18). So, we need to identify a *great city* that *sits* on seven mountains or hills. Before we go further, we must acknowledge that the number *seven* is used throughout Scripture (and in the book of Revelation) as a figure of completeness. It is possible, therefore, that the number seven may not be used literally, but as a figure of the complete depravity of the harlot. With that said, if this is a clue to help the reader understand the symbolism of the woman seated on the beast, we might expect it to be a more literal description in order to understand the figurative symbolism. If so, what can we find regarding great cities on seven hills?

Scripture uses the term "great city" in reference to a number of cities. These include: Gibeon (Josh. 10:2); Jerusalem (Jer. 22:8; Rev. 11:8—spiritually called "Sodom and Egypt"; cf. Lam. 1:1 "great among the nations"); the New Jerusalem (Rev. 21:10); Nineveh (Jonah 1:2; 3:2; 4:11); and the Babylon of Revelation (Rev. 14:8; 16:19; 18:10, 16, 18, 21). Unfortunately, there is no other Scripture that specifically identifies a city by saying it has seven "mountains" or "hills." Neither Rome nor Jerusalem are ever described that way in Scripture.

Mountains of Jerusalem

From the list of cities called "great" we see that this description was applied to Jerusalem, but also to Gentile cities. Is Jerusalem ever said to *sit* on seven hills? Most often it is associated with one hill—Mount Zion. At first this is the term applied to the portion of Jerusalem known as the "City of David" (2 Sam. 5:7; 1 Kings 8:1). Eventually, even when the city expanded to encompass other areas, the term "Zion" (or "Mount Zion") was still used to refer to Jerusalem as a whole (Isa. 24:23; 30:19; 31:9; 32:20; 37:22; 52:1; 62:1; 64:10; Jer. 26:18; Lam. 1:17; Joel 2:32; 3:16-17; Amos 1:2; Micah 3:12; 4:2).

There are other mountains associated with Jerusalem, but the words of the Psalmist are informative—"As the mountains surround Jerusalem, so the LORD surrounds His people from this time forth and forever" (Ps. 125:2). To *surround* something is not the same thing as to *sit on* something. Some lists of Jerusalem's so-called seven hills often mistakenly include surrounding mountains. For example, the Mount of Olives and Mount Scopus, which formed a high ridge along the eastern side of Jerusalem were never enclosed within the ancient walls of the city. Luke says the Mount of Olives was "a Sabbath day's journey" from Jerusalem (Acts 1:12). The first century Jewish historian Josephus said the Mount of Olives was a "distance of six furlongs from Jerusalem" (*Jewish Wars*, 5.2.3) and Mount Scopus was "seven furlongs from the city" (Ibid., 2.19.4). To be true to the text, these must be excluded from any attempt to associate seven hills with Jerusalem.

Josephus actually claimed, "The city was built upon two hills" (Ibid., 5.4.1), but then goes on to describe four hills. The main two hills he calls "the Citadel" on which the temple was built[2] and "Arca" (meaning "highest"). According to Josephus, during the Hasamonean period "Arca" (a high crescent shaped ridge) was reduced in order to fill-in a valley known as the Tyropoeon (or "Cheesemakers") Valley that ran south as far as the Pool of Siloam. Before this, the Tyropoeon Valley separated "Arca" from a third hill that Josephus does not name. That seems to suggest that in the first century Arca had been reduced making the lower third hill indistinguishable from it. (Ibid., 5.4.1-2). Today most sources refer to simply an eastern and western ridge. The fourth hill, Josephus calls "Bezetha" (a name also applied to the northern walled additions to the city called the "New City"). He describes Bezetha as a hill north of the temple running toward the Antonia Fortress which had a man-made valley carved to separate it from the Antonia Fortress (Ibid., 5.4.2). Josephus does not lend support to the idea that Jerusalem would have been readily recognized as a city that *sits on seven hills.*

Faulty Preterist Claims

Some preterist sources make the undocumented claim "The seven hills of Jerusalem are Mount Gared; Mount Goath; Mount Acra; Mount Bezetha; Mount Moriah; Mount Ophel; Mount Zion." Sadly this is a flawed and deceptive statement that counts different names applied to the same hill or names that may not refer to hills at all.

The first two mentioned in this list are drawn from Jeremiah 31:39. After the beautiful promise of the New Covenant, the Lord promises the rebuilding

---

[2] Many scholars understand Josephus to locate the "Citadel" of David on the western ridge culminating in the hill now called "Zion" in Jerusalem. See Peter J. Leithart, "Where Was Ancient Zion? *Tyndale Bulletin* 53.2 (2002): 161-175. If so, Josephus was mistaken in his identification. We have not seen evidence in his writings to support their conclusion.

and expansion of Jerusalem. Its connection with the New Covenant promises may suggest that it is to be understood in a figurative spiritual sense, but it declares: "The surveyor's line shall again extend straight forward over the hill Gareb; then it shall turn toward Goath" (Jer. 31:39).

We should note that Gareb is called a "hill," but Goath is not. The word itself means "bellowing" and under its lexicon entry it states, "a place near Jerusalem, site unknown" (BDB). It is pure supposition to call this a mountain! Gareb is called a hill, but under its entry we learn that it is "a hill near Jerusalem, apparently southwest" (Ibid.). Is this Josephus' unnamed third hill? Perhaps, we don't know. This hill is never referred to again in Scripture.

Perhaps it was the hill now identified as Zion, but if so that would raise more problems to any seven-hill identification. Today visitors to the Old City of Jerusalem are shown a hill just outside the southernmost walls of the city, and told that it is "Mount Zion." As noted above, however, the "stronghold" of the original city of Jerusalem (on the southern end of the eastern ridge) was known synonymously as "Zion" and "the City of David" (2 Sam. 5:7; 1 Kings 8:1). This was the oldest portion of Jerusalem, south of the temple mount and west of the Kidron Valley. This also appears to be synonymous with the portion of Jerusalem later called simply the "Ophel," meaning "hill" or "stronghold" (2 Chon. 33:14; Josephus, *Jewish Wars* 5.2.1-2 called "Ophlas"). Yet, the Bible tells us that the temple was built on Mount Moriah (2 Chron. 3:1; cf. Josephus, *Antiquities* 1.13.2)—the mountain where Abraham was commanded to sacrifice Isaac (Gen. 22:2)—but this place is also called Mount Zion (1 Macc. 4:37). So, from the preterist list above where is Mount Zion? Is it the Ophel (which can =Zion) or Mount Moriah (which can also =Zion)? Is it Mount Gareb? If so, we cannot count it twice.

Some will try to identify mounds on the two ridges as the separate mountains. On the east they will identify Zion, Ophel, Moriah, and Bezetha and on the western ridge Arca and perhaps Gareb, but where is the third (and thus seventh hill)? It is clear that if there is this much ambiguity (and synonymous application) over the names used throughout history for the hills associated with Jerusalem, Christians in first century Asia Minor could not have been expected to automatically identify Jerusalem as the city of seven-hills.

Evidence for Roman Identification

So, if it is not Jerusalem, what city is it? Unlike the ambiguity associated with names used for hills in Jerusalem the city of Rome had a long and consistent history of identifying itself as a seven-hilled city. Since as early as 575–535 BC the city walls of Rome encircled its seven hills (Aventinus, Caelius, Capitolinus, Esquilinus, Palatinus, Quirinalis, Viminalis). During those years the sixth king of Rome, Servius Tullius, expanded the walls to encircle the seven hills (Livy, *History of Rome* 1.44). The Romans celebrated an annual festival called the *Septimontium* (i.e., "Seven Hills" or "Seven Mountains"). Plutarch tells us it was to celebrate the inclusion of a seventh hill into the city limits of Rome, granting it the nickname in Greek *heptalophos* (ἐπτάλοφος) "seven-hilled city" (*Roman Questions* 69), or in Latin *septicollis*. This way of referring to Rome is well-attested in ancient sources (Virgil, *Aeneid* 6.782-783; *Georgics* 2.535; Martial, *Epigrams* 4.64.11-12; Cicero, *To Atticus* 6.5.2; Horace, *Carmen Saeculare* 7). Suetonius tells us that on this festival Domitian distributed food and provisions to the poor and wealthy Roman citizens (*Domitian* 4).

In AD 71 the mint in Rome issued a bronze coin that was a "sestertius" in value, which was one quarter of a denarius (a day's wage in New Testament times, cf. Matt. 20:2). The front of the coin featured a profile of the Roman emperor Vespasian, and the back fea-

A Roman Sesterius, with Roma seated on seven hills

tured a reclining figure of a woman sitting on seven hills, under which was the Latin word *ROMA*—the name of the personified figure of *Dea Roma*, the goddess of Rome.[3] The similarity between this image and John's vision of the harlot on a seven-headed beast is inescapable. If residents of Asia Minor possessed such coins the connection with Rome would have been immediate and unquestioned.

We should acknowledge that the cities of Asia Minor would have had a close association with Rome. The Jewish pseudepigraphical work known as *4 Ezra* claimed that Asia shared in the "glamour" and "glory" of Rome (15.46) For example, in 133 BC Attalus III, the king of Pergamum had willed the city to Rome (Livy, *Periochae* 58). It was for all intents and purposes a Roman city! In 41 BC Mark Antony and Cleopatra combined their forces at Ephesus (Plutarch, *Antony* 56). In 195 BC, Smyrna was the first city to build a temple to *Dea Roma*, the personified goddess of Rome. In AD 23 she had competed

---

[3] http://www.icollector.com/Roman-Empire-Vespasian-69-79-Sestertius-71-28-39g_i9258028

with ten other cities in Asia Minor to build the first temple to the godhead of Tiberias (Tacitus, *Annals* 4.56). These cities were very familiar with Rome and would have been well aware of her identification as the *urbs septicollis* (the Latin name for her meaning "the seven hilled city").

Two Texts Used for a Jerusalem Identification

Can we find anything like this when it comes to Jerusalem? Outside of Scripture there are two examples preterists cite as examples of Jerusalem being referred to in this way. The first comes in an apocryphal work known as 1 Enoch. It is believed to have been written between 170 and 64 BC. It contains a passage that is also included in the book of Jude (Jude 14-15; cf. 1 Enoch 1:9; 60:8). Many scholars make the assumption that Jude quoted from 1 Enoch, but it is not clear whether Jude used 1 Enoch or if both drew from information regarding an actual prophecy made by Enoch that is not recorded elsewhere in Scripture. Scholars have observed that 1 Enoch bears some similarity to the book of Revelation. That does not necessarily indicate that John patterned his text after 1 Enoch. It may simply indicate that this was a familiar genre to first century Jews. Fragments of 1 Enoch have been found among the Dead Sea Scrolls.

In 1 Enoch, there is a passage in which the narrator (speaking as Enoch) is shown "seven magnificent mountains" (24:2). The seventh of these mountains is said to be "in the midst of these, and it excelled them in height, resembling the seat of a throne" (24:3). The angel Michael is portrayed as explaining, "This high mountain which thou hast seen, whose summit is like the throne of God, is His throne, where the Holy Great One, the Lord of Glory, the Eternal King, will sit, where the Holy Great One, the Lord of Glory, the Eternal King, will sit" (25:3). We should note that this does not portray a city *sitting on* seven mountains. It is describing one mountain. Further, while we might assume that this text is talking about Jerusalem (as the throne of God) it does not explicitly speak of it in this way. At the most, we could compare this to visions of an eschatological spiritual throne (like the New Jerusalem of Revelation). This does not prove that a first century audience would relate this to John's reference to a city of seven hills, nor does it prove that if an audience connected it with 1 Enoch they would understand it to refer to Jerusalem.

The second, and only known instance we could find of a Jewish source speaking of the seven hills of Jerusalem, comes in an Midrashic text known as *Pirke De-Rabbi Eliezer*. Although this text claims to date to rabbis that lived from the first to the third centuries AD, modern scholars have demonstrated that references it makes to three stages of the Muslim conquest as late as AD 830, demand that it be dated to the mid-ninth century.

In a rather odd exposition on Jonah 2:6, this text declares that Jonah's words, "I went down to the moorings of the mountains," lead to the following interpretation: "Hence we may learn that Jerusalem stands upon seven (hills')" ("History of Jonah" 71). Not only is this an odd, forced, and twisted interpretation of Jonah 2:6, it doesn't prove that Jerusalem would have been identified as a "city of seven hills" in the first century. The late composition of this work makes it highly unlikely that it preserves an identification of Jerusalem that would have been understood by John's readers in the first-century.

3. The Temple in Revelation

In Revelation 11:1-2 John writes:

> Then I was given a reed like a measuring rod. And the angel stood, saying, "Rise and measure the temple of God, the altar, and those who worship there. But leave out the court which is outside the temple, and do not measure it, for it has been given to the Gentiles. And they will tread the holy city underfoot for forty-two months."

Advocates of an early dating argue that this is proof that Revelation could not have been written after AD 70 because it describes the temple still standing. Let us consider the problems with this argument.

First, it is unclear what temple is being described in this text. At the beginning of the book Jesus promised the faithful in the church in Philadelphia, "He who overcomes, I will make him a pillar in the temple of My God, and he shall go out no more. And I will write on him the name of My God and the name of the city of My God, the New Jerusalem, which comes down out of heaven from My God. And I will write on him My new name" (Rev. 3:12). Christians are now considered part of God's temple. Peter told his readers, "you also, as living stones, are being built up a spiritual house, a holy priesthood, to offer up spiritual sacrifices acceptable to God through Jesus Christ" (1 Pet. 2:5). Paul wrote to the Corinthians:

> Do you not know that you are the temple of God and that the Spirit of God dwells in you? If anyone defiles the temple of God, God will destroy him. For the temple of God is holy, which temple you are (1 Cor. 3:16-17).

After Revelation 11:1-2, in the same chapter John writes, "Then the temple of God was opened in heaven, and the ark of His covenant was seen in His temple" (11:19). If this is the same temple mentioned in 11:1-2 it is clearly not the physical temple in Jerusalem, because it contains the ark of the covenant.

After the Babylonian Exile and destruction of the temple by Nebuchadnezzar there is no further biblical record of the location of ark of the covenant. The apocryphal book of 1 Esdras claims the Babylonians took the "vessels of the ark," (1:54), but says nothing about the ark itself. The apocryphal book of 2 Maccabees preserves a legend that Jeremiah hid the ark in an unmarked cave (2:4-8), but the biblical Jeremiah had prophesied:

> "Then it shall come to pass, when you are multiplied and increased in the land in those days," says the LORD, "that they will say no more, 'The ark of the covenant of the LORD.' It shall not come to mind, nor shall they remember it, nor shall they visit it, nor shall it be made anymore" (Jer. 3:16).

At any rate, the Jerusalem temple in the first century did not house the ark of the covenant.

We should note, however, that the temple seen in Revelation 11:19 is said to have been "in heaven." The same is said of later visions John sees in the book: "the temple which is in heaven" (Rev. 14:17); "the temple of the tabernacle of the testimony in heaven" (Rev. 15:5); and "the temple of heaven" (Rev. 16:17). In these cases the temple is representative of conditions in heaven and the ark itself likely represents the holiest access to the presence of God. If this is the same temple as that described in 11:1-2, it tells us nothing about the status of the Herodian temple at the time Revelation was written.

When John sees the temple in 11:1-2 he is told, "leave out the court which is outside the temple, and do not measure it, for it has been given to the Gentiles. And they will tread the holy city underfoot for forty-two months." This has lead some to assume it must be describing the physical temple in Jerusalem. As one entered the Herodian temple he first came to a colonnaded court surrounding the temple known as the "Court of the Gentiles." Blocks from this have survived with inscriptions warning Gentiles not to enter any further into the temple. I photographed one in Istanbul. This is likely what is called the "middle wall of separation" between Jew and Gentile (Eph. 2:14). It is assumed that this is what John was shown.

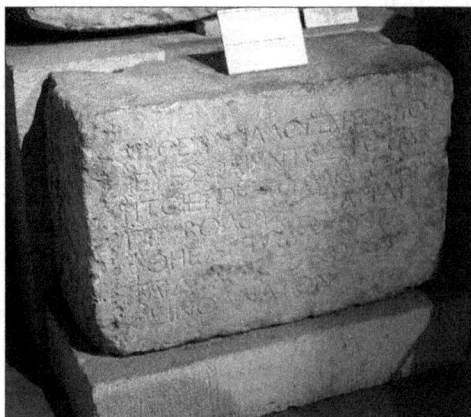

Inscription from the temple in Jerusalem warning Gentiles not to go further

We should note, however, that this is said to be "outside the temple" and the Gentiles are said to "tread the Holy City underfoot" for a time. After the testimony and resurrection of the two witnesses (which appear to represent the Law and the Prophets, see 11:6), it is declared, "The kingdoms of this world have become the kingdoms of our Lord and of His Christ, and He shall reign forever and ever!" (Rev. 11:15). If the resurrection of the two witnesses leads to the acknowledgement of Christ's reign having come to earth, why would we not assume that the temple at the beginning of the chapter represents the spiritual *stones* and *pillars* of the true temple of believers in Christ? This is how the temple is first referred to in the book (Rev. 3:12).

What then is the "court" that is tread underfoot by the Gentiles? In the next series of visions when the woman who gives birth to the One who "was to rule all nations with a rod of iron" (Rev. 12:5) is taken into heaven the dragon makes "war with the rest of her offspring, who keep the commandments of God and have the testimony of Jesus Christ" (Rev. 12:17). The church is a *temple* of God living for a time in a world surrounded by *nations* (= "Gentiles") who tread underfoot the "Holy City" (i.e., the people of God, cf. Heb. 12:22), but this will not last forever.

Preterists might disagree with this interpretation, but they must acknowledge that there are too many unanswered questions about the identity of the temple described in 11:1-2 to use it as a proof-text for claiming that the Herodian temple still stood when the book was written.

4. The Figure of Babylon

According to the preterist view, Babylon in the book of Revelation does not refer to Rome, but to Jerusalem. Preterists have objected to describing this as a "code word" for Rome. Perhaps that is not the best way to describe it. Instead, this may be the figure of speech known as *antonomasia*, or "name change." Scripture uses this in instances when the character of one person is reflected in another. Malachi, for example prophesied, "Behold, I will send you Elijah the prophet before the coming of the great and dreadful day of the LORD" (Mal. 4:5). This was not a promise of a reincarnation. Jesus said that Elijah had come in John, who was the "Elijah who is to come" (Matt. 11:13-14). John came "in the spirit and power of Elijah" (Luke 1:17), that is, he was like him in character. Jesus, in the letter to the church in Thyatira did the same thing, rebuking them for tolerating "that woman Jezebel" (Rev. 2:20). This woman wasn't really the Jezebel of the Old Testament. Instead, she behaved like her. She was doing to Thyatira what Jezebel had done to Ahab and Israel. Whether we say Babylon is Rome or Jerusalem clearly, John used "Babylon" as an antonomastic pseudonym for some other city. So, let's see which conclusion best fits the evidence. Six times in the book of Revelation the apostle refers to Babylon:

1. Revelation 14:8. The first comes after a vision of Christ as the Lamb who is said to be standing on "Mount Zion" with the 144,000 virgins sealed from the tribes of Israel (14:1). An angel declares, "Babylon is fallen, is fallen, that great city, because she has made all nations drink of the wine of the wrath of her fornication" (Rev. 14:8). As noted above, "Mount Zion" was a common way of referring to Jerusalem (Isa. 24:23; 30:19; 31:9; 32:20; 37:22; 52:1; 62:1; 64:10; Jer. 26:18; Lam. 1:17; Joel 2:32; 3:16-17; Amos 1:2; Micah 3:12; 4:2). As we will see below, the connection with the 144,000 likely describes a spiritual condition (cf. 7:14-17). So as Christ stands in the midst of spiritual Jerusalem, a declaration is made regarding the fall of Babylon. If Babylon is physical Jerusalem the picture is spiritual Jerusalem exalted over physical Jerusalem. This is certainly possible, but it would be an odd mixture of metaphors. Typically the spiritual condition is characterized as the true condition. Paul, for example, declared, "they are not all Israel who are of Israel" (Rom. 9:6) and "as many as walk according to this rule, peace and mercy be upon them, and upon the Israel of God" (Gal. 6:16). If it is Rome there is no mixed metaphor.

In this text, Babylon is also called "that great city." Preterists have cited this to argue that it connects Babylon with 11:8, "the great city which spiritually is called Sodom and Egypt, where also our Lord was crucified." The same phrase is used in 18:10 and 21; in 17:5 and 18:2 she is called "Babylon the Great;" and in 16:19 "great Babylon." Does that prove that Babylon is Jerusalem? Not necessarily. Remember, the same was said of Nineveh (Jonah 1:2; 3:2; 4:11) and Gibeon (Josh. 10:2). It only proves that both cities are said to be "great." If the city of 11:8 is the same as the city of 14:8 (and other references to Babylon) why is it identified with different names? It is called "Sodom and Egypt." Does the Holy Spirit lead John to use three figures (i.e., Sodom, Egypt, and Babylon) to describe Jerusalem? Perhaps, but that would certainly lead to greater possibility for confusion on the part of the reader. Again, if Babylon is Rome there is no confusion of metaphors.

2. Revelation 16:19. The second reference to Babylon comes after the seventh bowl of wrath is poured out. It is explained, "Now the great city was divided into three parts, and the cities of the nations fell. And great Babylon was remembered before God, to give her the cup of the wine of the fierceness of His wrath" (16:19). We should note here, similar to the first example, Babylon is said to fall, but here it is added, "the cities of the nations fell." We will consider some things later about the word *nations*, but we should note that this word is *ethnos* (ἔθνος), most often translated "Gentiles." Campbell's *Living Oracles* translation put this, "the cities of the Gentiles fell down." Does that tell us anything about who Babylon might be? Did the fall of Jerusalem in anyway cause Gentile cities (or even cities of the nations in general) to fall? No. On the other hand, the fall of the capital of the Roman Empire would affect all Roman colonies, provinces, and subjugated cities.

3. Revelation 17:5. As John is shown the judgment of the great harlot, he records, "And on her forehead a name was written: MYSTERY, BABYLON THE GREAT, THE MOTHER OF HARLOTS AND OF THE ABOMINA-TIONS OF THE EARTH" (17:5). Preterists have pointed out in the past that Jerusalem is often described as a harlot. For example, in Isaiah we see the lament, "How the faithful city has become a harlot!" (Isa. 1:21). Jerusalem is frequently rebuked for harlotry (Jer. 2:20; 3:1-11; Ezek. 16:1-43; 23, et al.), but so are other nations (e.g., "Onolah" Ezek. 23:5), even Gentile cities (e.g., Tyre, Isa. 23:17; Nineveh, Nahum 3:4).

We should note that Babylon is called the "mother of harlots." While the book of Hosea certainly describes a mother who commits harlotry (Hos. 2:2), that applies to the Israelites in general—not just to Jerusalem. To be a "mother of harlots" is not the same as being a mother who commits harlotry. In addition to this, G. Biguzzi has observed that there is a difference in the way Israel's harlotry is described in the Old Testament, and what is said of Babylon. He writes, "In the Old Testament Jerusalem is accused of letting itself be corrupted by the idolatry of the nations, in Revelation, on the contrary, Babylon is corrupting them with its own idolatry" (381).[4] As an example he cites Ezekiel 23:27, "She has never given up her harlotry brought from Egypt." By contrast, Babylon is said to be the "great harlot who corrupted the earth with her fornication" (Rev. 19:2; cf. 14:8; 17:2, 4; 18:3). If we understand Babylon as a pseudonym for Rome this language is perfectly applicable.

4. Revelation 18:2. In the same vision, the fourth reference comes when an angel cries out, "And he cried mightily with a loud voice, saying, 'Babylon the great is fallen, is fallen, and has become a dwelling place of demons, a prison for every foul spirit, and a cage for every unclean and hated bird!'" (18:2). This is very similar to the first reference, in declaring the fall of Babylon (cf. 14:8). The unusual phrase "a dwelling place of demons" is not found elsewhere in Scripture. A non-biblical text found among the Dead Sea Scrolls offers a rebuke to Babylon, declaring it will become a "dwelling place for demons" (4Q836). It is worth noting that while many Dead Sea Scrolls found

---

[4] G. Biguzzi, "Is the Babylon of Revelation Rome or Jerusalem?" *Biblica* 87. 3 (2006): 371-386.

at Qumran rail against the wickedness of Jerusalem they do not speak of her as "Babylon."

This text comes three verses after another key verse. 17:18 explains, "And the woman whom you saw is that great city which reigns over the kings of the earth." Preterists argue that Jerusalem could be described in this way. Certainly we can look at passages such as Psalm 68:29—"Because of Your temple at Jerusalem, Kings will bring presents to You." Or, Psalm 146:10—"The LORD shall reign forever—Your God, O Zion, to all generations. Praise the LORD!" Or texts with Messianic overtones, like Isaiah 24:23—"For the LORD of hosts will reign On Mount Zion and in Jerusalem," but to say that the Lord reigns is not the same as saying Jerusalem reigns. If this is meant to describe Jerusalem it is wholly figurative of Jerusalem's influence. Especially in the time of John, Jerusalem did not *reign over* any kings, but was a subjugated city.

There are many things that are said about Babylon and the Harlot that must also be considered if we are to make the proper identification. For example, Biguzzi observes the following regarding geographic and political descriptions:

> The Beast of Revelation 13, which rises from the sea (13:1), has authority over, or is adored by "all the earth" (13:3), "every tribe and people and tongue and nation" (13:7), and "all the inhabitants of the earth" (13:8). The Babylon of Revelation 17-18 has corrupted, or has enriched, or is mourned by "all the nations" (18:3), "the kings and merchants of the earth" (18:3b, 9, 11, 17), and "all those who had ships at sea" (18,19). Such a sea, that bathes many regions with their many peoples of different languages and cultures, is recognizable as the Mediterranean sea, whereas the multi-ethnic reign and its capital city, are recognizable as the Roman empire and Rome, much more conveniently than as Jerusalem (Ibid.).

He is absolutely right. These descriptions could never describe Jerusalem. Her fall would not be mourned by "all those who had ships at sea"—but the fall of Rome would.

5 and 6. Revelation 18:10 and 18:21. Finally, in the same section John sees the kings of the earth, "standing at a distance for fear of her torment, saying, 'Alas, alas, that great city Babylon, that mighty city! For in one hour your judgment has come'" (18:10). Later, he records, "Then a mighty angel took up a stone like a great millstone and threw it into the sea, saying, "Thus with violence the great city Babylon shall be thrown down, and shall not be found anymore." (18:21). Before this verse, the cry is offered, "Rejoice over her, O heaven, and you holy apostles and prophets, for God has avenged you on her!" (18:20).

One of the strongest arguments we have heard preterists make on this question concerns the "judgment" that was to be brought upon the harlot. The chapter ends with the ominous proclamation, "And in her was found the blood of prophets and saints, and of all who were slain on the earth" (18:24). They have connected this with the Lord's words upon leaving the temple, before the Olivet Discourse. As Luke records it He declares:

> . . . I will send them prophets and apostles, and some of them they will kill and persecute, that the blood of all the prophets which was shed from the foundation of the world may be required of this generation, from the blood of Abel to the blood of Zechariah who perished between the altar and the temple. Yes, I say to you, it shall be required of this generation (Luke 11:49-51).

Matthew adds the Lord's lament:

> O Jerusalem, Jerusalem, the one who kills the prophets and stones those who are sent to her! How often I wanted to gather your children together, as a hen gathers her chicks under her wings, but you were not willing! See! Your house is left to you desolate (Matt. 23:37-38).

Their conclusion is that Christ's pronouncement of judgment echoes Revelation 18:24, so it must mean that Babylon is Jerusalem. They then conclude that this judgment is carried out in the destruction of Jerusalem in AD 70. Let's look closer at this.

First, does Jesus say blood will be required of Jerusalem, or of "this generation"? Yes, Jesus laments Jerusalem (Matt. 23:37), declaring her "house" (probably the temple) "desolate." And yes, after this Jesus foretells the destruction of the temple (Matt. 24:1-2), but a "generation" is a people. In other words, although the destruction of Jerusalem would certainly be a major judgment on the wickedness of the Jewish people of Jerusalem, did that punish the entirety of the "wicked and adulterous generation" (Matt. 16:4) who rejected Jesus? What of Capernaum? What of Chorazin and Bethsaida? Were they not a part of the same *generation* (cf. Luke 10:13-15; Matt. 11:21-24). Were there no Gentiles that were a part of that *generation?* Jesus said, "And Jerusalem will be trampled by Gentiles until the times of the Gentiles are fulfilled" (Luke 21:24). What does that mean? Is He talking about a time until Gentiles no longer *trample* Jerusalem, or a time when judgment will come upon the Gentiles (cf. Gen. 15:16)?

Second, how far can we take this idea of *requiring blood* from this generation? Is Jesus saying that God is holding the inhabitants of Jerusalem *guilty* of the blood of all prophets killed in the past? The Law of Moses commanded, "Fathers shall not be put to death for their children, nor shall the children be put to death for their fathers; a person shall be put to death for his own sin." (Deut. 24:16). The Lord told Ezekiel, "The soul who sins shall die. The son shall not bear the guilt of the father, nor the father bear the guilt of the son. The righteousness of the righteous shall be upon himself, and the wickedness of the wicked shall be upon himself" (Ezek. 18:20). Jesus is not saying that the inhabitants of first century Jerusalem are being held guilty for the sins of their ancestors. He is talking about a consequence that will finally play out. They will not be spared the growing conflict with Rome, and it will be allowed as a punishment for their rejection of the Messiah.

Finally, notice something about the wording in Revelation 18:24. It is not the same judgment proclaimed by Jesus. The Lord spoke of "the blood of all the prophets," but in Babylon is found "the blood of prophets and saints, and of all who were slain on the earth." That is much broader than Jesus's rebuke before leaving the temple. Whoever Babylon is she is figured as having a share in the deaths of "all who were slain on the earth." That is not what the Lord said in His lament over Jerusalem.

So, if Rome is Babylon is John saying God holds her citizens *guilty* of every murder ever committed? No, as mentioned above with Jerusalem, eventually the cumulative nature of her sins will *find her out* (Num. 32:23). While the connection with Jesus's words is compelling, it does not prove that the Babylon of Revelation is Jerusalem.

The Figure of Babylon in Jewish and Early Christian Sources

Having considered where the figure of Babylon is used in the book of Revelation, we must also consider how this figure was used outside of Scripture and in the first writings by those who commented on John's Apocalypse.

Unfortunately, we do not have preserved examples of Babylon as a figure of Jerusalem or Rome before the destruction of Jerusalem or the writing of the book of Revelation. However, after the destruction of Jerusalem it is clear that Jewish sources begin to use Babylon as a pseudonym for Rome.

Two of the most compelling examples of this come in Jewish pseudepigraphical works written late in the first century or early in the second century after the destruction of the temple. The first, called *Second Baruch*, claims, "But the king of Babylon will arise who has now destroyed Zion, and he will boast over the people, and he will speak great things in his heart in the presence of the Most High." (67.7). We note here that the Jewish author of this work calls the Roman emperor "the king of Babylon."

In a similar way, in the second text known as *Fourth Ezra*, the writer claims to have written, "In the thirtieth year after the destruction of our city" (3.1), yet in sadness he asks "Are the deeds of Babylon better than those of Zion?" (3:31), asking "Is that why she has gained dominion over Zion?" (31:28). As previously mentioned, the writer also claimed Asia shared in the "glamour" and "glory" of Babylon (15:46), warning Asia, "You have imitated that hateful harlot in all her deeds and devices" (15:48) These demonstrate early evidence of Jews identifying Rome with the pseudonym "Babylon," characterizing her as a "harlot," and even considering Asia Minor as sharing in Roman idolatry (as noted earlier).

The clear and overwhelming interpretation among the earliest writers that comment on the book of Revelation interprets Babylon as a reference to Rome. Tertullian (ca. AD 160-220) declares this repeatedly in terms like this, "Babylon, in our own John, is a figure of the city Rome, as being equally great and proud of her sway, and triumphant over the saints" (*An Answer to the Jews* 9; cf. *Against Marcion* 3.13; *Scorpiace* 12). Victorinus (–AD 303) throughout his commentary equates Rome with Babylon. He speaks of "the fall of Babylon, that is, of the Roman state" (Comments on 7:8; cf. on 17:9). Eusebius (ca. 260-341) wrote, "And Peter makes mention of Mark in his first epistle which they say that he wrote in Rome itself, as is indicated by him, when he calls the city, by a figure, Babylon, as he does in the following words: 'The church that is at Babylon, elected together with you, salutes you; and so does Marcus my son' [1 Pet. 5:13]" (*Ecclesiastical History* 2.15.2). Preterists have objected to interpreting Peter's words "She who is in Babylon, elect together with you, greets you; and so does Mark my son" (1 Pet. 5:13) as a reference to Babylon, but isn't it interesting that Eusebius interpreted this way? The earliest claims regarding the Gospel of Mark call him the "interpreter of Peter," claiming that he wrote the Gospel after Peter's death in Rome (*Against Heresies* 3.1.1). This has to tell us something. It all adds up. It all harmonizes. The evidence is far more compelling that Babylon is Rome rather than Jerusalem.

5. "Nations"

Finally, as noted above, the word "nations" is translated from the Greek word *ethnos* (ἔθνος), from which our English word "ethnic" is derived. It is used 164 times in the New Testament, and 94 of those instances it is translated "Gentile(s)." Thayer defines it as follows:

> (1) a multitude (whether of men or of beasts) associated or living together; 1a) a company, troop, swarm; (2) a multitude of individuals of the same nature or genus; 2a) the human family; (3) a tribe, nation, people group; (4) in the OT, foreign nations not worshipping the true God, pagans, Gentiles; (5) Paul uses the term for Gentile Christians.

The preterist assumption is that "nations" must indicate political entities, as they now exist in the form of distinct geographical, ethnic, and governmental entities—but is that a certain conclusion? How is this word used throughout the book of Revelation?

We see that those who overcome in Thyatira are promised "power over the nations" (2:26)—does that mean France, Germany, or Italy? The Lamb is considered worthy to open the book and the seals because He has, "redeemed us to God by Your blood out of every tribe and tongue and people and nation" (5:19). This is interesting—they are redeemed "out of" *tribes, tongues, peoples,* and *nations,* but that speaks of the origin of the people not the present condition or status of the "nations" from which they came. In John's vision of heaven, after seeing the 144,000 sealed from the tribes of Israel, he then is shown, "a great multitude which no one could number, of all nations, tribes, peoples, and tongues, standing before the throne and before the Lamb, clothed with white robes, with palm branches in their hands" (7:9). This is very interesting! Once again it speaks of *nations, tribes, peoples,* and *tongues,* but where are these people? They are "before the throne." Is this on earth or in heaven? The elder explains to John, "These are the ones who come out of the great tribulation, and washed their robes and made them white in the blood of the Lamb" (7:14). The fact that they have "come out of the great tribulation" points to a condition of deliverance from the tribulation of earth. He continues:

> Therefore they are before the throne of God, and serve Him day and night in His temple. And He who sits on the throne will dwell among them. They shall neither hunger anymore nor thirst anymore; the sun shall not strike them, nor any heat; for the Lamb who is in the midst of the throne will shepherd them and lead them to living fountains of waters. And God will wipe away every tear from their eyes (7:15-17)

This uses some of the same language used at the end of the book (cf. God dwelling with them—21:3; wiping away tears—21:4; fountains to satisfy all thirst—21:6). Yet notice, they are said to be "before the throne" serving God "day and night." The church on earth might be said to be *before the throne,* but none of us serve God "day and night." It is true that Christ leads us now and we are now His temple, but we do not yet enjoy a condition of *no hunger* or *thirst* (spiritually or physically). This is a heavenly condition, and yet "nations" are said to exist. This is simply a way of speaking of *peoples,* it is not a proof that political and geographic entities still exist on earth under the conditions described in 7:14-17. This is demonstrated in the other examples when *ethnos* is used in Revelation as well (10:11; 11:2, 9, 18; 12:5; 13:7; 14:6,

8; 15:4; 16:19; 17:15; 18:3, 23, 19:15; 20:3, 8). There is no reason we should apply it differently in 21:4, 6, or 22:2.

Conclusion

Brother Dan King has written a thematic commentary on the book of Revelation entitled "*I Saw the Heaven Opened*" (Athens, AL: Truth Publications Inc., 2018). I had the privilege of helping with its editing and final preparation. In his introduction he offers eight points that lead him to reject an early dating of the book. Two of these were new to me, but quite compelling.

1. "The church at Smyrna did not exist as early as the theory of the early date of Revelation would require" (52). In the second century, a bishop from Smyrna lived named Polycarp (ca. AD 69-155). He personally knew the apostle John while he was still alive (Eusebius, *Ecclesiastical History* 5.24). Before his own martyrdom, Polycarp wrote a letter to the church in Philippi that has survived. In it he discusses Paul's love for them as expressed in the biblical epistle of Philippians. He writes, "For he boasts of you in all those churches which alone then knew the Lord; but we [of Smyrna] had not yet known Him" (*To the Philippians* 11.3). Scripture does not record the establishment of the church in Smyrna, but when Christ's epistle is addressed to them in Revelation they had existed at least long enough that He could say, "I know your works, tribulation, and poverty, but you are rich" (Rev. 2:9). Philippians was written during Paul's imprisonment (Phil. 1:16). Early date advocates try to date Philippians to Paul's Caesarean imprisonment from 56-58, but Paul extends a greeting from "those of Caesar's household" which lends more support to dating it to his Roman imprisonments 60-62 or 66/67. If Polycarp says no church existed in Smyrna when Philippians was written it makes a pre-AD 70 date of Revelation highly unlikely.

2. "The church at Laodicea is depicted in the letter to them (3:17) as being rich and well situated" (53). The epistle Jesus directs to Laodicea says to the Christians in this city, "you say, 'I am rich, have become wealthy, and have need of nothing'—and do not know that you are wretched, miserable, poor, blind, and naked" (Rev. 3:17). During the reign of Nero, in 60 or 61 an earthquake virtually destroyed Laodicea, but they recovered without the aid of Rome (Tacitus, *Annals* 14.27). While this likely relates to the confidence echoed in Jesus's words "you say, 'I am rich, have become wealthy, and have need of nothing,'" it also becomes a factor in any conclusions regarding dating. While repairs certainly could have been well underway, if we accept a pre-AD 70 date of Revelation, it is hard to imagine the Lord characterizing their situation as *rich* and *wealthy*. Would we call New Orleans (even now 14 years after Hurricane Katrina) as *rich, wealthy, with need of nothing*? The later we date Christ's words from this event the more His words become applicable.

If any of the facts we have considered in support of an identification of Rome as Babylon and a date for the writing of the book during the persecution of Domitian were taken alone, we might be able to question this conclusion. When all the facts are considered together it establishes a preponderance of evidence that makes any alternatives untenable.

CONSEQUENCES

*I*n Ecclesiastes 7:16, Solomon warns the reader not to be "overly righteous" nor "overly wise" then balances it in the next verse by warning against being "overly wicked" or "foolish" (7:17). The Holy Spirit is not teaching that *a little bit of sin* is ok—He is cautioning against excessive reactions by which one might "destroy yourself" (7:16). The translation known as *Good News for Today,* rather loosely translates the first part of the sense, "avoid both extremes" (7:18b).

At the beginning of our study we noted how the rise of premillennialism contributed to the rise of a partial-preterist understanding among most members of churches of Christ who take a non-institutional view of things. I believe that was appropriate. By interpreting *everything* literally premillennialists have continually shown themselves to offer erroneous predictions, false identifications, and a system of biblical exegesis that cannot be sustained. Clearly, many prophecies in Old and New Testaments, carry with them a figurative sense in their immediate application that does not always demonstrate literal cosmological events. However, the warning of Solomon is fitting here. We must be careful to avoid "both extremes." Simply because premillennialism errs in going to one extreme, we should not allow it to cause us to overreact to the other extreme in saying *everything* is figurative.

Why Does All of This Matter?

Having taken an in-depth look at these issues we must conclude by asking some questions. Is this just an issue of different ways of looking at a subject that are inconsequential to the mutual faith and fellowship Christians share with one another? What influence do these things have on our service to God, those we teach, and the body of Christ? Allow us to conclude this study by offering some consequences we fear result if we accept this view.

1. It changes our view of Scripture.

A fundamental conviction that brethren have long held is that God revealed His word in a way that can be easily understood without the need for additional direct operation on the part of the Holy Spirit or explanation from any religious authority. We appeal to Paul's words to the Ephesians—"when you read, you may understand my knowledge in the mystery of Christ" (Eph. 3:4). We consider Jesus's words, "I thank You, Father, Lord of heaven and earth, that You have hidden these things from the wise and prudent and revealed them to babes. Even so, Father, for so it seemed good in Your sight" (Luke 10:21).

After studying this doctrine now for years I must say, this is not an easy view of Scripture to understand. It demands continually looking at the simple statements of Scripture and concluding that they do not mean what they say, but carry a different sense dependant upon conclusions drawn about Scriptures remotely separated from the text in question. It demands assuming that we can know what men and women long ago thought and how they would have understood things. It demands connecting concepts and texts distinct from one another in context, genre, background, and covenantal placement in order to make sense of even basic doctrines. That could hardly be described as a revelation given to "babes" so that they might "understand" it simply by reading it.

Now, certainly there are principles taught in Scripture that are characterized as "solid food" in contrast to "milk" (1 Cor. 3:2; Heb. 5:12, 14), and "hard to understand" (2 Pet. 3:16). But, we must recognize that this view of end times makes *all of Scripture* hard to understand—even principles the Holy Spirit counts as "elementary principles" (Heb. 6:1-2). This is a consequence that must be recognized if we accept this view.

2. It changes how we view our brethren.

If this view is correct, those who do not understand Scripture the same way that preterists do are ignorant, uninformed, or deliberately unwilling to accept the truth of God's word. Isn't that how one must view those of us who reject full-preterism? Those who see it as they do are the only ones who have truly grasped these things, and thus the only ones whom they can truly view as sound in their understanding of God's word.

John taught:

> Whoever transgresses and does not abide in the doctrine of Christ does not have God. He who abides in the doctrine of Christ has both the Father and the Son. If anyone comes to you and does not bring this doctrine, do not receive him into your house nor greet him; for he who greets him shares in his evil deeds (2 John 9-11).

If this realized eschatology is correct, these are fundamental elements of the doctrine of Christ. Let's remember how Preston described it? "It is an extensive treatment of ALL of Israel's promises" that "should be seen as the uncovering of the eternal purpose of God."[1] If that's true, those who do not adopt it are not *abiding in* the doctrine of Christ. Won't that inevitably force one to come to the point that he or she can no longer maintain fellowship with those of us who don't see it their way lest they share in their "evil deeds"?

I don't want to see that happen to any of my brethren, but how can it not be the consequence? Those who lean this way start to speak negatively of "traditional views" or what the "church of Christ" has always taught. That reflects a view of one's brethren that demands that the person change those of us who reject the AD 70 doctrine, or we must change him or her. Now, obviously, dear reader if you are leaning this direction we want you to change your mind. I pray that you will not look down on those of us who have seriously studied this, but do not accept this false view. If that cannot happen, please recognize that to accept this view will change how you speak about, respond to, and view those with whom you may have been in fellowship for years.

3. It changes how we view ourselves.

Those of us who preach full-time or even those who preach when the opportunity arises, are a strange lot! We must be convinced enough of the convictions we hold that we have the confidence to stand before a congregation of Christians—some who may have been Christians longer than we have been alive—and tell them what we understand the word of God to say about how they should live, what they should believe, and what they should do.

This is an honor and a privilege. We who do this are "stewards of the manifold grace of God" (1 Pet. 4:10). We are to, "speak as the oracles of God" (1 Pet. 4:11). Yet, with this privilege comes a great danger. Confidence can easily become pride. When we become so certain of our convictions we can easily imagine that we have seen something no one else has ever seen before.

Solomon warns, "Pride goes before destruction, and a haughty spirit before a fall" (Prov. 16:18). I have thought about this often as I have written this material. It would be very easy for me to be so confident in my own view that I allow pride to prevent me from honestly and fairly considering preterist views (and the Scriptures that preterists have looked to in support of their convictions). It would be easy for me to imagine that I have a wisdom or knowledge superior to theirs and allow my own arrogance to color my views. I pray that I have not done that, and hope that I have not communicated my convictions in a way that is prideful, condescending, or arrogant.

---

[1] Don K. Preston, "Why the Study of Covenant Eschatology Is Important," *Bible Prophecy,* November 28, 2012, http://www.bibleprophecy.com/why-the-study-of-covenant-eschatology-is-important-guest-article/.

Dear reader, this may be a danger that you face as well. It takes courage to hold a view that is so different from what you may have been taught, and which runs opposite to what is held by so many people. Yet, with that courage can also come a view of yourself that leads you to imagine that you have found something that others have not. In Scripture and in the years after the New Testament the Gnostics developed this problem. They embraced "what is falsely called knowledge" (1 Tim. 6:20), and looked down on those that just didn't have that wisdom, insight, and secret knowledge which they believed they had attained. If you are not careful, you too could come to see yourself in that way. That is a dangerous possibility that could well be a consequence of adopting this view.

4. It changes how brethren will view us.

We believe, for the most part, brethren are very patient with one another. In the years I have been preaching I have encountered brethren that have personally held unusual views on particular issues or Scriptures. Generally these things did not compromise our ability to work with one another and maintain fellowship. When that was not the case it was because the views they held involved fundamental issues of faith, about which there could be no compromise.

In the book of Galatians, if we understand the problem the churches in that region were facing, it involved efforts on the part of Judaizing teachers to turn believers back to Mosaic Law. While the Old Law had been God's revealed will for the Jews, when these teachers tried to compel believers to bind it under Christ, Paul described it as turning to a "different gospel" (Gal. 1:6). If one goes to the point that he adopts a view that teaches Jesus has already come (and there will be no future, literal second coming of Jesus), the resurrection has already passed (and there will be no future, literal, bodily resurrection), collective judgment took place when Jerusalem was destroyed (and there will be no future, collective judgment of all those who have ever lived), and that the material universe is unending (and there will never be a destruction of this universe and a creation of a new place called "the heavens and the earth") he has adopted a "different gospel."

Now please understand, if one adopts all of these views and they are correct, then he is the one following the true gospel and all of us who reject it have followed a false gospel. But, either way, it must be recognized that these conflicting views of such fundamental concepts of the Christian faith cannot coexist for long. Eventually, (as mentioned above) either those who accept them will be forced to see those of us who do not as being in error, or their brethren will come to see them as preaching a "different gospel." I cherish fellowship with my brothers and sisters in Christ and I want to do all that I can to keep that from happening. That is why I offer this material to persuade those who are considering full-preterism to reject it, or to change the minds of those who have already adopted it. Please recognize, however, that if that can't happen this may be an unavoidable consequence as these conflicting concepts of biblical teaching inevitably collide with one another.

5. Where will it lead you?

Some Christians who first accept some of these views continue, for a time to believe in the resurrection, final judgment, and a literal end of the world. As time goes on, it becomes harder and harder to cling to these fundamental beliefs. What happens is the more they interpret passages that have generally been understood to apply to the end of time to AD 70, the harder it becomes for them to continue to believe in a bodily resurrection, final judgment, and a literal end of the world. If these things are not taught in those Scriptures, where are they taught?

We saw in our examination of Hebrews 6 that the writer considered the doctrines "of resurrection of the dead, and of eternal judgment" (Heb. 6:2) to be fundamental "elementary principles of Christ" (Heb. 6:1). Paul described Hymenaeus and Philetus as "having strayed from the truth," because they claimed, "the resurrection is already past," and the result of their influence served to, "overthrow the faith of some" (2 Tim. 2:18).

If the preterist view is truly what the Bible teaches it must be affirmed and all who truly follow the Bible must accept it as the truth. If it is not, would it not be that the one who accepts it is denying "elementary principles of Christ"? If it is not, doesn't a figurative view of the resurrection say, "the resurrection is already past," and thus make one guilty of having "strayed from the truth" and (heaven forbid) overthrowing the "faith of some"?

Some who accept a few preterist views may be able to continue to feel a sense of accountability to God, fellowship with His people, and faithful service to God, but not everyone who adopts these views can. We know of those who have accepted these views and slowly begun to lose any sense of accountability at all. Fellowship becomes unimportant, because gradually all those who don't hold to their view are seen as ignorant and uninformed. Every song that is sung, prayer that is offered, and sermon preached no longer measures up, because it doesn't match their view. As a result, they must discredit and undermine "traditional" beliefs or even (God forbid) break fellowship with all others. I know a man who used to preach and now holds these views, but worships with no one! How ironic that a view that claims that we now live in the "New Jerusalem" in our relationship with God in the church, could actually lead a person to have no association with a local church at all. Dear reader, don't let that happen to you!

Others have split off from congregations with whom they have long been associated and formed "preterist churches." Some advocates of this view envision it as "the next reformation." They are very evangelistic about their convictions, and believe firmly that everyone should view Scripture as they do. Others quietly try to infiltrate non-preterist churches and lead its members to accept their views. In these cases, they don't come out and openly reveal their convictions—they slowly influence the unsuspecting to become full-preterists.

Among those holding these views who have come out of churches of Christ, a strange ecumenical posture is sometimes adopted. Shared preterist convictions have led some to overlook error that others teach on salvation, the organization of the church, scriptural worship, and the work of the church. They identify themselves with others in these new "preterist churches" in spite of their acceptance of denominational errors. May that never happen to you!

6. How will it affect others?

When a person adopts preterist views, it inevitably becomes very public. He will teach them in classes, preach them from the pulpit, and offer comments in classes that articulate his convictions. We understand that. When we believe something is the truth we want to share it and should talk about it, but what impact will that have on others?

As we mentioned at the beginning of our study, some may misunderstand the views a person holds and exaggerate in their own minds what they understand the person to be saying. Others may be confused and struggle with faith altogether as a result. In other words, let's say I am a teenager or immature Christian. I hear preterist views and it causes me to conclude that Scripture cannot be understood. Could the result be that I turn from faith altogether? Could it cause me to say, "If I can't understand things like the judgment, why try to understand anything?"

Others might be persuaded by preterist views, but take them in directions that the one who first accepts only some preterist tenets does not. One young woman might say, "If there is not really going to be a judgment day, what's the use! I'll just live however I want to live!" Another young man might say, "If the end of the world is figurative, maybe baptism is figurative!" A young couple might say, "If we can't understand Scripture at face value, we are never going to try to impose our views on our children." As unlikely as these things might seem, people are a curious lot. Our influence can have unexpected consequences. We must be very certain that all that we say and do is based on scriptural convictions about which we are absolutely certain.

All of us are accountable for our own decisions. Even when we are following Scripture to the very best of our understanding we may clash with those around us, "rub someone the wrong way," or lead someone to reject faith although we have done absolutely nothing wrong. Even so, Jesus taught, "whoever causes one of these little ones who believe in Me to sin, it would be better for him if a millstone were hung around his neck, and he were drowned in the depth of the sea" (Matt. 18:6). To avoid this, we must be willing to cut off a hand or gouge out an eye rather than risk causing someone else to stumble (Matt. 18:7-9).

Again, if a person is absolutely convinced of the validity of the preterist view he cannot (and should not) remain silent. He must shout it from the "housetops" (Luke 12:3). On the other hand, if there is even an ounce of doubt, one must consider the danger he risks in expressing these views. What may be considered an intriguing possibility could have consequences we don't want.

My prayer is that in this study we have done all that is within our power to turn those who stand outside of Christ away from this heresy and to bring brothers and sisters in Christ together in the "same mind" and the "same judgment" (1 Cor. 1:10). The false doctrines of preterism are a rejection of "elementary principles of Christ" that compromise the fellowship Christians should enjoy with one another. I firmly believe that this doctrine is in error and I pray that you, dear reader, will carefully consider the points offered in these studies and change your mind (if you are a preterist) or turn the other direction if you have been leaning toward accepting the AD 70 doctrine. Please receive these pages in the spirit of love for God and for my brethren in which they were intended. May God bless our labors unto His glory.

APPENDIX: THE ESCHATOLOGY OF EZEKIEL

*I*n March of 2019 I was asked to participate in a yearly preacher's study organized by brother Kevin Kay in Bowling Green, KY known as *Studies in the Scriptures* (SITS - http://sitsconference.com/). The focus of that year's study was the book of Ezekiel. Kevin asked me to close the two-day study with a lecture on the Eschatology of Ezekiel. While the scope of that study covered issues much broader than only realized eschatology, I offer it as an appendix to this present study in order to supplement the material we have covered. Readers will find in this lecture some areas that deal directly with answers to preterism, but also some additional material on eschatology in general, and some interpretations they might find challenging.

Ezekiel and Eschatology

Introduction

I have been asked to address the topic of eschatology and Ezekiel. As I have worked on this assignment, I have come to recognize what a formidable task it truly is. Much of the issue depends on how we define *eschatology.* Much of it depends on how we interpret some of the things revealed in the book. Broadly speaking, eschatology is defined as, "the part of theology concerned with death, judgment, and the final destiny of the soul and of humankind" (*New Oxford American Dictionary*). Does the book of Ezekiel use end-times language? Does it reveal principles that address *death, judgment, and the final destiny of the soul?* Certainly. Yet, does it deal with things that are actually discussing what will happen at the end of the world? That is the question.

A Playground for Speculation

One doesn't have to look far into what is written on Ezekiel to recognize that for many it has become a playground for speculation. This is not a new development. In Judaism an entire school of mystical philosophy began to develop well before the time of Christ drawn largely from the opening visions of Ezekiel. Applying the Hebrew word *merkabah* (מֶרְכָּבָה), meaning "chariot," to the creatures Ezekiel saw, fantasy and speculation led to the development of a body of texts known as Hekhalot literature. These works imagined fanciful ascents into heaven. This so-called Merkabah Mysticism, figured prominently in a type of Jewish Gnosticism that ultimately grew in the Middle Ages into the speculations of Jewish Kabbalistic philosophy. It is little wonder that Jerome claimed, "The beginning and ending" of Ezekiel "are wrapped in such obscurity that among the Hebrews… these parts are not read before [one is] thirty years [old]" (*Epistle to Paulinus* 8, Pope).

In more recent times, most of us are familiar with the use premillennialists have made of this book. Particularly, the temple visions of the last chapters have figured into their false concepts that the temple described there must one day be literally built (with sacrifices and all) before Jesus returns to establish His physical kingdom from a restored Israel sitting on His throne in Jerusalem.

Most of us have always thought that the first airplane to achieve flight was the Kitty Hawk, operated by Orville and Wilbur Wright in 1903. What we may not have known was that a year earlier, in 1902, Burrell Cannon, a Baptist preacher and sawmill operator claimed to have flown a craft 160 feet, 10 feet off the ground. Cannon claimed that the ship, known as Ezekiel's Airship, was inspired by studying the vision described in the opening chapter of Ezekiel. A full-size replica can still be viewed at the Northeast Texas Rural Heritage Center and Museum in Pittsburg, Texas.

Perhaps the most sensational examples of these speculations flourish in our own time. So-called "Ancient Alien" theorists see Ezekiel's visions of "living creatures" within the book, not as chariots, but alien spaceships. David J. Halperin, Professor Emeritus of Religious Studies at the University of North Carolina, Chapel Hill, who has authored scholarly texts on Ezekiel and been published in a number of peer-reviewed religious journals, is also the host of a blog and website named for his book, *Journal of a UFO Investigator* (New York: Viking Press, 2011).

While our study may present some ideas that are different than we may have heard before, we will try our best to avoid veering into this playground of speculation, and sincerely seek simply to explore what Ezekiel reveals to us about eschatological issues.

I. Impact of the Opening Vision

The first vision revealed to Ezekiel introduces some features that will appear throughout the book. How we understand this initial vision has an impact on the eschatological significance of these repeating elements.

A. The Four Living Creatures

The book begins with a vision, Ezekiel later summarizes as "the glory of the LORD... like the glory which I saw by the River Chebar" (Ezek. 3:23). A significant element of this vision is what Ezekiel calls "four living creatures" (Ezek. 1:5). Like many other elements within the book, this immediately reminds us of John's words in the book of Revelation. He also sees "four living creatures" (Rev. 4:6, 8; 5:6, 14; 6:1, 6; 7:11; 14:3; 15:7; 19:4). In John's vision, they surround the throne of God (Rev. 4:6), praise the worthiness of the Lamb with the twenty-four elders (Rev. 5:8-9), rejoice at the fall of Babylon (Rev. 19:1-4), and are said to *have* bowls filled with the "prayers of the saints" (Rev. 5:8).

Not only are these creatures identified in the same way, but they share other similarities. Ezekiel writes, "As for the likeness of their faces, each had the face of a man; each of the four had the face of a lion on the right side, each of the four had the face of an ox on the left side, and each of the four had the face of an eagle" (Ezek. 1:10). John writes, "The first living creature was like a lion, the second living creature like a calf, the third living creature had a face like a man, and the fourth living creature was like a flying eagle" (Rev. 4:7). The likeness of a lion, calf (or ox), man, and eagle are shared, but unlike the vision shown to John, the four creatures Ezekiel sees have "four faces" with these likenesses (Ezek. 1:6). That raises several questions: (1) Are these visions of the same creatures? (2) Are these literal characteristics of these creatures, or are they figurative ways of describing what these creatures represent? (3) If they are figurative, what are they intended to represent?

In Revelation they surround the throne in heaven, with the twenty-four elders (who clearly represent the tribes and the apostles). Near the end of Ezekiel, as he receives a vision of the temple, the Lord declares, "Son of man, this is the place of My throne and the place of the soles of My feet, where I will dwell in the midst of the children of Israel forever" (Ezek. 43:7). The writer of Hebrews declared that the arrangement of the tabernacle (and the temple after it) were a "copy and shadow of the heavenly things" (Heb. 8:5). Do we see anything in the arrangement of the tabernacle in the wilderness that might relate to these "living creatures"?

The tabernacle was surrounded by the tribes who encamped around it. The Lord commanded:

> And the LORD spoke to Moses and Aaron, saying: "Everyone of the children of Israel shall camp by his own standard, beside the emblems of his father's house; they shall camp some distance from the tabernacle of meeting" (Num. 2:1-2).

The arrangement of people around the tabernacle was to be according to their tribe. On the east side were Judah, Issachar, and Zebulun (Num. 2:3-9). On the south side were Reuben, Simeon, and Gad (Num. 2:10-17). On the west side were Ephraim, Manassah, and Benjamin (Num. 2:18-24). On the north side were Dan, Asher, and Naphtali (Num. 2:25-31). The Levites formed a circle "in the middle of the camps" (Num. 2:17). The Lord commanded:

> . . . the Levites shall camp around the tabernacle of the Testimony, that there may be no wrath on the congregation of the children of Israel; and the Levites shall keep charge of the tabernacle of the Testimony (Num. 1:53).

In many ways the camp of the Levites is very similar to the position held by the "twenty-four elders" in the throne scene of Revelation. They serve to guide and direct the people in their service to God.

The Standards of the Tribes of Israel

Notice what is said about the encampment of the other tribes—each tribe was to "camp by his own standard, beside the emblems of his father's house" (Num. 2:2). What were these standards? We are not told. They appear to have been flags or banners that identified each tribe's camp on sight. Do we know what was on these standards? Not with any certainty, but there are some biblical clues and claims found in Jewish Rabbinical tradition. Genesis ends with Jacob's prophecy regarding the fate of each of his children (Gen. 49:1-33). In this prophecy we see Judah described "as a lion" (Gen. 49:9).

The Bamidbar (or Numbers) Rabbah (ca. AD 1200) commenting on Numbers 2:2, claimed that the color of the standards corresponded to the colors of the precious stones on Aaron's breastplate. It claimed that the following figures were on each standard: Rueben – a mandrake (cf. Gen. 30:14-16); Simeon – Shechem (the man or city, cf. Gen. 33:18; 34:1-30); Levi – the Urim and Thummim (cf. Exod. 28:30); Judah – a lion (cf. Gen. 49:9); Issachar – the sun and the moon; Zebulun – a ship (cf. Gen. 49:13); Dan – a serpent (cf. Gen. 49:17); Gad – a camp (cf. Gen. 49:19); Naphtali – a deer (cf. Gen. 49:21); Asher – an olive-tree (cf. Gen. 49:22); Ephraim – an ox; Manasseh – a unicorn (from a word likely referring to a gazelle, antelope, or even a rhinoceros; and Benjamin – a wolf (Gen. 49:27).

When the book of Numbers describes the movement of the tribes it speaks of the three tribes on each side following the first tribe, mentioning only one standard. It lists the eastern tribes first, following Judah (Num. 10:14), then the southern tribes following Reuben (Num. 10:18), the western tribes following Ephraim (Num. 10:22), and the northern tribes following Dan (Num. 10:25). Some have described the standards that led these groups as *super-standards*, calling the four groups of three tribes together. What were these standards?

Both the Jerusalem (or Pseudo-Jonathan) Targum (ca. AD 700s) and the Babylonian (or Onkelos) Targum (ca. AD 200s) in their commentary on Numbers 2:2 only describe four standards. The Jerusalem Targum claims that each standard bore the names of three tribes on each side on them. It claims Judah's standard bore the figure of a "young lion," and Ephraim the figure of a "young man." We note, that differs from the Numbers Rabbah mentioned above, which said the tribal flag of Ephraim was an ox. The Jerusalem Targum makes some interesting claims about the other two *super-standards.* Concerning Reuben, it reads:

> . . . upon it shall be set forth the figure of a stag. Some would have thought there should have been upon it the figure of a young ox; but Moses the prophet altered it, that the sin of the [golden] calf might not be remembered against them.

We may remember that the tribal standard of Reuben was said to be a mandrake (in memory of him giving mandrakes to his mother, which she bartered with Rachel – Gen. 30:14-16), but why does it say it "should have been a young ox." It is unclear. What is clear is that Jewish tradition at one point associated an ox with the tribe of Reuben.

Concerning Dan, the Jeruslem Targum claims, "upon it shall also be set forth the figure of a basilisk serpent." Basilisk is a term used in the LXX for a "cobra" (Ps. 91:13) or a "viper" (Isa. 59:5). That echoes Jacob's prophecy (Gen. 49:17), as well as the claim of the Numbers Rabbah. However, at least since the 16th century, a Latin commentary on Ezekiel written by Juan Bautista Villalpando preserves a tradition that Ahiezer (the chief of Dan – Num. 2:25) changed the figure to the image of an eagle eating a serpent (*De postrema Ezechielis prophetæ visione*, 467). That is interesting in light of the Jerusalem Targum's claim that it was a "basilisk serpent." In the LXX this word was used of snakes generally, but as time went on, a "basilisk" came to be considered a mythical flying dragon or snake. Is it possible that the image of an eagle eating a snake became confused with a flying snake? What is clear is that a tradition existed that associated the image of an eagle with the fourth *super-standard.*

Identity of the Living Creatures: Human, Non-Human, or Both?

So, if this is correct, it would mean that four figures would have been visible on the standards raised on four sides of the Israelite camp: a lion, an ox, a man, and an eagle. Is it possible that the visions in Ezekiel and Revelation are intended as figurative ways of picturing those who worship God surrounding His throne? In Revelation chapter five, John writes:

> Now when He had taken the scroll, the four living creatures and the twenty-four elders fell down before the Lamb, each having a harp, and golden bowls full of incense, which are the prayers of the saints. And they sang a new song, saying: "You are worthy to take the scroll, And to open its seals; For You were slain, And have redeemed us to God by Your blood Out of every tribe and tongue and people and nation, And have made us kings and priests to our God; And we shall reign on the earth (Rev. 5:8-10).

Verse nine has an important textual issue. The overwhelming majority of manuscripts (including Codex Sinaiticus [ℵ]), and most ancient translations) put it "redeemed us" or "redeemed us to God." Yet, on the basis of the reading adopted by the UBS/Nestle Aland critical text— a reading based upon evidence Bruce Metzger himself acknowledged was "slight" (i.e., Codex Alexandrinus [A] and the Ethiophic version) —most newer translations render this simply redeemed "unto God" (ASV) or "for God" (RSV, NASB, NIV, ESV). What difference does it make? It tells us something about how to identify these "living creatures." Scripture reveals nothing to us about Christ redeeming any other created beings (Heb. 2:5-10), but He has redeemed human beings.

Does this interpretation mesh with what we see in Ezekiel? There are some challenges to this interpretation. First, the "living creatures" of the first chapter are equated with "cherubim" in chapter ten, which says—"And the cherubim were lifted up. This was the living creature I saw by the River Chebar" (Ezek. 10:15). Second, although Ezekiel says these were the same creatures he saw by the Chebar, the appearance of their faces is slightly different. Instead of an ox, one is said to be "the face of a cherub" (Ezek. 10:14). The Babylonian Talmud claimed that Resh Lakish taught, "Ezekiel entreated concerning it and changed it into a cherub. He said before Him: Lord of the universe, shall an accuser become an advocate!" (*Chagigah* 13b). As we saw in the Jerusalem Targum, they believed that the image of an ox served as a reminder of Israel's sin with the gold calf.

So, does that mean we should reject any interpretation of the "living creatures" as including human beings worshipping God? Perhaps, but we should note that in the book of Ezekiel itself the term "cherub" is used of the king of Tyre (Ezek. 28:11-16). Throughout both Old and New Testaments there are times that words for angelic beings are also applied to human beings (e.g., 1 Sam. 11:1-4; Luke 8:18-24). Later in Ezekiel, the cherubim on the walls of the temple were said to have only two faces: that of a man and a lion (41:18-19). In Revelation the "living creatures" had only one face (Rev. 4:7). Are these descriptions of the anatomy of different species of angelic beings or figurative and spiritual ways of describing those (human or angelic) surrounding God in worship?

Let's notice some further characteristics of the "living creatures" in Ezekiel. They are seen as "a whirlwind . . . coming out of the north" (Ezek. 1:4). Remember, the vision is by the Chebar (believed to be near the Euphrates not far from Babylon). North would be how anyone coming from Israel would come to them. They are said to have "the likeness of a man" (Ezek. 1:5), even though they are also said to have four faces and four wings (Ezek. 1:6). "The hands of a man were under their wings" (Ezek. 1:8). "Their appearance *was* like burning coals of fire, like the appearance of torches going back and forth among the living creatures" (Ezek. 1:13). They are radiant in appearance—a quality often ascribed to spiritual beings generally (cf. 2 Kings 6:17).

"A Wheel in the Middle of a Wheel"

At this point, Ezekiel begins the descriptions of the wheels. We should note that in spite of the mountain of speculation that has grown up interpreting this as a *merkebah* "chariot" (or "throne-chariot"), the Hebrew word *merkebah* is never used in Ezekiel! The prophet sees, "a wheel . . . on the earth beside each living creature" (Ezek. 1:15). We notice it sits "on the earth." The Babylonian Talmud described this as having, "one wheel at the bottom hard by the living creatures" (*Chagigah* 13b). They are further described as having, "a wheel in the middle of a wheel" (Ezek. 1:17).

So-called "Ancient Alien" theorists in our day see in this a description of an extra-terrestrial spaceship. In 1974 Josef Blumrich, a NASA engineer, wrote a book entitled *The Spaceships of Ezekiel* (New York: Bantam Books, 1974) suggesting that these visions were actually alien visitations. The same year, influenced by the descriptions of Ezekiel, Blumrich patented a wheel that could move in multiple directions known as the "Omnidirectional wheel" (US patent 3789947). Is that what Ezekiel saw—alien or advanced technology? No.

Notice some things about the "wheels." Yes, they move "toward any one of four directions" (Ezek. 1:17), but they are "full of eyes, all around the four of them" (Ezek. 1:18). When the creatures move, the "wheels went beside them" or "hard by them" (Ezek. 1:19, JPS), but he also tells us twice, "the spirit of the living creatures was in the wheels" (Ezek. 1:20-21). These wheels are described as animate. This is not inanimate technology. Ezekiel is not misinterpreting engines and mechanical propulsion. He is describing something living, yet calling it "wheels."

When they move it is said to be "a tumult like the noise of an army" (Ezek. 1:24). Is that a clue that this is not talking about a science fiction type creature, but the company of God's faithful hosts spiritually personified as a living creature? If so, these aren't literal "wheels" but a way of describing the company of God's worshippers encircling the throne of God. What is the "wheel in the middle of a wheel"? Remember the arrangement of the Levites? They encircled the tabernacle in the middle of the other tribes, which encircled them.

Ezekiel sees a firmament above the creatures (Ezek. 1:22) and above it was "the likeness of a throne" (Ezek. 1:26), which Ezekiel explains was, "the appearance of the likeness of the glory of the LORD" (Ezek. 1:28). Throughout the book, the "living creatures" move with God's glory as it is manifested in different places.

The Spiritual Hosts of God

Does Scripture ever describe God's people in similar terms? Speaking to living Christians, the Hebrew writer declares:

> . . . You have come to Mount Zion and to the city of the living God, the heavenly Jerusalem, to an innumerable company of angels, to the general assembly and church of the firstborn who are registered in heaven, to God the Judge of all, to the spirits of just men made perfect, to Jesus the Mediator of the new covenant, and to the blood of sprinkling that speaks better things than that of Abel (Heb. 12:22-24).

Living Christians are said to be part of a "general assembly" and "innumerable company of angels" together with the "spirits of just men made perfect." Yes, the Scriptures speak of all the dead this side of judgment as residing in the realm of Hades or Sheol (Luke 16:19-31; Rev. 20:13-14), but if the Hebrew writer envisions living saints as already a part of the spiritual assembly of God's people, why would it surprise us if the same are pictured in the visions of Ezekiel and John?

Historically, among Jews and Christians most have interpreted the "living creatures" as simply a class of angelic beings, and their identification in Ezekiel with cherubim could certainly justify this. However, that is not the only way these visions have been interpreted. Irenaeus (ca. 125-202) was the first to interpret them as figures representing the four gospels (Against Heresies 3.11.8). This speculative allegorical view was later adopted and expanded by later writers and within Catholicism. It came to be featured prominently in Western religious art (see figure 1). While interpreting them in correlation to the standards of the Israelite camp is not an interpretation original to me, I acknowledge that it has not been a majority view. Martin Luther, however, came very near to this conclusion, writing, "This vision in the first part of Ezekiel . . . is nothing else, as I understand it . . . than a revelation of the kingdom of Christ in faith, here on earth, in all four quarters of the whole world . . ." (A New

Figure 1: This wooden box from the early 13th century which is in the Musée de Cluny in Cologne is overlaid with carved ivory portraying Christ surrounded by the "four living creatures"—The man (Matthew), the eagle (John), the lion (Mark), and the ox (Luke). It reflects the allegorical interpretation still common in Catholicism.

Preface to the Book of Ezekiel). We would not limit it by saying "here on earth," but his view reflects a recognition of the figurative nature of these visions that we appreciate.

So, if the "living creatures" figuratively and spiritually represent God's worshippers, what does their use in Ezekiel and Revelation teach us? Whether we understand them to be angelic non-human cherubim or a spiritual representation of God's people one thing is clear—even when God's glory departs from Jerusalem, His faithful worshippers maintain their service to Him. What a comfort this would be to exiles who will learn before the book ends that Jerusalem had fallen, and the temple was destroyed. What a comfort it would be to those in John's day who faced persecution from Rome, and had also seen the temple in Jerusalem destroyed once again. God's glory remained and His hosts worshipped Him wherever they were transplanted.

Some may question this interpretation, and choose to see the "living creatures" as non-human angelic beings. That has certainly been the most common interpretation, but if my suggestion is correct it influences how we see their appearance throughout the book. God's people are given promises of judgment on the ungodly. They are given a vision of a future of hope, peace, and restoration following their transplanted status. This influences how we interpret what is, in fact eschatological and what has already been fulfilled.

B. Three Key Scenes

Let's notice three key scenes in the book in which the "living creatures" with the "glory of the LORD" are seen. Each of these portray three different conditions.

Scene One: The first comes in the opening vision. Ezekiel is "among the captives by the River Chebar" (1:1), yet he is shown the "glory of the LORD" (1:28). In this scene the throne, with the "living creatures" is independent of the temple—seven years before its destruction (1:2; cf. 33:21). Ezekiel is then sent to prophesy (2:1-10), and commanded to eat the scroll of God's revelation (3:1-27), during which time the "living creatures" and the "glory of the LORD" take him to Tel Abib by the River Chebar (3:13-14). At this point, he identifies the "glory of the LORD" as the same thing he saw at the beginning (3:23). In many ways this is just an extension of the first scene, portraying God's glory independent of the temple.

Scene Two: The next scene is much different. It comes six years before the destruction of the temple (8:1; cf. 32:21). Ezekiel is taken to see the abominations in Jerusalem (8:1-18), and shown six men who slay those in the city not marked on the forehead (9:1-11). He later describes this as "when I came to destroy the city" (43:3), but this does not seem to be literal. He spiritually observes what would happen when Babylon literally destroyed the city. In this frightening scene, Ezekiel three times mentions that what he saw were the same manifestations he saw at the beginning. He writes, "And the cherubim were lifted up. This was the living creature I saw by the River Chebar" (10:15). It is interesting that here he speaks in the singular—"the living creature," as he does when he mentions it again—"This is the living creature I saw under the God of Israel by the River Chebar, and I knew they were cherubim" (10:20). Notice, he says "living creature" (singular), but "they were cherubim." Specific identity is treated collectively. Nonetheless, this is the same manifestation. He says a third time, "And the likeness of their faces was the same as the faces which I had seen by the River Chebar, their appearance and their persons" (10:22). But, notice the condition of this scene—"Then the glory of the LORD departed from the threshold of the temple and stood over the cherubim" (10:18). The temple had not yet been destroyed, but Ezekiel sees God's glory *riding* on the hosts of His cherubim leaving the temple.

Let's notice some things in the context of this scene. When describing the "living creatures" Ezekiel writes, "And their whole body, with their back, their hands, their wings, and the wheels that the four had, were full of eyes all around. As for the wheels, they were called in my hearing, 'Wheel'" (10:12-13). In this vision the prophet doesn't just describe the wheels with eyes, but says body, back, hands, wings, and wheels "were full of eyes all around." This is the same thing said of the "living creatures" in Revelation as well (Rev. 4:6). That is a ghastly image, if it is literal. What if it is figurative? It is the "general assembly" and "innumerable company of angels"—"the spirits of just men made perfect" (cf. Heb. 12:22-24) in the company of God regardless of the wickedness of Jerusalem and the Lord's departure from the temple.

Consider this odd passage, "they were called in my hearing, 'Wheel'" (10:13). What does this mean? The word "wheel" in Hebrew is *galgal* (וְּלְגַּל), but we should remember that it was not until centuries after the New Testament that Hebrew began to be written with vowel pointing. Modern Hebrew is still often written with only consonants. Another word for "wheel" (or "rolling") would have been spelled exactly the same way when this was first written. We say it Gilgal (וְּלְגָּל). What was Gilgal? It is where Israel first camped when they crossed the Jordan (Josh. 4:19), where the twelve stones were set up (Josh. 4:20), where God "rolled away the reproach of Egypt" (Josh. 5:9), where they kept their first Passover (Josh. 5:10), where Samuel made a circuit as a judge (1 Sam. 7:16), and where Saul was set up as king (1 Sam. 11:15) when Samuel called to the people, "Come, let us go to Gilgal and renew the kingdom there" (1 Sam. 11:14). Imagine if we translated this literally—"Come, let us go to Wheel and renew the kingdom there." Could this have any correlation to the words of Ezekiel? Could these "living creatures" that represent the camp of God's people be named after the memory of their first camp, and the camp where they *renewed* the kingdom? As the "glory of the LORD" departs the temple, is this an appeal to recall a past renewal that must happen once more in their exile. After this scene of the glory departing the temple, God tells Ezekiel, "Although I have cast them far off among the Gentiles, and although I have scattered them among the countries, yet I shall be a little sanctuary for them in the countries where they have gone" (11:16). Yes, the "glory of the LORD" had departed from the temple in Jerusalem, but God is not limited by geography (or even the unfaithfulness of His people). Wherever His faithful are taken He is to them "a little sanctuary."

So the cherubim lifted up their wings, with the wheels beside them, and the glory of the God of Israel was high above them. And the glory of the LORD went up from the midst of the city and stood on the mountain, which is on the east side of the city. Then the Spirit took me up and brought me in a vision by the Spirit of God into Chaldea, to those in captivity. And the vision that I had seen went up from me. So I spoke to those in captivity of all the things the LORD had shown me (11:22-25).

Scene Three: Finally, the prophet sees the "living creatures" and the glory of the LORD" in one final scene. In the glorious image of a rebuilt temple in Jerusalem, Ezekiel records:

And behold, the glory of the God of Israel came from the way of the east. His voice was like the sound of many waters; and the earth shone with His glory. It was like the appearance of the vision which I saw—like the vision which I saw when I came to destroy the city. The visions were like the vision which I saw by the River Chebar; and I fell on my face. And the glory of the LORD came into the temple by way of the gate which faces toward the east. The Spirit lifted me up and brought me into the inner court; and behold, the glory of the LORD filled the temple. Then I heard Him speaking to me from the temple, while a man stood beside me" (43:2-6).

He tells us "The visions were like the vision which I saw by the River Chebar," but the condition is much different. Fourteen years after the temple had been destroyed (40:1; cf. 32:21), in a hopeless and helpless time, the prophet is given a picture of a time when God's glory is not confined to the "little sanctuary" among His scattered people, but in a glorious restored temple. God's glory is said to come "from the east," the direction one would return from Babylon. The "living creatures" who accompany the Lord's glory in all conditions at all times serve as a picture of the true spiritual condition of those faithful to God.

II. Eschatological Elements within Ezekiel

With the opening visions of Ezekiel as an introduction, and the "living creatures" accompanying the "glory of the LORD" as recurring figures, throughout the book we find numerous passages with eschatological implications.

A. Ezekiel 7:2—"The End Has Come"

Following the opening visions given to Ezekiel, he is called to illustrate the siege and destruction of Jerusalem in various ways (4:1-6:14). After this, the Lord declares, "And you, son of man, thus says the Lord GOD to the land of Israel: 'An end! The end has come upon the four corners of the land" (7:2). This is restated a few verses later, "An end has come, the end has come; it has dawned for you; behold, it has come!" (7:6). Obviously, this is eschatological language, but to what "end" is the Lord referring?

The context makes it clear that the "end" that is under consideration is not the end of time, but the fall of Judah and Jerusalem to Babylon. The Lord tells Ezekiel:

> . . . the land is filled with crimes of blood, and the city is full of violence. Therefore I will bring the worst of the Gentiles, and they will possess their houses; I will cause the pomp of the strong to cease, and their holy places shall be defiled. Destruction comes; they will seek peace, but there shall be none (7:23-25).

This illustrates a fact that runs throughout Scripture—when the Holy Spirit speaks of "the end" it does not always refer to the end of time. The context must be considered to determine the application.

Brother Kevin Kay, in some material he shared with me, lists seven different events identified as "the end" in Scripture. Consider his list (which I have modified slightly):

- Israel in 722 BC (Amos 8:1-3, 10)
- Nineveh in 612 BC (Nah. 1:8-9)
- Jerusalem in 586 BC (Ezek. 7:1-9; Hab. 2:2-3)
- Babylon in 539 BC (Dan. 5:26)
- Jewish persecution in 165/164 BC (Dan. 8:17, 19)
- Kings of the North and South (Dan. 11:27, 35, 40; 12:4, 8-9, 13)
- Jerusalem in AD 70 (Dan. 9:26)

Preterist Rejection of an End of Time

Sadly, this fact has led some to argue that Scripture does not teach an end of time or destruction of this present universe. An oft repeated statement made by preterists to defend their position is—"the Christian age has no end." Their argument is drawn from promises regarding the kingdom, that it, "shall stand forever" (Dan. 2:44). This assumes that the conditions of the kingdom once established cannot continue on into a changed new and heavenly existence. The assertion also fails to explain how Paul could speak of showing the "riches of His grace" in the "ages [plural] to come" (Eph. 2:7). Their argument is that the Christian age came after AD 70 and "has no end." Yet, like the Hebrew writer, Paul said of the accounts in the Old Testament, "Now all these things happened to them as examples, and they were written for our admonition, upon whom the ends of the ages have come" (1 Cor. 10:11). Here, not only is "ages" plural, but also "ends." How can they explain multiple "ends of the ages" if their limited concept of the "Christian age" has no end? This preterist argument doesn't work.

"The End of the Age"

Much of their argument is focused on interpreting the phrase "end of the age" in Matthew 24:3 as a reference to the end of the Jewish age (as they argue it) in AD 70, rather than as a reference to the end of time. Many brethren who are not full-preterists have adopted this conclusion, but we contend that this fails to take into account how the phrase is used throughout the entire book of Matthew.

The phrase "end of the age" translates the phrase *tēs sunteleias tou aiōnos* (τῆς συντελείας τοῦ αἰῶνος). Most modern translations have rejected the KJV rendering "end of the world," because the Greek word *aiōn* (αἰών) carries a basic conceptual idea of time. Thayer defines it, "(1) for ever, an unbroken age, perpetuity of time, eternity; (2) the worlds, universe; (3) period of time, age." We should note from Thayer's second definition that it can refer to the *world,* as is reflected at times in Scripture. The Hebrew writer tells us God through Christ, "made the worlds (*aiōn*)" (Heb. 1:2) and the "worlds (*aiōn*) were framed by the word of God" (Heb. 11:3). Even so, we agree that "age" is the preferable sense in the phrase *tēs sunteleias tou aiōnos.*

This phrase is used six times in Scripture and five of them are in Matthew. This helps us see the scope of its use in the book. Three instances are found in parables in chapter 13. In the Parable of the Wheat and Tares, as Jesus offered the explanation He declared, "The enemy who sowed them is the devil, the harvest is the end of the age, and the reapers are the angels. Therefore as the tares are gathered and burned in the fire, so it will be at the end of the age" (Matt. 13:39-40). In the Parable of the Dragnet, He offers a similar explanation, "So it will be at the end of the age. The angels will come forth, separate the wicked from among the just, and cast them into the furnace of fire. There will be wailing and gnashing of teeth" (Matt. 13:49-50). In all three of these examples we see it as a time that involves angels, separation of the just from the wicked, and the assignment of punishment. The preterist tries to identify this with AD 70, but it must be acknowledged that if so any separation of the just and the wicked could only be seen in spiritual terms. Sin, wickedness, and evil still continue to function. That hardly seems like it would fit Jesus's description of separating "the wicked from among the just."

The final example in Matthew poses the greatest challenge to the preterist position. At the close of the Great Commission, Jesus promised, "lo, I am with you always, even to the end of the age" (Matt. 28:20). If the "end of the age" is the end of the Jewish Age, how can we understand this promise? The world continued after AD 70. Preterists argue that Christ dwells with His people in the church, applying the promise of Revelation 21:3 to the age of

Christ. Yet, was Jesus only promising to be with His people until the end of the Jewish Age? No. He was promising to be with them "always." Now, the preterist might respond by arguing, "if this means the end of the universe, would that mean He won't be with Christians after that?" The difference has to do with the view we take of Christ living with His people. If "age to come" means end of the world, the Christian is promised a literal, rather than a spiritual presence of God with His people. If the preterist view is correct, the problem remains the same—how can they hope for His continued presence with them? How is it any different from His dwelling with us now in the church?

The final example is equally challenging to the preterist position. The Hebrew writer speaks of Christ's sacrifice of Himself, "now, once at the end of the ages, He has appeared to put away sin by the sacrifice of Himself" (Heb. 9:26). We should note that the Hebrew writer says Christ's sacrifice came "at the end of the ages," so, within the first century, before AD 70 the Holy Spirit described the time of Jesus's death as coming at "the end of the ages." Unlike the phrases in Matthew, this is in the plural. If Jesus died in the Jewish Age, and (as preterists argue) the age of Christ began at AD 70, what "ages" are being described here? Just as God described the fall of Jerusalem in Ezekiel as "the end," there are many ages that have come to an end. But, this foreshadows the fact that one day, all things in this present universe will come to an end (2 Pet. 3:1-13).

We can also, learn the sense of "the end of the age" by looking at some texts that speak of the "age to come." As Jesus speaks of those who sacrifice to serve Him, He contrasts, "this present time" with the "age to come" (Luke 18:30). In Mark's account He promises they shall, "receive a hundredfold now in this time—houses and brothers and sisters and mothers and children and lands, with persecutions—and in the age to come, eternal life" (Mark 10:30). Preterists argue that after AD 70 Christians now have eternal life, but notice the contrast here infers that the "persecutions" in "this time" (which they would identify as the Jewish Age) do not carry over into the "age to come." Have persecutions truly ended? No.

The End of Time in the Old Testament

It is often falsely asserted that the Old Testament never taught that this present universe would end. That is a question to which we could devote considerable time. Yet, for the purposes of this study, let's notice only a few passages. After the flood, God declared, "While the earth remains, seedtime and harvest, cold and heat, winter and summer, and day and night shall not cease" (Gen. 8:22). Most English translations render this text with dynamic equivalency rather than literal wording. The Hebrew uses the adverb *ad* (עַ) meaning "as long as," before the words "all the days" (YLT, DBY). God literally promises "as long as all the days of the earth" seasons and day and night will not cease. To refer to something with the qualifier "while" or "as long as" necessarily implies that there will be a time when the earth will not remain (or literally) when "all the days" of earth will be completed. This sets the stage for things that will be further revealed as time goes on. We believe that has to play a role in how we must interpret the wording in Daniel 12:13—"the end of the days." If the implication has been made as early as Genesis 8:22 that "all the days of the earth" are a limited number, Daniel can properly understand "the end of the days" to point to that time. While this differs from "the end" of Ezekiel 7:2, which is not pointing to the end of "all the days," that doesn't mean we should reject the clear teaching of Scripture that there will be an "end of the age" in its final and ultimate sense (as it relates to this universe).

B. Ezekiel 32—Those Who Go Down to the Pit

It is commonly asserted that the Old Testament is silent regarding the afterlife. Modern reformed Jews often lean on this in their uncertainty (or denial of life after death). While we would agree that there is much less revealed in the Old Testament than in the New, evidence for it runs throughout its pages. A clear example of this is found in Ezekiel chapter 32. After pronouncing judgment on Ammon, Moab, and Edom (25:1-17), Tyre and Sidon (26:1-27:36; 28:1-26), and Egypt (29:1-31:18), in the twelfth year of Jehoiachin's captivity (32:1), the prophet is commanded to pronounce a lament of judgment on Pharaoh (32:2). This lamentation calls Pharaoh to consider his future contact with "those who go down to the pit" (32:18). While this is certainly poetic language, it offers some profound facts about the after-life. Referring to Pharaoh, Ezekiel is told, "The strong among the mighty shall speak to him out of the midst of Sheol" (32:21a, ASV). Although some might take this to mean that the dead *speak* to him through their example—they were powerful, but now lie in shame—this apparently refers to what Pharaoh and his multitudes will see and hear *after death*. The Lord promises him, "I will lay your flesh on the mountains, and fill the valleys with your carcass" (32:5, NKJV).

Pharaoh is then told who will be in Sheol. These include, Assyria (32:22-23), Elam (32:24-25), Meshach and Tubal (32:26-28), Edom (32:29), and the Sidonians (32:30). Although these, like Pharaoh "caused terror in the land of the living" (32:25; cf. 32:24, 26, 27, 32), when Pharoah is said to *see* them they "bear their shame with those who go down to the Pit" (32:24, 25, 30). Ezekiel is told, "Pharaoh will see them and be comforted over all his multitude"—that is, he will be consoled to see they have died as his multitudes have died—"Pharaoh and all his army, slain by the sword" (32:31). This clearly shatters any picture of the life of man ending upon death. If Pharaoh ceases to exist upon death there is no way he could "see" those listed here. If these sinful souls pass out of existence they do not "bear their shame," and could not "speak to him out of the midst of Sheol" (ASV).

C. Ezekiel 34:13; 37:21-22; 36:25-28; 39:25-29—
The Preterist Doctrine of "the Gathering"

Numerous times in Scripture Ezekiel is told about a re-gathering of the Israelites following their exile. A fundamental teaching espoused by preterists is the argument that passages in the Old Testament that speak of God gathering Israel back together with the Gentiles under the Messiah should be harmonized with the wording in the Olivet Discourse promising, "And He will send His angels with a great sound of a trumpet, and they will gather together His elect from the four winds, from one end of heaven to the other" (Matt. 24:31). The conclusion is then drawn that this is not talking about final judgment, but God's coming in judgment upon Jerusalem in AD 70. It is asserted that this was when the promised *gathering* took place—not at the cross. Oddly enough, some advocates of this view even apply this to Hebrews 10:25, arguing that it is not talking about faithfulness in gathering (or assembling) in the local church, but anticipation of this AD 70 *gathering*.

Preterists often exercise a major flaw in their approach to scriptural interpretation. They choose a definition within a particular passage of Scripture. Often, little attention is given to the context or background of the passage. Then, their definition is applied throughout any other passages of Scripture that use the same wording. Certainly, it is important to harmonize Scripture with Scripture, but if our initial definition is flawed, we will carry this flawed definition with us to all other Scriptures we encounter. This flawed approach is seen in their flawed doctrine of an AD 70 *gathering*. Just because a gathering is referred to in one passage doesn't mean it automatically apples to all other texts that mention a gathering.

A number of preterist sources offer lists of Old Testament passages describing *gatherings*. Don Preston has written a series of seven articles entitled, "The Re-Gathering of Israel."[1] A preterist author named Tina Rae Collins has published an entire book entitled *The Gathering in the Last Days* advocating

---

[1] This series started began April 29, 2013 and ran through May 14, 2013. They can be viewed on his website: http://donkpreston.com/articles/.

this view.[2] Among the passages Collins offers to defend her position are two from Ezekiel. Let's consider these texts.

The first is Ezekiel 34:13, which reads, "And I will bring them out from the peoples and gather them from the countries, and will bring them to their own land; I will feed them on the mountains of Israel, in the valleys and in all the inhabited places of the country" (Ezek. 34:13). This clearly has Messianic overtones, but when was it accomplished? As the gospel was being preached (before AD 70), Paul wrote:

> Now all things are of God, who has reconciled us to Himself through Jesus Christ, and has given us the ministry of reconciliation, that is, that God was in Christ reconciling the world to Himself, not imputing their trespasses to them, and has committed to us the word of reconciliation. Now then, we are ambassadors for Christ, as though God were pleading through us: we implore you on Christ's behalf, be reconciled to God (2 Cor. 5:18-20).

If God, in Christ at the cross and in the spreading of the gospel of Jesus Christ had already reconciled "the world to Himself," and the apostles as His ambassadors could already make the appeal "be reconciled to God," this *gathering* foretold by the prophets had already occurred.

The second passage Collins cites reads:

> Thus says the Lord God: "Surely I will take the children of Israel from among the nations, wherever they have gone, and will gather them from every side and bring them into their own land; and I will make them one nation in the land, on the mountains of Israel; and one king shall be king over them all; they shall no longer be two nations, nor shall they ever be divided into two kingdoms again" (Ezek. 37:21-22).

This text comes in a prophecy the Lord revealed to Ezekiel of two sticks—one representing Judah and the other representing Ephraim (the son of Joseph), often used to refer to the northern kingdom of Israel (Ezek. 37:16). The Lord

---

[2] In the introduction to her book, Collins doesn't tell much about her religious background, but extends personal thanks to Arthur Ogden, whom she says started her on "this journey" and "patiently listened to my questions," and Sam Dawson whom she says "nudged me over a hump that was holding me back." She also thanks Dawson for proofreading her manuscript. Arthur Ogden's book, *The Avenging of the Apostles and Prophets: Commentary on Revelation*, has been widely read among our brethren. Although he did not accept full-preterism, it is interesting that she says he *started* her in this direction. Sam Dawson, used to preach among non-institutional brethren and is now a full-preterist. Realized eschatology is often a progressive path that begins with accepting a few faulty premises. When these are adopted certain logical consequences follow.

promises a reunion of the two kingdoms (37:17-20). This foreshadows a reunion under the Messiah. Ezekiel is told, "David My servant shall be king over them, and they shall all have one shepherd; they shall also walk in My judgments and observe My statutes, and do them" (Ezek. 37:24). This would not be David reincarnated, but Jesus, a descendent of David, who would reign on David's throne. Before Mary's conception, the angel announced to her, "He will be great, and will be called the Son of the Highest; and the Lord God will give Him the throne of His father David" (Luke 1:32).

Ezekiel's prophecy helps us determine some things about when this *gathering* would happen. Ezekiel is told, "I will make them one nation" and "one king shall be king over them all." When did the Messiah have a "nation" and when did Jesus reign as "king over them all"? Peter told Christians (before AD 70), "But you are a chosen generation, a royal priesthood, a holy nation, His own special people, that you may proclaim the praises of Him who called you out of darkness into His marvelous light" (1 Pet. 2:9). Ezekiel was told these reunited peoples would be "one nation," yet Peter says it was already *gathered* before AD 70. Before His ascension, Jesus proclaimed that He had "all authority" both "in heaven and on earth" (Matt. 28:18). We have used this for years to show premillennialists that Jesus already reigns over His kingdom. The preterist must see the same thing. Jesus was already the "one king" reigning over the promised "one nation" that was gathered of both Jews and Gentiles through the gospel long before AD 70.

Other Gathering Passages in Ezekiel

This concept of *gathering* arises frequently in Ezekiel echoing the same sense. Following Ezekiel's vision of the glory of the LORD departing the temple, Ezekiel is told:

> Therefore say, "Thus says the Lord GOD: 'Although I have cast them far off among the Gentiles, and although I have scattered them among the countries, yet I shall be a little sanctuary for them in the countries where they have gone.'" Therefore say, "Thus says the Lord GOD: 'I will gather you from the peoples, assemble you from the countries where you have been scattered, and I will give you the land of Israel'" (11:16-17).

In the prophecy to the mountains of Israel, God promised to "sanctify My great name" so that "the nations shall know that I am the LORD" (36:23). He then declared, "For I will take you from among the nations, gather you out of all countries, and bring you into your own land" (36:24). This is further explained by offering additional elements of this promise that directly correspond to things fulfilled in the gospel. He promises:

Then I will sprinkle clean water on you, and you shall be clean; I will cleanse you from all your filthiness and from all your idols. I will give you a new heart and put a new spirit within you; I will take the heart of stone out of your flesh and give you a heart of flesh. I will put My Spirit within you and cause you to walk in My statutes, and you will keep My judgments and do them. Then you shall dwell in the land that I gave to your fathers; you shall be My people, and I will be your God (36:25-28).

This parallels Jeremiah's prophecy of a new covenant with "the house of Israel and with the house of Judah" (Jer. 31:31) and Joel's prophecy of an outpouring of the Holy Spirit in the "last days" (Joel 2:28, as quoted in Acts 2:17). God promised, "I will put My law in their minds, and write it on their hearts; and I will be their God, and they shall be My people" (Jer. 31:33)—the same promise here in Ezekiel. When did He put His Spirit within His people to do His laws—as Joel and Ezekiel prophesied? Peter confirmed its fulfillment in Acts 2:16. When was the new covenant in place? The Hebrew writer said that Jesus was already the "Mediator of the new covenant" (Heb. 12:24). This shows us the gathering promised in Ezekiel 36:24 was accomplished in the gospel—not something that awaited fulfillment in AD 70.

Finally, at the close of the prophecy against Gog and Magog (which we shall discuss below), the Lord speaks of bringing back "the captives of Jacob" and "the whole house of Israel" (39:25), but again speaks of it as when He "shall have poured out My Spirit on the house of Israel" (39:29). If this pouring out of the Spirit was fulfilled in the gospel—if the definition of being a Jew was changed to mean those who are of faith and a circumcised heart (Rom. 2:28-29; Gal. 3:7), defining them as "the Israel of God" (Gal. 6:16) since, "they are not all Israel who are of Israel" (Rom. 9:6)—it tells us that the time when the Lord brings "back from the peoples" and has "gathered them out of their enemies' lands" and is "hallowed in them in the sight of many nations" (Ezek. 39:27) is accomplished in the gospel, not the destruction of Jerusalem in AD 70. It may also help us understand how to interpret the prophecy against Gog and Magog in general (as we shall see).

D. Ezekiel 34:23—"One flock and One Shepherd"
One of the most clearly Messianic prophecies in the book comes immediately after Ezekiel learns that Jerusalem has fallen, in the twelfth year of their captivity (33:21). Ezekiel is told to prophesy against the "shepherds of Israel" (34:1). After rebuking the Jewish leaders, as we briefly noticed above, Ezekiel is told:

As a shepherd seeks out his flock on the day he is among his scattered sheep, so will I seek out My sheep and deliver them from all the places where they were scattered on a cloudy and dark day. And I will bring them out from the peoples and gather them from the countries, and will bring them to their own land; I will feed them on the mountains of Israel, in the valleys and in all the inhabited places of the country. I will feed them in good pasture, and their fold shall be on the high mountains of Israel. There they shall lie down in a good fold and feed in rich pasture on the mountains of Israel (34:12-14).

This picture of a shepherd seeking out his lost and scattered sheep immediately calls to mind Jesus's parable of the shepherd leaving his ninety-nine sheep to seek out his lost lamb to bring it back into the fold (Luke 15:4-7; Matt. 18:12-14). When Jesus sent out the Twelve, they were not yet to go to the Gentiles, but only to "the lost sheep of the house of Israel" (Matt. 10:6). Unlike the wicked shepherds whom Ezekiel is called to rebuke, Jesus would be the "good shepherd" who "gives His life for the sheep" (John 10:11).

As the Lord speaks further to Ezekiel, He declares, "O My flock, thus says the Lord GOD: Behold, I shall judge between sheep and sheep, between rams and goats" (34:17)—a striking similarity to Jesus's own promise of His role in final judgment. He declared:

When the Son of Man comes in His glory, and all the holy angels with Him, then He will sit on the throne of His glory. All the nations will be gathered before Him, and He will separate them one from another, as a shepherd divides his sheep from the goats (Matt. 25:31-32).

The Lord goes on to promise Ezekiel, "I will establish one shepherd over them, and he shall feed them—My servant David. He shall feed them and be their shepherd. And I, the LORD, will be their God, and My servant David a prince among them; I, the LORD, have spoken" (34:23-24). Much of how we interpret the eschatological significance of various prophecies within Ezekiel hinges upon when we consider this prophecy to have been fulfilled. If it is fulfilled in Jesus, this and the kingdom over which He rules is not awaiting an end times establishment. If it is not, with modern Conservative and Orthodox Jews one must believe it is still to come, and is therefore to be an eschatological event.

Premillennialists face a dilemma—if Jesus is the "one shepherd" and the "David" who reigns as "prince among them" how can they treat this prophecy as eschatological? That is to place oneself, with modern Jews, in a position of denying Jesus's present shepherding of His people. Hal Lindsey, in his book, *The Late Great Planet Earth* argued, "The real issue between the amillennial and the Premillennial viewpoints is whether prophecy should be interpreted literally or allegorically" (165). That may be true in many instances, but we would ask—is Christ now *literally* the "good Shepherd"? Yes. If so, He now reigns as "David a prince among" His people.

E. Ezekiel 37:1-14—The Valley of Dry Bones

Following Ezekiel's prophecy to the "mountains of Israel" (36:1-38), Ezekiel is taken "in the Spirit of the LORD" to a valley filled with dry bones (37:1). The Lord asks Ezekiel, "can these bones live" (37:3). Ezekiel is commanded:

> . . . Prophesy to these bones, and say to them, "O dry bones, hear the word of the LORD! Thus says the Lord GOD to these bones: 'Surely I will cause breath to enter into you, and you shall live. I will put sinews on you and bring flesh upon you, cover you with skin and put breath in you; and you shall live. Then you shall know that I am the LORD'" (37:4-6).

Ezekiel obeys (37:7-9) and the bones "lived, and stood upon their feet, an exceedingly great army" (37:10). This is a spiritual vision much like Ezekiel's vision of the slaughter of the inhabitants of Jerusalem (9:1-11). He is told, "Son of man, these bones are the whole house of Israel" (37:11a). Like the "sour grapes" proverb (18:2), the Lord quotes the attitude of the people as they are in captivity—"Our bones are dry, our hope is lost, and we ourselves are cut off!" (37:11b). Like other prophesies in the book offered to illustrate spiritual conditions this remarkable vision is offered to bring hope to the captives. The Lord explains:

> Therefore prophesy and say to them, "Thus says the Lord GOD: 'Behold, O My people, I will open your graves and cause you to come up from your graves, and bring you into the land of Israel. Then you shall know that I am the LORD, when I have opened your graves, O My people, and brought you up from your graves. I will put My Spirit in you, and you shall live, and I will place you in your own land. Then you shall know that I, the LORD, have spoken it and performed it,' says the LORD" (37:12-14).

Jesus would declare, "the hour is coming in which all who are in the graves will hear His voice and come forth—those who have done good, to the resurrection of life, and those who have done evil, to the resurrection of condemnation" (John 5:28-29). Is this the same resurrection shown to Ezekiel? No. Remember the attitude that motivated this vision—the captives felt like hopeless dry bones. Yet, the Lord promised them new life. They were not literally dry bones, nor literally in "graves," but they were displaced from their land. This is foretelling the return from exile that would be fulfilled in the days of Ezra and Nehemiah.

This is further reinforced by the vision of two sticks reunited (discussed above) that immediately follows this vision (37:15-28). This vision moves beyond simply the return from exile to discuss the Messianic age. It promises a reunion of Judah and Ephraim, i.e., Israel (37:19), but associates this with the time when "one king shall be king over them all; they shall no longer be two nations" (37:22). The Lord uses the same language we saw in the prophesy to the shepherds of Israel—"David My servant shall be king over them, and they shall all have one shepherd" (37:24; cf. 34:23-24). This was fulfilled in the coming of Jesus and the establishment of His church, so the resurrection of the dry bones vision that precedes this vision is not talking about "resurrection at the last day" (John 11:24), but the spiritual resurrection after the Babylonian exile that would set the stage for the coming of Christ's kingdom.

F. Ezekiel 38-39—Prophecy against Gog and Magog

Premillennialists have long argued that Ezekiel's reference to "Gog, the prince of Rosh" (38:3) foretells a future Russian invasion of Israel. Like the prophecies against other nations the Lord gives a prophetic condemnation to Gog and Magog (38:1-39:29), but it is important for us to recognize how this text relates to historical events and how it came to be used in the New Testament and Jewish literature after the New Testament. The warning addresses, "Gog, of the land of Magog, the prince of Rosh, Meshech, and Tubal," (38:2). Speaking to Gog, the text foretells:

> . . . you will come from your place out of the far north, you and many peoples with you, all of them riding on horses, a great company and a mighty army. You will come up against My people Israel like a cloud, to cover the land. It will be in the latter days that I will bring you against My land, so that the nations may know Me, when I am hallowed in you, O Gog, before their eyes (38:15-16).

We first must ask whom the Lord is addressing? Magog, Meshech, and Tubal are all sons of Japheth listed in Genesis 10:2. Josephus claimed, "Magog founded those that from him were named Magogites, but who are by the Greeks called Scythians" (*Antiquities of the Jews* 1.6). This identification is still widely accepted among scholars. Rosh is handled in different ways in various translations because the Hebrew word *ro'sh* (ראש) means "head" or "chief." So while some will render this "prince of Rosh" (ASV, NASB, NKJV, YLT, GLT) others translate it "chief prince of Meshech" (KJV, RSV, NIV, ESV, HCSB). Either way there is no basis for equating this with Russia. Nevertheless, this continues to be taught. Edwin Yamauchi, who has written extensively on the subject, bemoaning the fact that this identification, which he calls "untenable," continues, writes:

> It is a reflection on evangelical scholarship when some of its spokesmen continue to adhere to the groundless identification of *rôš* as Russia, and the association of Meshech with Moscow and of Tubal with Tobolsk, when we

have had cuneiform texts and discussions of them that provided the true clarification of these names since the end of the 19th century ("Meshech, Tubal, and Company: A Review Article," 243, 245).

It is unclear exactly when this prophecy was given to Ezekiel. The last time indicator was mentioned when word came to the prophet of Jerusalem's fall (33:21). That would put this around 586 BC. Some forty years earlier, history records that Scythians had swept into Palestine intent on marching into Egypt. In his *Histories*, Herodotus records that in pursuit of the Cimmerians, the Scythians had moved into Asia Minor taking control away from the Medes for twenty-eight years (4.1), becoming "masters of all Asia" (1.104). Around 630 BC they swept through Palestine towards Egypt as far as Ashkelon, stopped only by gifts sent to them from the Pharaoh. During this invasion they looted and plundered as they went (1.105).

Earlier in Ezekiel these peoples were mentioned in the prophecy against Tyre. Tubal and Meshech, together with Javan, another son of Japheth (Gen. 10:2), were said to have traded with Tyre, bartering "human lives and vessels of bronze for your merchandise" (27:13). In the prophecy to Pharaoh, as he was told of those he would see in Sheol, he was told, "There are Meshech and Tubal and all their multitudes, with all their graves around it, all of them uncircumcised, slain by the sword, though they caused their terror in the land of the living" (32:26). This "terror in the land of the living" undoubtedly hearkens back to the invasion recorded by Herodotus.

"The Latter Years"

Ezekiel's prophecy of an invasion by Gog does not refer to the incident Herodotus records, but when was it to occur? The prophet is told, "After many days you will be visited. In the latter years you will come into the land of those brought back from the sword and gathered from many people on the mountains of Israel, which had long been desolate; they were brought out of the nations, and now all of them dwell safely" (38:8). Remember, this is revealed at a time when the Israelites are scattered to many nations and the land is "desolate." The term "latter" is translated from the Hebrew word 'acharith (אַחֲרִית) defined to mean, "after part, end; (a) end, issue, event; (b) latter time (prophetic for future time); (c) posterity; (d) last, hindermost" (BDB). The KJV translates it "end" thirty-one times, "latter" twelve times, "last" seven times, and "posterity," "reward," "hindermost," "uttermost parts," "at the length," "remnant," or "residue" in the other instances of its sixty-one uses in the Old Testament.

We might assume that the use of this word automatically points to the end of time, but as we noticed above with the phrase "the end," the specific application of a word's meaning is influenced (if not determined) by its context. Perhaps the best way to conceptualize the meaning of *'acharith* is to take it in the sense of *after-times*—always taking into consideration what is being considered as preceding it and approaching an end. For example, the return of the Babylonian exiles will be said to happen "in the latter (*'acharith*) days" (Jer. 49:39). The same word is used of the return of Moabite captives (Jer. 48:47). This was not the end of time, but later than when Jeremiah wrote, and after the captivity. It can refer simply to the outcome of something. Isaiah wrote, "Let them bring forth and show us what will happen; let them show the former things, what they were, that we may consider them, and know the latter end (*'acharith*—"outcome" NASB) of them; or declare to us things to come" (Isa. 41:22). It will be used of the last portion of nations under Babylon's control (Jer. 50:12), of someone's "posterity"—i.e., those who come *after* them (Amos 4:2), and of the last portion of people slain in battle (Ezek. 23:25; Amos 9:1). While it can point to the ultimate *latter time* (e.g., "Declaring the end (*'acharith*) from the beginning, and from ancient times things that are not yet done," Isa. 46:10), its conceptual sense is just *the things that come after*.

When this invasion is said to occur, the Lord uses eschatological language, declaring, "there shall be a great earthquake in the land of Israel," (38:19). The fish, birds, and "all creeping things that creep on the earth, and all men who are on the face of the earth shall shake at My presence. The mountains shall be thrown down, the steep places shall fall, and every wall shall fall to the ground" (38:20). The slain multitudes of Gog are said to fill a valley called "Hamon Gog" (39:11), and it will take seven months for the Israelites to bury all of them (39:12), and their bodies will also become a feast for "every sort of bird and to every beast of the field" (39:17-22). We should note, however, that similar wording was used before this of Pharaoh. Ezekiel records:

> Thus says the Lord GOD: "I will therefore spread My net over you with a company of many people, and they will draw you up in My net. Then I will leave you on the land; I will cast you out on the open fields, and cause to settle on you all the birds of the heavens. And with you I will fill the beasts of the whole earth. I will lay your flesh on the mountains, and fill the valleys with your carcass. I will also water the land with the flow of your blood, even to the mountains; and the riverbeds will be full of you. When I put out your light, I will cover the heavens, and make its stars dark; I will cover the sun with a cloud, and the moon shall not give her light. All the bright lights of the heavens I will make dark over you, and bring darkness upon your land," Says the Lord GOD (32:3-8).

The Lord is using the language of judgment. His enemies will not succeed, but will be called to account for their sin. Whether it is Egypt or Gog, none will escape. While the literal end will come, the Lord frequently uses judgment language that foreshadows it even in describing acts of judgment that do not literally involve these types of cosmic events.

Gog and Magog in Jewish Thought

While it is now generally accepted that the prophecy against Gog and Magog was motivated by the frightening march of the Scythians into Palestine in 630 BC,[3] it is interesting to see how the predictive allusions to a future invasion came to be used in Jewish literature. While "Gog and Magog" are frequently used in reference to opponents of the Messiah in the latter days, it seems to stand as a metaphor for opponents of God generally rather than a literal and specific reference to a resurgence of the Scythians in the last days. This becomes clear in the fact that it is no longer referred to as "Gog, of the land of Magog" (38:2), but simply "Gog and Magog."

For example, in one document from the Dead Sea Scrolls we see "Magog" used as a generic term for enemies of the Messiah. 4Q161 (4QpIsaᵃ), a Pesher (or interpretation) of the book of Isaiah, commenting on Isaiah 11:1-5, and the phrase "a shoot will spring from the stem of Jesse" (NASB) reads:

> . . . shoot] of David which will sprout in the fi[nal day since with the breath
> of his lips he will execute] his [ene]my and God will support him with [the
> spirit of c]ourage [. . . thro]ne of glory, h[oly] crown and multi-colour[ed]
> vestments [. . .] in his hand. He will rule over all the pe[ople]s and Magog
> [. . .] his sword will judge [al]l the peoples (Frags. 8-19 [Column III] lines
> 18-21).

Just before this, in commenting on Isaiah 10:34-35, it explains, "«And Lebanon, with its gran[deur], [will fall». They are the commanders of the] Kittim…" (Ibid., lines 7-8). Kittim is the term used repeatedly in the scrolls to refer to Rome and its armies. This likely suggests that "Magog" was not referring specifically to Scythians, but to opponents of Israel generally.

This is echoed in the Babylonian Talmud. Although compiled after the New Testament, it preserves many rabbinical teachings before and concurrent with it. At least three tractates speak of the "war of Gog and Magog" in the same way. Commenting on the meaning of Psalm 115:1, one claims, "Rabbi Johanan . . . said: [Ps. 115:1] 'Not unto us, O Lord, not unto us' refers to the servitude to [foreign] powers. Others state, Rabbi Johanan said: [Ps.

---

[3] See Yamauchi, Edwin M. "The Scythians: invading hordes from the Russian steppes." *Biblical Archaeologist* 46.2 (Spring 1983): 90-99.

115:1] 'Not unto us, O Lord, not unto us' refers to the war of Gog and Ma-gog" (*Pesachim* 118a). In two tractates, the messianic declarations of Psalm 2 are said to apply to the Gog-Magog war. One claims, "... when the battle of Gog-Magog will come about they will be asked, 'For what purpose have you come?' and they will reply: [Ps. 2:2] 'Against God and His Messiah' as it is said, [Ps. 2:1] Why are the nations in an uproar, and why do the peoples mutter in vain ..." (*Abodah Zarah* 3b). The second declares:

> Rabbi Johanan further said in the name of Rabbi Simeon ben Yohai: A bad son in a man's house is worse than the war of Gog and Magog. For it is said: [Ps. 3:1] A Psalm of David, when he fled from Absalom his son, and it is written after that: Lord, how many are mine adversaries become! Many are they that rise up against me. But in regard to the war of Gog and Magog it is written: [Ps. 2:1] Why are the nations in an uproar? And why do the peoples mutter in vain ... (*Berachoth* 7b).

It is likely that John's use of "Gog and Magog" in Revelation reflects this same usage. Describing Satan's brief release at the end of his 1000 years of bondage, John writes:

> Now when the thousand years have expired, Satan will be released from his prison and will go out to deceive the nations which are in the four cor-ners of the earth, Gog and Magog, to gather them together to battle, whose number is as the sand of the sea. They went up on the breadth of the earth and surrounded the camp of the saints and the beloved city. And fire came down from God out of heaven and devoured them. (Rev. 20:7-9).

This is not predicting a literal Scythian (or Russian) invasion of Israel, nor was Ezekiel. It is describing God's judgment upon any who exalt themselves against God, and His anointed Christ. Dan King, in his commentary on Rev-elation writes:

> ... In the Rabbinical writings Gog and Magog had ... come to be identified with the future enemies of the Messiah. Likewise, it seems that John also uses these symbols to picture the last fierce enemies of God and Christ, and of their people, the Church. According to Ezekiel, God uses sword (38:21), fire (39:6), and burning sulfur (38:22) to execute judgment against Gog and Magog. John also employs these same instruments of divine judgment in his vision to describe their downfall ... (324).

G. Ezekiel and Revelation

We have noticed throughout our study the many similarities that exist between the book of Ezekiel and the book of Revelation. I wish to draw once again from the material mentioned above that brother Kevin Kay shared with me in which he charts these numerous similarities. For example, Ezekiel starts with a declaration that he looked as "the heavens were opened" (1:1). John says, "I saw heaven opened" (Rev. 19:11). Both see "four living creatures" with similar features (1:5, 10; Rev. 4:6-7). Above the "living creatures" (beneath the throne), Ezekiel sees a firmament "like the color of an awesome crystal" (1:22), while John sees before the throne "a sea of glass, like crystal" (Rev. 4:6). For Ezekiel the sound of the "living creatures" was "like the noise of many waters" (1:24), while for John this is the sound of the voice of the Son of Man (Rev. 1:13, 15). To Ezekiel, the sight of the throne was "the appearance of a rainbow in a cloud on a rainy day" (1:28), while John saw "a rainbow around the throne, in appearance like an emerald" (Rev. 4:3). Ezekiel sees one scroll (2:9), while John sees seven (Rev. 6:1). Both eat a scroll that tastes like "honey" (3:1-3), but for John it becomes "bitter" in his stomach (Rev. 10:10). Both describe the marking (or sealing) on the "forehead" of God's people for protection (9:4; Rev. 7:3). Both feature coals and fire that is before God being cast upon the city or the earth (10:2; Rev. 8:5). In Ezekiel, judgment upon Jerusalem involves "sword and famine and wild beasts and pestilence" (14:21), while in John it comes on one fourth of the earth by "sword, with hunger, with death, and by the beasts" (Rev. 6:8). Ezekiel is told music will cease in Tyre (26:13), while John is told it will cease in Babylon [i.e., Rome] (Rev. 18:22). The sea traders are also said to mourn for both of these cities (27:28-30; Rev. 18:17-19). Both describe their authors being taken places "in the Spirit of the LORD" (37:1; cf. Rev. 17:3; 21:10). Both feature a type of spiritual resurrection. For Ezekiel it is the dry bones—representing Israel (37:10), for John it is the two witnesses—representing the Law and the Prophets (Rev. 11:11). Both promise a time when God's tabernacle—"shall be with them; indeed I will be their God, and they shall be My people" (37:27; cf. Rev. 21:3). Both speak of Gog and Magog (38:2-3; Rev. 20:8). Both are shown Jerusalem from a "high mountain" (40:2; Rev. 21:10). Both make use of a "measuring rod" to measure things within the temple visions (40:3; Rev. 11:1). Ezekiel is shown a glorious temple from which water flows for healing (47:1, 12). In Revelation it flows from the throne and the Lamb and is called the "water of life" (Rev. 22:1-2). Ezekiel's temple has twelve gates bearing the names of the twelve tribes (48:31-34) as does the New Jerusalem shown to John (Rev. 21:12-13). Like the Israelite camp in the wilderness in both there are three on each side (although Ezekiel puts them in a different arrangement than the encampment in the wilderness).

Interpreting the Similarities

Clearly, it is more than coincidence that these two books share so many similarities, but how may we account for this relationship between the two books? The critic of faith would charge that John creatively borrowed from the work of Ezekiel and crafted his own vision of the last days following the dictates of his own imagination. While there is no doubt that John's Jewish upbringing would have made him familiar with this important book of prophecy, we must reject this naturalistic explanation of these similarities. John, like Ezekiel was moved by the Holy Spirit to write what he did (2 Pet. 1:21). This fact alone could account for much of the resemblance. The same God who inspired one book equally inspired the other. It is also possible, however, that the fact that Ezekiel would have been so well known to John established a type of *prophetic vocabulary* (so to speak) that influenced the way he chose to express what the Spirit led him to write. This is only to be expected. When one sees similar things that he has heard others describe, it is only to be expected that he will describe them in similar ways.

It is important to recognize, however, that similarities in wording, motifs, and imagery do not necessarily constitute synonymous subjects, interpretations, or purpose. Simply because Ezekiel prophesied against Jerusalem, doesn't demand that we understand the book of Revelation as a prophecy against Jerusalem. Just because Ezekiel's temple bears similarities with John's New Jerusalem, doesn't demand that we conclude the two represent the same thing—as we shall see below.

III. Concluding Temple Visions

Having taken us from the years of warning before the fall of Jerusalem, through the ominous reality of Israel's sinfulness and the destruction of the temple, the book of Ezekiel ends with a vision of a glorious rebuilt temple that spans the last eight chapters of the book. There are many eschatological issues that hinge on how we interpret these final visions.

A. Challenges in Interpreting the Temple Visions of Ezekiel 40-48

Perhaps one of the most challenging things about the study of Ezekiel is how to interpret the temple visions at the end of the book. Is it a reconstructed Mosaic temple? It certainly pictures a return to the land (39:27-28) and a restoration of worship (43:22, 23, 27; 45:13). However, it also portrays acts of worship that were different from what the Law of Moses taught. For example, Mosaic Law commanded that on Passover, "you shall present an offering made by fire as a burnt offering to the LORD: two young bulls, one ram, and seven lambs in their first year . . . also one goat as a sin offering, to make atonement for you" (Num. 28:19, 22). In Ezekiel, the Lord commands, "On the seven days of the feast he shall prepare a burnt offering to the LORD, seven bulls and seven rams without blemish, daily for seven days, and a kid of the goats daily for a sin offering" (45:23). Concerning grain offerings made with daily sacrifices, Mosaic Law required, "one-tenth of an ephah of fine flour as a grain offering mixed with one-fourth of a hin of pressed oil" (Num. 28:5), while in Ezekiel the Lord requires, "a sixth of an ephah, and a third of a hin of oil" (46:14).[4] Plumptre observes correctly, "There is no trace in the after history of Israel of any attempt to carry Ezekiel's ideal into execution. No reference is made to it by the Prophets Haggai and Zechariah, who were the chief teachers of the people at the time of the rebuilding of the temple" (422-423).

So, is it a premillennial Messianic temple? The dispensationalist sees Ezekiel's temple visions as a literal blueprint for a temple that must be rebuilt before the Messiah can return to establish His kingdom. But, they struggle with how to explain the continuation of animal sacrifices.[5] Is it a figure representing the church? Martin Luther drew this conclusion. He wrote, "this building of Ezekiel is not to be understood to mean a physical building, but like the chariot, so the building at the end is nothing else than the kingdom of Christ, the Holy Church, or Christendom, here on earth until the last day" (*A New Preface to the Book of Ezekiel*). Yet, once again, if this is a figure of the spiritual kingdom that exists in the church, why are there sacrifices, priests, and holy days? If this represents life under the Messiah, why are Gentiles prohibited from entering it (44:9)? Preterist Steve Gregg recognizes:

> Some Christian commentators have understood the content of these chapters as an apocalyptic vision, which is best interpreted spiritually. They point out that the church, in the New Testament, is often referred to as God's 'temple' or habitation . . . . If this is the correct view, we would be required either to see many of the tedious details as being either superfluous or as corresponding to spiritual ideas that would be very difficult to identify with confidence ("Making Sense of Ezekiel's Temple Vision").

If these interpretations do not fit, is the vision a figure for eternal life in heaven? Some of the same problems arise if we interpret the vision in

---

[4] Reuven Chaim Klein, in his article, "Reconciling the Sacrifices of Ezekiel with the Torah," *Jewish Bible Quarterly* 43.4 (Oct - Dec 2015): 211-222, explores numerous examples such as these along with the efforts Jewish commentators have made to explain this.

[5] Jerry M. Hullinger has devoted considerable attention to this dilemma in the following articles: "The Problem of Animal Sacrifices in Ezekiel 40-48" *Bibliotheca Sacra* 152 (July-September 1995) 279-89; "The Divine Presence, Uncleanness, and Ezekiel's Millennial Sacrifices" *Bibliotheca Sacra* 163 (October-December 2006): 405-22; "The Function of the Millennial Sacrifices in Ezekiel's Temple, Part 1" *Bibliotheca Sacra* 167 (January-March 2010): 40-57; "The Function of the Millennial Sacrifices in Ezekiel's Temple, Part 2" *Bibliotheca Sacra* 167 (April-June 2010): 166-79.

terms of a future description of eternal life, in a heavenly condition with God, after resurrection, final judgment, and the destruction of this universe. Why are there still burnt offerings (40:42), including sin and trespass offerings (44:29)? In the heavenly Jerusalem nothing shall enter that causes an abomination (Rev. 21:27). Why are the Levites and sons of Zadok still serving (40:46). The New Jerusalem of Revelation has no temple (Rev. 21:22). In the heavenly temple portrayed in Revelation prior to final judgment, while it does refer to an "altar" (Rev. 6:9; 8:3, 5; 9:13; 11:1; 14:18; 16:7), it is associated with incense and prayers (Rev. 8:3). Nothing is mentioned about sacrifices (Rev. 11-16)—other than that of Christ, the Lamb.

B. The Temple Vision Analyzed

To sort through these problems and determine the appropriate interpretation, let's carefully analyze the vision, considering its context, timing, and clues that may help us reach some conclusions. First, we should note when this vision is given to Ezekiel. It begins, "In the twenty-fifth year of our captivity, at the beginning of the year, on the tenth day of the month, in the fourteenth year after the city was captured, on the very same day the hand of the LORD was upon me; and He took me there." (40:1). This is thirteen years after Jerusalem had been taken and the temple had been destroyed. The faithful Jews in exile had to face the fact that the temple—the place where their worship was to be directed—no longer existed. Ezekiel's visions began when the temple still stood. Twenty years earlier, he was called to tell the people this would happen before it actually did (1:2; 4:1-17). Nineteen years earlier, he was given a vision of the glory of the Lord departing from the temple (10:18; cf. 8:1). Thirteen years earlier, word had come from one who escaped Jerusalem, reporting, "The city has been captured!" (33:21). 2 Kings describes this, saying, "they burned the house of God, broke down the wall of Jerusalem, burned all its palaces with fire, and destroyed all its precious possessions" (2 Chron. 36:19; cf. 2 Kings 25:19). How helpless, and hopeless this must have felt!

In the midst of this dark time, Ezekiel is carried away in the spirit from his exile to the land of Israel and shown a glorious scene—not of ruins and rubble, but "something like the structure of a city" (40:2). He is not told, like Daniel to conceal what he sees (Dan. 12:4). He is told, "Declare to the house of Israel everything you see" (40:4). Then he is shown a beautiful vision of a temple—not as it was, but far more glorious. Unlike the temple filled with abominations, from which the glory of the Lord had departed (10:18), the glory of the Lord returns to this temple. Ezekiel writes:

And behold, the glory of the God of Israel came from the way of the east. His voice was like the sound of many waters; and the earth shone with His glory. It was like the appearance of the vision which I saw—like the vision which I saw when I came to destroy the city. The visions were like the vision which I saw by the River Chebar; and I fell on my face. And the glory of the LORD came into the temple by way of the gate which faces toward the east. The Spirit lifted me up and brought me into the inner court; and behold, the glory of the LORD filled the temple (43:2-5).

What a revelation! What was lost could be restored. What was in ruins could again be filled with the glory of the Lord.

Did this glory wait for the coming of the Messiah? We saw earlier the promise of a time when the Lord would, "establish one shepherd over them, and He shall feed them—My servant David" (34:23), promising, "And I, the LORD, will be their God, and My servant David a Prince among them" (34:24). This clearly points to Jesus, the Son of David, but does that "Prince" reign over the temple shown to Ezekiel? No.

Princes in the Temple Visions

Princes are mentioned frequently in the temple visions, but "David" is never mentioned. What is said about these "princes"? The prince is granted the right to "eat bread before the Lord" (44:3). He is assigned a dwelling place beside the "holy district" (45:7; 48:21). Instruction is given to him where and how to enter the temple (46:2, 8, 10). He is allowed to give some of his property "to his sons" (46:17), and forbidden from taking the property of others to give it to his sons (46:18). He is assigned an allotment of land between the land allotted to Judah and Benjamin (48:22).

The people of the land were to make offering "for the prince in Israel" (45:16), but specific instructions are given regarding the offerings the prince was to make (45:17; 46:4, 12, 16). It is unclear if this is speaking of him making the sacrifices himself, or through the priests. This led some Jews to conclude the term "prince" here refers to the High Priest. The medieval Jewish commentator Rashi (ca. 1040-1105), commenting on Ezekiel 45:7, wrote, "I say that this 'prince' as well as every [mention of] 'the prince' in this section means the High Priest; but I heard in the name of Rabbi Menahem that it means the king."[6]

---

[6] Klein takes Rashi's reference to "the king" to refer to the Messiah and cites statements in the Babylonian Talmud that apply Ezekiel's instructions to the prince to a Messianic future age (*Baba Batra* 122a) (222).

The vision doesn't only speak of "the prince" in the singular. After commanding an allotment for him by the holy district, the Lord commands:

> The land shall be his possession in Israel; and My princes shall no more oppress My people, but they shall give the rest of the land to the house of Israel, according to their tribes. Thus says the Lord GOD: "Enough, O princes of Israel! Remove violence and plundering, execute justice and righteousness, and stop dispossessing My people," says the Lord GOD (45:8-9).

Would Jesus be charged to "remove violence and plundering"? Would He be told to "stop dispossessing" God's people? No. Would He be included in a promise that the sinful oppression "princes" once carried out would be "no more"? This is speaking of human princes, charging them to practice proper behavior. It echoes the rebuke offered earlier in the book (see 19:1-14). This becomes even clearer in an instruction given regarding sacrifice. The Lord commands, "the prince shall prepare for himself and for all the people of the land a bull for a sin offering" (45:22). Jesus was without sin (Heb. 4:15). He makes offering for the people (Heb. 9:24), but He does so "by the sacrifice of Himself." (Heb. 9:26)—He does not need to "prepare for Himself" (as in Ezekiel's vision) "a sin offering."

C. Ezekiel and Isaiah's Visions Compared

We might compare Ezekiel's temple vision with some elements of Isaiah's vision of "new heavens and a new earth" (Isa. 65-66). The Lord declares, "For behold, I create new heavens and a new earth; and the former shall not be remembered or come to mind" (Isa. 65:17). Then after describing conditions in this new existence He concludes, "'For as the new heavens and the new earth which I will make shall remain before Me,' says the LORD, 'So shall your descendants and your name remain'" (Isa. 66:22). How are we to understand this? We might be inclined to see this as a reference to final judgment (cf. 2 Pet. 3:1-13), but there are elements within the prophecy that affirm the continuation of conditions in this life, as well as conditions under Mosaic Law.

For example, in this "new earth" eating of "swine's flesh" is still forbidden (66:17), worship from "Sabbath to Sabbath" continues (66:23), and there are "Levites" (66:21). In Christ all foods are clean (1 Tim. 4:4), the Sabbath is no longer binding (Col. 2:16), and all believers are priests (1 Pet. 2:9). In the new earth of Isaiah there is death (Isa. 65:20). In the new earth of the New Testament there is no death (Rev. 21:4). In the new earth of Isaiah there is a temple (Isa. 66:6). In the new earth of Revelation there is no temple (Rev. 21:22). These differences make it clear that the new heavens and earth of Isaiah cannot be wholly equated with New Testament descriptions that are called the *new heaven* and *new earth*.

Isaiah is likely using a figurative description of some type of restoration of Israel following a judgment from the Lord. The imagery of the wolf feeding alongside the lamb, and the lion eating straw are common figures for peace and safety (66:25; cf. 11:6). This has led full-preterists to argue that there will never be a destruction of the present heavens and earth. We must recognize, however, that there is nothing in the wording of the text that would preclude seeing an element of prophetic foreshortening (i.e., comparing a present event with a future literal event). In Isaiah 65:17, the Lord uses the Hebrew Qal perfect verb form, expressing simple completed action, "I create new heavens and a new earth," leaving the time when this creation occurs unspecified. In Isaiah 66:22, although it is usually translated as a future, "I will make," the Lord actually uses a Hebrew Qal participle there, which also expresses simple completed action—"I make" (GLT) or "I am making" (YLT). In other words, Isaiah's vision does not describe the church or heaven, but foreshadows some elements that will be true of both. In this respect it is similar to Ezekiel's temple vision—it may not describe the church or heaven, but foreshadows elements that will also be true of both.

The River Flowing from the Temple

One element of the temple vision that leads many to conclude that it must refer to the Messianic Age is the river Ezekiel sees flowing from the temple (47:1-12). It begins as a shallow flow only to "the ankles" (47:3), then swells up to the knees and waist (47:4), until it grows into a river one must swim to cross (47:5). The river flows to the east (down toward the Dead Sea) where it heals the waters, making them capable of sustaining fish like the "Great Sea," i.e., the Mediterranean (47:8-10). On its banks are said to be "all kinds of trees" whose "fruit will be for food" and "leaves for medicine" (47:12). This is obviously similar to John's vision in Revelation, where he writes:

> And he showed me a pure river of water of life, clear as crystal, proceeding from the throne of God and of the Lamb. In the middle of its street, and on either side of the river, was the tree of life, which bore twelve fruits, each tree yielding its fruit every month. The leaves of the tree were for the healing of the nations (Rev. 22:1-2).

In John's vision the water flows "from the throne," but we should remember that as Ezekiel's vision is further explained the Lord tells him, "this is the place of My throne" (43:7). Yet, unlike John's vision where there is "no more curse" (Rev. 22:3), in Ezekiel's vision not all things are healed. Ezekiel writes, "But its swamps and marshes will not be healed; they will be given over to salt" (47:11).

What Might Have Been

In 1993, the musical group Little Texas, released a song entitled *What Might Have Been,* that urges two former lovers who have moved on not to think about "what might have been." When my brother Curtis and I were talking about how to interpret the temple vision of Ezekiel, one thought he suggested reflected the same idea. Is it possible that Ezekiel is not talking about conditions of eternal life with God, the spiritual Messianic temple, or a premillennial temple (as dispensationalists conceive it), but an idealized picture of what might have been? Gregg echoes this thought, in suggesting:

> . . . one might reasonably refer to the vision as that which "might have been," had the Jewish exiles in Babylon exhibited a more thorough repentance than they did. There is an indication that the realization of this vision in Israel's future was contingent on the people being sufficiently ashamed, or repentant, of their past sins . . . ("Making Sense of Ezekiel's Temple Vision").

He goes on to quote a portion of Ezekiel's instructions to show the vision to the Jews in exile. The prophet is told:

> Son of man, describe the temple to the house of Israel, that they may be ashamed of their iniquities; and let them measure the pattern. And if they are ashamed of all that they have done, make known to them the design of the temple and its arrangement, its exits and its entrances, its entire design and all its ordinances, all its forms and all its laws. Write it down in their sight, so that they may keep its whole design and all its ordinances, and perform them (43:10-11).

We must note the conditional elements of this instruction. Ezekiel is to describe the design, "that they may be ashamed of their iniquities." This revelation is intended to produce shame, however, the extent to which he is to "make known to them the design" also depends on "if they are ashamed of all that they have done." The temple of Ezekiel offers to the Jews in exile (and afterwards) a possible picture of what their life after the exile could have been like.

Objections Answered

If this is a correct interpretation, why do the offerings differ from Mosaic ordinances? As noted above, many of the differences reflect an augmentation, rather than a reduction—i.e., seven versus two, etc. This may have been symbolic of the completeness of their restoration, an indication of affluence they could one day enjoy, or even a Divine change of the Law. At any rate, the presence of animal sacrifices precludes interpreting this as Messianic or heavenly (Heb. 9:11-14; 10:1-6).

If this is correct, how do we explain the river flowing from the temple? Certainly, when the gospel went forth from Jerusalem after Christ's ascension a fountain was "opened for the house of David and for the inhabitants of Jerusalem, for sin and for uncleanness" (Zech. 13:1). This differs from Ezekiel's vision, in that in the next chapter it is described as "living waters" that "flow from Jerusalem, half of them toward the eastern sea and half of them toward the western sea" (Zech. 14:8)—Ezekiel's river flows only to the eastern sea. In Zechariah's fountain, the prophecy of Micah was fulfilled that declared, "Many nations shall come and say, 'Come, and let us go up to the mountain of the LORD, To the house of the God of Jacob; He will teach us His ways, And we shall walk in His paths.' For out of Zion the law shall go forth, and the word of the LORD from Jerusalem" (Micah 4:2). Yet, even before the Messiah would come, Jeremiah was told the Jews had forsaken "the fountain of living waters"—identified as the Lord (Jer. 2:13; 17:13). A return to faithfulness to Him would bring them back to this source of life and healing. While Ezekiel's vision does not picture the ultimate healing river of John's heavenly vision, nor even the fountains of Zechariah, it promises God's word flowing forth from His faithful people. The flow of living water that could offer healing to all nations, would begin through the trickle of faithfulness that began well before Christ came.

Conclusion

The book of Ezekiel is a wondrous series of diverse visions that span the beginnings of the Babylonian exile, up to the fall of Jerusalem, and well into years of captivity that followed. Its visions of the "glory of the LORD" surrounded by "living creatures" that worship Him in truth regardless of where they may be, offered hope, purpose, and a picture of a brighter future to His people who desperately needed it. Although it has become a raucous playground of speculation to those who wish to find in it panoramic stairways to angelic ascents into heaven, or alien spaceships and flying machines, at its heart we see the mind of God speaking to rebellious or hurting people in figures intended to move them to obedience and comfort. The wise student will avoid the hyper-literalistic extremes of dispensationalism as well as the dismissive, and disjointed fog of full-preterism. While it clearly contains many elements that are eschatological in nature, much of it focuses on the near future that would come to those in exile, or the somewhat more remote coming of Christ and His establishment of the church. It does not foreshadow a future Russian invasion of Israel, nor a rebuilt temple in Jerusalem prior to the establishment of an earthly Messianic kingdom. It offers promises of condemnation to God's enemies and the assurance of God's deliverance to those faithful to Him. This message is a declaration of encouragement and truth as important today as it was when it was first revealed to Ezekiel.

Works Cited

Blumrich, Josef . *The Spaceships of Ezekiel.* New York: Bantam Books, 1974.

Collins, Tina Rae. *The Gathering in the Last Days.* New York: M. F. Sohn Publications, 2012.

Comfort, Philip W. *New Testament Text and Translation Commentary.* Carol Stream, IL: Tyndale House Publishers, Inc., 2008.

Gregg, Steve. "Making Sense of Ezekiel's Temple Vision" *Christian Research Institute* June 1, 2012. https://www.equip.org/article/making-sense-eze-kiels-temple-vision/.

Greek New Testament, produced at Tyndale House, Cambridge. Wheaton: Crossway, 2017.

Halperin, David J. *Journal of a UFO Investigator.* New York: Viking Press, 2011.

Hullinger, Jerry M. "The Divine Presence, Uncleanness, and Ezekiel's Millennial Sacrifices" *Bibliotheca Sacra* 163 (October-December 2006): 405-22.

———. "The Function of the Millennial Sacrifices in Ezekiel's Temple, Part 1" *Bibliotheca Sacra* 167 (January-March 2010): 40-57.

———. "The Function of the Millennial Sacrifices in Ezekiel's Temple, Part 2" *Bibliotheca Sacra* 167 (April-June 2010): 166-79.

———. "The Problem of Animal Sacrifices in Ezekiel 40-48" *Bibliotheca Sacra* 152 (July-September 1995) 279-89.

King, Daniel H., Sr. *I Saw the Heaven Opened.* Athens, AL: Truth Publications, Inc., 2018.

Klein, Reuven Chaim. "Reconciling the Sacrifices of Ezekiel with the Torah," *Jewish Bible Quarterly* 43.4 (Oct - Dec 2015): 211-222.

Lindsay, Hal with C. G. Carlson. *The Late Great Planet Earth.* New York: Bantam Books, 1974.

Metzger, Bruce M. *A Textual Commentary on the Greek New Testament.* Stutgartt: United Bible Society, 1971.

Ogden, Arthur M. *The Avenging of the Apostles and Prophets: Commentary on Revelation.* Pinson, AL: Ogden Publications, 1985.

Plumptre, E. H. "Ezekiel: an Ideal Biography, VIII." *The Expositor 2nd Series* 8.6 (Dec. 1884): 419-430.

Preston, Don K. "The Re-Gathering of Israel" *DonK.Preston.com.* No. 1-7, April 29, 2013 – May 14, 2013. http://donkpreston.com/articles/.

Villalpando, Juan Bautista and Jerome de Prado. *De postrema Ezechielis prophetæ visione,* vol. 2, In *Ezechielem Explanationes et Apparatus.* Rome, 1605.

Yamauchi, Edwin M. "Meshech, Tubal, and Company: A Review Article." *Journal of the Evangelical Theological Society* 19.3 (Sum 1976): 239-247.

———. "The Scythians: invading hordes from the Russian steppes." *Biblical Archaeologist* 46.2 (Spring 1983): 90-99.

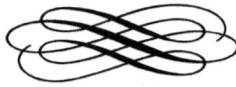

SCRIPTURE INDEX

220 • Thinking about AD 70

John

Acts

Romans

Biography

Kyle Pope (1963—) has preached the gospel since 1987 for churches in Missouri, Arkansas, Alabama, Kansas, and Texas. He currently preaches for the Olsen Park church of Christ, in Amarillo, TX. In 1982, he and his wife, Toni, were married. They have three children and four grandchildren. Kyle earned his BA from the University of Alabama (1997) in Humanities and MA from the University of Kansas (2000) in Greek and Latin. Truth Publications has published a number of his books including: *Biblical Guidance Through the Stages of Life; The "Gender-Inclusive" Movement Among Churches of Christ; The Hardening of Pharaoh's Heart; Harmony of 2 Samuel, Kings and Chronicles; Hope, the Anchor for the Soul; How Does the Holy Spirit Work in a Christian?; How We Got the Bible; The Matthew Commentary* in the Truth Commentary series; *"Ready to Give a Defense"—Answering Our Friends' Religious Questions;* and *Romans* in the Bible Text Book series. He edited *The Changing Face of Denominationalism* and co-edited two books with Mark Mayberry: *"In the Beginning" : Studies in Genesis* and *Taking Hs Hand, Helping Each Other Home.* Kyle is a board member of Truth Publications, Inc. and serves on its Publications Committee. He can be reached at kyle@truth-publications.com (or kmpope@att.net).

CREDITS

www.ingramcontent.com/pod-product-compliance
Lightning Source LLC
Chambersburg PA
CBHW070032100426
42740CB00013B/2664